JESUS SPEAKS

A SERIES OF VISIONS AND MESSAGES FROM JESUS AND MARY TO CATALINA

Tim Francis
Editor

Jesus Speaks

Published by 21st Century Press
Springfield, MO 65807

21st Century Press is a Christian publisher dedicated to publishing books that have a high standard of family values. We believe the vision for our company is to provide families and individuals with user-friendly materials that will help them in their daily lives and experiences. It is our prayer that this book will help you discover Biblical truth for your own life and help you meet the needs of others. May God richly bless you.

21st Century Press
2131 W. Republic Rd, MB 211
Springfield MO 65807
email: lee@21stcenturypress.com

ISBN TP: 978-1-951774-47-9
ISBN Ebook: 978-1-951774-48-6

Printed in the United States of America

21stCENTURY PRESS
READING YOU LOUD AND CLEAR

Contents

Introduction

As detailed in my book, *FROM THE CRACKHOUSE to GOD'S HOUSE, THE POWER OF A MOTHER'S PRAYER,* God answered my mother's prayer to bring me back from the dark web of addiction to the loving and protective heart of Christ. How did he do this? He used a "common and ordinary woman," a housewife like my own mother. A lady named Catalina (Katya Rivas). He used a successful attorney along with the father of investigative journalism in Australia. Putting them together led to the making of what has never been filmed in history. The Fox TV Special, Signs from God-Science Tests Faith was the first time a person was filmed before, during, and after receiving the stigmata. The special was a significant success, with 29 million people watching it across North America. As one journalist said:

> "Put it this way – this is either the biggest hoax of the 20th century, in which case it would have to be a fairly huge conspiracy or the most important moment of the century if not the whole millennium."

My mother recorded it and sent it to me. Hoping to get the ATTENTION of her "prodigal son." I was blown away by what I witnessed! (Go to www.ScienceTestsFaith.com to watch it)

It took me ten years to discover the meaning behind the miracle witnessed on that show. In 2009 I was led to the messages given by Jesus & Mary to Catalina. She has a seventh-grade education with no theological training. She has written over eighty books. At times, she has written in Greek, Polish, and Latin. These are languages she cannot read, write, or speak. The attorney, Ron Tesoriero, filmed her writing for almost one hour without pausing. Quoting Ron:

"She started with a blank page in her notebook. She wrote the first sentence and without stopping, the next sentence, then paragraph after paragraph, and then page after page, without one pause. She did not refer to any other material or book to write those 14 pages"

> "You do not know how holy, how misunderstood and how maltreated is that unique Sacrament in which I give Myself to you. That is the reason for these books, because a large part of the laity in My Church are ignorant of so many things that for the other part are common and even ordinary."

Well, that described me perfectly, IGNORANT! After reading these messages I immediately started attending daily Mass, regular confession, along with bible, prayer, holy hour, rosary, etc. Everything my mom prayed I would do when she was alive on earth. Now that she is in heaven, her prayers were answered. My recommendation is to take this book with you to the weekly Holy Hour. Allow Jesus & Mary to speak to you while you sit in front of Jesus Himself.

Speaking about one of the chapters in this book, Catalina's Archbishop states:

> "Each phrase of the Seven Words is profound in its contents, which leads me to recommend that the reading of this book be done slowly; thinking that we are beside the Lord, in order to feel the Divine Love of Jesus Christ in our lives. It is possible that some may want to rate this book as "just another pious writing." That is not so. Besides the fact that this text contains no dogmatic error, it leads us into the presence of Christ to unite us all in faith, love, and hope of a perfect life in God."
>
> Mons. René Fernández A. ARCHBISHOP EMERITUS OF COCHABAMBA

Outside of the catechism and the Bible this will be your most prized possession for spiritual growth. Keep it close and share with many.

May our Lord and Lady cover you with many graces and protect you from the enemy that likes to divide & depress!

—Tim Francis

> ***Special note**: My new friend and brother in Christ, Lee Fredrickson, came up with the idea to put all seven of these booklets into one book. How about that, a Baptist wants to take these Catholic messages to the world. Jesus is smiling and so is my mother.

IMPRIMATUR

Imprimatur given for the original Spanish text from:
Bishop Jose Oscar Brahona C.
Obispo de San Vicente, El Salvador, C. A.
March 2, 2004

They said therefore unto him: Lord, give us always this bread. And Jesus said to them: I am the bread of life: he that cometh to me shall not hunger: and he that believeth in me shall never thirst.
(John 6:34-35 DRV)

Then Jesus said to them: Amen, amen, I say unto you: Except you eat the flesh of the Son of man, and drink his blood, you shall not have life in you. He that eateth my flesh, and drinketh my blood hath everlasting life: and I will raise him up in the last day.
(John 6:54-55 DRV)

Chapter 1

The Holy Mass

In a marvelous catechesis, the Lord and the Virgin Mary have been instructing us, in the first place, about the way to pray the Holy Rosary, to pray with our hearts, meditating and enjoying the moments of our encounter with God and our Blessed Mother. They have also taught us the way to make a good Confession, and [in this testimony] they have shown us what takes place during the celebration of the Holy Mass and the way to live it with our hearts.

This is the testimony that I must and want to give to the whole world, for the greater Glory of God and for the salvation of all those who want to open their hearts to Him. It is given so that many souls who are consecrated to God may rekindle the fire of their love for Christ; those who own the hands that have the power to bring Christ to earth to be our nourishment [the priestly souls] and the others [the religious souls] that they may break loose of the habit of receiving Him as a "routine practice" and relive the amazement of the every day encounter with Love. And it is given so that my lay brothers and sisters the world over may live the greatest of Miracles, the celebration of the Holy Eucharist with their hearts.

It was the vigil of the Annunciation and the members of our group and I had gone to the Sacrament of Reconciliation. Some of the ladies of the prayer group were not able to do it then, and they left their Confession for the next day before Holy Mass.

When I arrived to Church the next day, a little bit late, His Excellency, the Archbishop and the priests were already coming out of the sacristy.

With that gentle and feminine voice that sweetens one's soul, the Virgin Mary said:

> "Today is a day of learning for you; and I want you to pay close attention because all that you witness today, everything that you experience on this day; you will have to share with all humanity."

I became awe struck and did not understand [the meaning of Her words] but I tried to be very attentive. The first thing I noticed was a choir of very beautiful voices that was singing as if from far away. At times the music would draw closer and then move farther away, like the sound of the wind.

His Excellency started Mass, and when he reached the Penitential Rite the Blessed Virgin said:

> "From the bottom of your heart ask the Lord's forgiveness for all your faults, for having offended Him. In this way you will be able to participate worthily in this privilege that is, to attend Holy Mass."

I must have thought for a split second: "But I am in the state of Grace. I just went to confession last night."

She answered:

> "Do you think you have not offended the Lord since last night? Let Me remind you of a few things. When you were leaving home to come here, the girl who helps you approached you to ask for something, and since you were running late, you answered her in a hurry and not in the best way. That was a lack of charity on your part, and you say that you have not offended God...?"
>
> "On your way here a bus crossed into your lane and almost hit you. You expressed yourself in an unfitting manner against that poor man, instead of coming saying your

prayers and preparing yourself for Mass. You showed lack of charity and you lost your peace and patience. And you say that you have not hurt the Lord…?"

"You arrive at the last minute when the procession of the celebrants to the Altar has begun… and you are going to participate in the Mass without previous preparation..."

"All right my Mother, say no more to me," I replied. "You do not have to remind me of more things because I am going to die of grief and shame."

"Why must you all arrive at the last moment? You should arrive earlier so that you can say a prayer and ask the Lord to send His Holy Spirit, that the Holy Spirit may grant you a spirit of peace and cleanse you of the spirit of the world, your worries, your problems and your distractions in order that you may be able to live this so sacred a moment. However, you arrive almost when the celebration is about to begin, and you participate in Mass as if it were an ordinary event, without any spiritual preparation. Why? This is the greatest of Miracles. You are going to live the moment when the Most High God gives His greatest gift and you do not appreciate it."

That was enough. I felt so bad that I had more than enough to ask for forgiveness from God. Not only for the offenses of that day, but also for all the times that, like so many other people, I had waited for the priest to finish his homily before I entered the Church. I asked forgiveness for the times when I did not know or refused to understand what it meant to be there, and for the times perhaps, when having my soul full of more serious sin, I had dared to participate in the Holy Mass.

It was a Feast day and the Gloria was to be recited. Our Lady said:

"Glorify and bless the Most Holy Trinity with all your love, in your acknowledgment of being the Trinity's creature."

How different was that Gloria! Suddenly I saw myself in a far off place full of light, before the Majestic Presence of the Throne of God. With how much love I went on thanking Him, as I repeated: "For your immense Glory we praise You, we bless You, we worship You, we glorify You, we give You thanks, Lord, God, Heavenly King, God the Father Almighty."

And I evoked the paternal countenance of the Father, full of kindness… "Lord Jesus Christ, only Son of the Father, Lord God, Lamb of God, You take away the sins of the world…"

And Jesus was in front of me, with that face full of tenderness and Mercy..." For You alone are the Holy One, You alone are the Lord, You alone are the most High Jesus Christ with the Holy Spirit..." the God of beautiful Love.... He, Who at that moment, was filling my entire being with joy…

And I asked: "Lord, deliver me from all evil spirits. My heart belongs to You. My Lord, send me Your peace so that I may obtain the best possible benefits from this Eucharist and that my life may produce the finest fruits. Holy Spirit of God, transform me, act within me, guide me. Oh God, give me the gifts that I need to serve you better…!"

The moment of the Liturgy of the Word arrived and the Virgin Mary had me repeat: "Lord, today I want to listen to Your Word and produce abundant fruit. Let Your Holy Spirit cleanse the soil of my heart so that Your Word may grow and develop in it. Lord, purify my heart so that it may be well disposed."

Our Lady said:

> "I want you to be attentive to the readings and to the entire homily of the priest. Remember that the Bible says that the Word of God does not return without having born fruit. If you are attentive, something of all that you have heard will remain in you. You must try to recall all day long those Words that have left an impression on you. Sometimes it may be two verses; other times the reading of the entire

Gospel or perhaps only one word. Savor them for the rest of the day and this will then become part of you, because that is the way to change one's life, by allowing the Word of God to transform you."

"And now tell the Lord that you are here to listen to what you want Him to say to your heart today."

Once again I thanked God for giving me the opportunity to hear His Word. And I asked Him to forgive me for having had so hard a heart for so many years, and for having taught my children that they should go to Mass on Sunday [only] because it was so commanded by the Church and not for love, for the need to be filled by God. For I, who had attended so many Eucharistic Celebrations, mostly to fulfill an obligation, and thus believed that I was saved, the thought of living the celebration had never entered my mind, much less that of paying attention to the readings or to the priest's homily!

What great sorrow did I feel about so many years of needless loss because of my ignorance!... How superficial is our attendance at Mass when we go only because it is a wedding Mass or a funeral Mass or because we want to be seen by society! What great ignorance about our Church and the Sacraments! How much waste in trying to educate ourselves and becoming cultured about the things of the world, things which can disappear in one moment leaving us with nothing. Things, which at the end of our lives, do not even serve us to prolong our existence by one single minute! And yet we know nothing of what will obtain for us a little bit of Heaven on earth and eventually, eternal life. And we call ourselves cultured men and women...!

A moment later came the Offertory, and the Holy Virgin said:

"Pray like this: (and I followed) Lord, I offer all that I am, all that I have, all that I can. I put everything into Your Hands. Build up Lord, with the little that I am. Transform me, God

> Almighty, through the merits of Your Son. I ask for my family, for my benefactors, for each member of our Apostolate, for all the people who persecute us, for those who commend themselves to my poor prayers… Teach me to lay my heart down on the ground before them, so that their walk may be less hard... This is how the saints prayed; this is how I want all of you to pray."

And this is how Jesus asks us to pray, that we lay our hearts on the ground so that they [for whom we intercede] may not feel its harshness, but rather that we give them relief through the pain caused by their stepping on our hearts. Years later, I read a prayer booklet by a Saint whom I love dearly, José María Escrivá de Balaguer, and in that booklet I found a prayer similar to that which the Virgin Mary taught me. Perhaps this Saint, to whom I entrust myself, pleased the Virgin Mary with those prayers.

Suddenly, some characters that I had not seen before began to stand up. It was as if from the side of each person present in the Cathedral another person emerged, and soon the Cathedral became full of young beautiful beings. They were dressed in very white robes and started to move into the central isle, on their way to the Altar.

Our Mother said:

> "Observe. They are the Guardian Angels of each one of the persons who are here. This is the moment in which your guardian angel carries your offerings and petitions before the Altar of the Lord."

At that point I was completely astonished because these beings had such beautiful faces, so radiant as one is unable to imagine. Their countenance was very beautiful, they had almost feminine faces; however, the structure of their body, their hands, their height were masculine. Their naked feet did not touch the floor, but rather they went as if gliding. That procession was very beautiful.

Some of them were carrying something like a golden bowl with something [inside] that shone a great deal with a golden white light.

The Virgin Mary said:

> "Observe. They are the Guardian Angels of the people, who are offering this Holy Mass for many intentions, those who are conscious of the significance of this celebration, those who have something to offer to the Lord…"
>
> "Make your offering at this moment… Offer up your sorrows, your pains, your dreams, your sadness, your joys. Offer your petitions. Remember that the Mass has infinite value. Therefore, be generous in your offering and in your asking."

Behind the first Angels came others who had nothing in their hands; they were going empty handed.

The Virgin Mary said:

> "Those are the angels of the people who, in spite of being here, never offer anything. They have no interest in living every liturgical moment of the Mass, and their Angels have no offerings to carry before the Altar of the Lord."

At the end of the procession came other Angels who were rather sad, with their hands together in prayer, but with their eyes downcast:

> "These are the Guardian Angels of the people who are here, yet they are not here. That is to say, they are the people who have seen themselves forced to come, who have come here out of obligation but without any desire to participate in the Holy Mass. Their Angels go forth in sadness because they have nothing to carry to the Altar, except for their own prayers.

"Do not sadden your Guardian Angels... Ask for much. Ask for the conversion of sinners, for peace in the world, for your relatives, your neighbors, for those who commend themselves to your prayers. Ask for much, not only for yourselves, but also for all the others.

"Remember that the offering which most pleases the Lord, is when you offer yourselves as a holocaust so that Jesus, upon His descent may transform you by His own merits. What do you have to offer the Father by yourselves? Nothingness and sin, but the offering of yourselves united to the merits of Jesus, is pleasing to the Father."

That spectacle, that procession was so beautiful, that it would be difficult to compare it to another. All those celestial creatures were bowing before the Altar, some leaving their offering on the floor, others prostrating themselves on their knees, their foreheads almost touching the ground. And upon reaching the Altar, they would disappear from my sight.

The final moment of the Preface had arrived, and suddenly, when the assembly was saying, "Holy, Holy, Holy," everything that was behind the celebrants disappeared. Behind the left side of the Archbishop appeared thousands of Angels in a diagonal line: small Angels, large Angels, Angels with immense wings, Angels with small wings, Angels with no wings. Like the previous Angels, all were dressed in tunics like the white albs of the priests and altar boys.

Everyone knelt down with hands placed together in prayer and bowed their heads in reverence. You could hear the most beautiful music, as if there were very many choirs harmonizing in different voices, all of them saying in unison with the people: Holy, Holy, Holy...

The moment of the Consecration had arrived, the moment of the most marvelous of Miracles... Behind the right side of the Archbishop appeared a multitude of people also in a diagonal line. They were dressed in the same kind of tunics as the Guardian Angels but in soft colors: rose, green, light blue, lilac, yellow; that is, in different and very soft colors. Their faces were also brilliant, full of joy. They all seemed to be of the same age. You could tell (and I cannot say why) that there were people of different ages but their faces looked the same, without wrinkles, happy. They all knelt down as well, at the singing of the "Holy, Holy, Holy Lord…"

Our Lady said:

> "These are all the Saints and the Blessed in Heaven, and among them are also the souls of your relatives and family members who already enjoy the Presence of God."

Then I saw Her. She was there, exactly to the right of His Excellency, the Archbishop… a step behind the celebrant. She was suspended a little off the floor, kneeling on some very fine fabrics, transparent but luminous at the same time, like crystalline waters. The Holy Virgin, Her hands joined together, was looking attentively and respectfully at the celebrant.

And She was speaking to me from there, but silently, directly to my heart, without looking at me:

> "It seems strange to you seeing Me a little behind Monsignor, does it not? This is how it should be... Notwithstanding how much My Son loves Me, He has not given Me the dignity that He gives a priest, of being able to bring My Son in My hands daily, as the priestly hands do. Because of this I feel such profound respect for a priest and for the whole miracle that God carries out through a priest, that I am compelled to kneel here."

My God, how much dignity, how much grace the Lord pours out over the priestly souls. And neither we, nor perhaps some of them, are aware of it.

There began to appear in front of the Altar some shadows in human form, gray in color, and they were raising their hands upwards. The Holy Virgin said:

> "These are the blessed souls of Purgatory who wait for your prayers to be refreshed. Do not stop praying for them. They pray for you but they cannot pray for themselves. It is you who have to pray for the blessed souls in order to help them depart [from Purgatory], that they may go to their encounter with God and enjoy Him eternally."
>
> "As you see, I am here all the time. People go on pilgrimages and look for My apparition sites, and that is good because of all the graces that they receive there. But during no apparition, nor in any other place am I present longer [over time] than at the Holy Mass. You will always find Me at the foot of the Altar where the Eucharist is celebrated. At the foot of the Tabernacle, I remain with the angels because I am always with Him."

To see that beautiful countenance of our Mother at that moment of the "Sanctus," together with all the others with their resplendent faces, their hands placed together, awaiting that miracle which repeats itself continuously, was to be in Heaven itself. And to think that there are people, that there are some of us who can be distracted, talking at that moment… I say with sorrow that many men, more than women, stand with their arms crossed, as if paying homage to the Lord from one equal to another.

The Virgin Mary said:

> "Tell everybody that never is a man more a man than when he bends his knees before God."

The celebrant said the words of the "Consecration." He was a person of normal height but suddenly he began to grow and become filled with light. A supernatural light between white and gold enveloped him and grew very strong around his face, in such a way that I could not see his features. When he raised the Sacred Form, I saw his hands. There were some marks on the back of his hands, from which emanated a great deal of light. It was Jesus!… It was He Who was wrapping His Body around the celebrant, as if He were lovingly surrounding the hands of His Excellency. At that moment the Host began to grow and became enormous, and upon it was the marvelous Face of Jesus, looking toward His people.

By instinct I was about to bow my head and Our Lady said:

> "Do not look down. Look up to view and contemplate Him. Cross your gaze with His and repeat the Fatima prayer: 'Lord, I believe, I adore, I trust and I love You. I ask pardon for those who do not believe, do not adore, do not trust and do not love You. Forgiveness and Mercy… Now tell Him how much you love Him and render your homage to the King of Kings.'"

I told it to Him. It seemed that I was the only one that He was looking at from the enormous Host. But I learned that this was how He gazed at each person, with love to the fullest. Then I bowed my head until I had my forehead on the floor, as did all the Angels and the Blessed from Heaven. I wondered, perhaps for a fraction of a second, what was all that about Jesus taking on the body of the celebrant, and at the same time being inside the Host, which upon being lowered by the celebrant, became small again. Tears were running down my cheeks. I was unable to let go of my astonishment.

Immediately afterwards, Monsignor said the consecratory words for the wine and, as the words were being said, lightning began to flash in the sky and in the background. There was no church ceiling and no walls. It was all in darkness, but for that brilliant light on the Altar.

Suddenly, I saw Jesus crucified suspended in the air. I saw Him from the head to the lower part of His chest. The cross beam of the Cross was sustained by some strong, large hands. From within the resplendent light, a much smaller, brilliant light came forth like that of a very small, very brilliant dove. It swiftly flew once around the entire Church and went to rest on the left shoulder of His Excellency who continued being Jesus, because I could make out His long hair, His luminous wounds and His large body, but I could not see His Face.

Above, was Jesus crucified, His head fallen upon His right shoulder. I was able to contemplate His face, His bruised arms and torn flesh. He had a wound on the right side of His chest and blood was gushing out toward the left; and what looked like water, but very brilliant, [gushed out] toward the right. They were more like jets of light coming forth towards the faithful, and moving to the right and to the left. I was amazed at the amount of blood that was flowing into the Chalice. I thought it would overflow and stain the whole Altar, but not a single drop was spilled!

At that moment the Virgin Mary said:

> "This is the miracle of miracles. I have repeated this to you. Time and space do not exist for the Lord, and at the moment of the Consecration all the assembly is taken to the foot of Calvary at the instant of the crucifixion of Jesus."

Can anyone imagine that? Our eyes cannot see it, but we all are there at the very moment when Jesus is being crucified, and He is asking for forgiveness to the Father, not only for those who are killing Him, but also for each one of our sins: "Father, forgive them for they know not what they do."

From that day on, I do not care if I am taken for a mad woman but I ask everyone to kneel and to try to live this privilege that the Lord grants us, with his or her heart and with all the sensitivity that she or he is capable.

When we were about to pray the Our Father, the Lord spoke for the first time during the celebration and said:

"Wait, I want you to pray with the deepest profundity that you can summon. At this moment I want you to bring to mind that person or persons who have done you the most harm during your life, so that you may embrace them close to your bosom and say to them from your heart: 'In the Name of Jesus, I forgive you and wish you peace. In the Name of Jesus, I ask for your forgiveness and wish you my peace.' If the person merits peace, he or she will receive it and greatly benefit from it; if that person is not capable of opening up to peace, then that peace will return to your heart. But I do not want you to receive or offer peace to others when you are not capable of forgiving and feeling that peace in your own heart first.

"Beware of what you do," continued the Lord "You repeat in the Our Father, forgive us our trespasses as we forgive those who trespass against us. If you are capable of forgiving and not forgetting, as some say, you are conditioning the forgiveness of God. You are saying: forgive me only as I am capable of forgiving but not further."

I do not know how to explain my pain at the realization of how much we can hurt the Lord. Also, how much we can injure ourselves by holding so many grudges, bad feelings and unflattering things, which stem from our own unconscious feelings and over-sensibilities. I forgave; I forgave from my heart, and asked for forgiveness from all the people whom I had hurt at one time or another, in order to feel the peace of the Lord.

The celebrant said, "...grant us peace and unity..." and then, "the peace of the Lord be with you..."

Suddenly I saw amid some (but not all) of the people who were embracing each other that a very intense light placed itself in between them. I knew it was Jesus and I practically threw myself to embrace the person next to me. I could truly feel the embrace of the Lord in that light. It was He Who was embracing me to give me His peace, because in that moment I had been able to forgive and remove from my heart all grief that others had caused.

The moment of the celebrants' Communion arrived. There I once again noticed the presence of all the priests next to Monsignor.

When he took Communion, the Virgin Mary said:

> "This is the moment to pray for the celebrant and the priests who accompany him. Repeat along with Me: 'Lord, bless them, sanctify them, help them, purify them, love them, take care of them and sustain them with Your Love. Remember all the priests in the world. Pray for all the consecrated souls...'"

Dear brothers and sisters, this is the moment in which we must pray for them, because they are the Church, as also are we, the laity. Many times we the laity demand much from the priests but we are incapable of praying for them, of understanding that they are human, and of comprehending and appreciating the solitude that many times can surround a priest.

We must understand that priests are people like ourselves, and that they are in need of our caring and understanding. They need affection and attention from us because in consecrating themselves to Jesus, they are giving their lives for each one of us, as He did.

The Lord wants that the people in the flock, who have been entrusted to him by God, pray and help in the sanctification of their Pastor. Someday, when we are on the other side, we will understand the wonder worked by the Lord in giving us priests to help us save our souls.

The people began to leave their pews to go to Communion. The great moment of the encounter in Holy Communion had arrived.

The Lord said to me:

> "Wait a moment. I want you to observe something..."

An interior impulse made me raise my eyes towards the person who was about to receive Communion on the tongue from the hands of the priest.

I must explain that this person was one of the ladies from our group who had been unable to get to Confession the previous night and had done so just that morning before Holy Mass. When the priest placed the Sacred Host on her tongue, something like a flash of light, that very golden-white light (that I had seen before) went right through this person's back first, and then continued to envelop her back, her shoulders and her head.

The Lord said:

> "This is how I am pleased to embrace a soul who comes with a clean heart to receive Me!"

The tone of Jesus' voice was that of a happy person. I was in awe, looking at my friend return to her pew, surrounded by light, embraced by the Lord. I thought of the wonder that we miss so many times by going to receive Jesus with our small or large offenses when it should be instead a celebration.

Many times we say that there are not always priests to hear our Confession. But the problem is not about always going to Confession. The problem rests in our ease of falling into evil again. On the other hand, in the same way that women make an effort to look for a beauty parlor, or that men, for a barber when we have a party, we also have to make an effort to seek a priest when we need all those dirty things removed from us. We must not have the audacity to receive Jesus at any time with our hearts full of ugly things.

While on my way to receive Communion, Jesus said:

> "The Last Supper was the moment of the greatest intimacy with My own. During that hour of love I instituted what in the eyes of mankind might be the greatest madness, to make Myself a prisoner of Love. I instituted the Eucharist. I wanted to remain with you until the end of time because My Love could not bear that you, whom I loved more than My Life, be left orphans…"

I received that Host which had a different flavor. It was a mixture of blood and incense that inundated me entirely. I felt so much love that the tears ran down my cheeks, prevailing over my efforts to hold them back.

When I returned to my seat and started to kneel down, the Lord said:

"Listen..."

And a moment later, I began to hear the prayers of the lady who was seated in front of me and who had just received Communion.

What she was saying without opening her mouth was more or less like this:

> "Lord, remember that we are at the end of the month and I do not have the money to pay the rent, the car and the children's school. You have to do something to help me... Please, make my husband stop drinking so much. I can no longer bear his drunken episodes, and my youngest son is going to be held back again this year if you do not help him. He has exams this week. And do not forget that my neighbor must move to another place. Have her do it at once because I cannot stand her any more... etc., etc.."

Then, His Excellency said: "Let us pray," and obviously all the assembly stood up for the final prayer.

Jesus said in a sad tone:

> "Did you notice? Not once did she tell Me that she loved Me. Not once did she give thanks for My gift to her of bringing My Divinity down to her poor humanity to elevate her toward Me. Not a single time did she say: 'Thank You Lord.' It has been a litany of requests... and almost all of those who come to receive Me are like that."

> "I have died for love and I am risen. For love I await each one of you, and for love I remain with you... But you do not realize that I need your love. Remember that I am the Beggar of Love in this sublime hour for the soul."

Do you realize that He, Love, is begging for our love and we do not give it to Him? Moreover, we avoid going to that encounter with the Love of Loves, with the only Love who gives Himself in a permanent oblation.

As the celebrant was about to impart the blessing, the Most Holy Virgin said:

> "Be attentive, be careful... [Many of] you make any old sign instead of the Sign of the Cross. Remember that this blessing could be the last one that you receive from the hands of a priest. You do not know if after leaving here you will die or not. You do not know if you will have the opportunity to receive a blessing from another priest. Those consecrated hands are giving you the blessing in the Name of the Holy Trinity. Therefore, make the Sign of the Cross with respect, as if it were the last one of your life."

How many things we forego by not understanding and not participating daily in Holy Mass! Why not make an effort to begin the day a half-hour earlier so as to hurry to the Holy Mass and receive all the blessings that the Lord wants to pour out on us?

I am aware that not everybody can go to daily Mass because of their obligations, but at least two or three times a week. And yet so many avoid going to Mass on Sunday, using the smallest excuse: that they have a child, or two or ten so they cannot go to Mass. How do people manage when they have other important types of commitments? They take all the children with them, or they take turns with the husband going at one hour and the wife at another, but they fulfill their duty to God.

We have time to study, to work, to entertain ourselves, to rest, but WE DO NOT HAVE TIME TO GO TO HOLY MASS AT LEAST ON SUNDAYS.

Jesus asked me to remain with Him a few minutes longer after Mass was over. He said:

> "Do not run out as soon as Mass is over; stay a moment in My company. Enjoy it and let Me enjoy yours..."

As a child I had heard someone say that the Lord remained with us for five or ten minutes, after Communion. I asked Him at this moment: "Lord, for how long do You really remain with us after Communion?"

I suppose that the Lord must have laughed at my silliness because He answered:

> "For as long as you want to have Me with you. If you speak to Me all day long, offering Me some words as you go about your chores, I will listen to you. I am always with all of you. It is you who leave Me. You come out of Mass and you are done with the day of obligation. You kept the day of the Lord and that is it. You do not think that I would like to share in your family life with you, at least on that day.
>
> "In your homes you have a place for everything and a room for each activity: a room to sleep, another to cook, another to eat, etc., etc.. Which is the place you have made for Me? It must be not just a place where you have an image that is dusty all the time, but a place where at least five minutes a day, the family meets to give thanks for the day and for the gift of life, to ask for their needs of the day, to ask for blessings, protection, health... Everything has a place in your homes, but Me.
>
> "Men plan their day, their week, their semester, their vacations, etc.. They know what day they are going to rest,

what day they will go to the movies or to a party, or visit grandmother or the grandchildren, their friends, the children, or go to their diversions. How many families say at least once a month: 'This is the day for our turn to go and visit Jesus in the Tabernacle, and the whole family comes to talk to Me? How many sit down before Me and have a conversation with Me, telling Me how it has been since the last time, telling Me their problems, the difficulties, asking Me for what they need… allowing Me to share in their things? How many times?

"I know everything. I read even the deepest secrets in your hearts and minds. But I enjoy your telling Me about your things, your allowing Me to share in, as a family member, as the most intimate friend. How many graces man fails to receive by not giving Me a place in his life!"

When I stayed with Him that day and on many other days, He continued to give us teachings, and today I want to share them with you on this mission that has been entrusted to me.
Jesus says:

"I wanted to save My creatures because the moment of opening the door to Heaven has been impregnated with too much pain…" "Remember that no mother has ever fed her child with her own flesh. I have gone to that extreme of Love in order to communicate My merits to all of you."

"The Holy Mass is Myself prolonging My life and My sacrifice on the Cross among you. Without the merits of My life and My Blood, what would you have to present yourselves before the Father? Nothingness, misery and sin…"
"You should exceed the Angels and Archangels in virtue, because they do not have the joy of receiving Me as nourishment like you do. They drink a drop from the spring, but you, who have the grace of receiving Me, have the whole ocean to drink."

The other thing that the Lord spoke about with sorrow concerned the people who go to their encounter with Him out of habit, those souls who have lost the awe of each encounter with Him. He said that routine turns some people so lukewarm that they have nothing new to tell Jesus when they receive Him.

He spoke of no small number of consecrated souls who lose their enthusiasm about falling in love with the Lord, and turn their vocation into a trade, a profession to which they give no more than what it demands of them, but without the sentiment…

Then the Lord spoke to me about the fruits that each Communion must yield in us. It does happen that there are people who receive the Lord daily but do not change their lives. They spend many hours in prayer and do many works, etc., etc., but their lives do not go on transforming, and a life that does not continue to transform itself cannot bear true fruits for the Lord. The merits we receive in the Eucharist should bear the fruits of conversion within us and fruits of charity toward our brothers and sisters.

We, the laity, have a very important role within our Church. We have no right to remain silent in the presence of the command that the Lord gives to us as baptized men and women to go forth and announce the Good News. We do not have any right to absorb all this knowledge and not share it with others, and allow our brothers and sisters to starve while we have so much bread in our hands.

We cannot watch our Church crumble while we are comfortably staying in our parishes and homes, receiving and receiving so much from the Lord: His Word; the priest's homilies; the pilgrimages; the Mercy of God in the Sacrament of Reconciliation; the marvelous union and nourishment of Holy Communion; and the talks given by such and such preachers.

In other words, we are receiving so much and do not have the courage to leave our comfort zone and go to a jail, to a correctional institution and speak to those who need it the most. To tell them not to give up, that they were born Catholic and that their Church needs them there, suffering, because this suffering will serve to redeem others, because that sacrifice will gain for them eternal life.

We are incapable of going to hospitals, to the terminally ill, and praying the Chaplet of Divine Mercy to help them with our prayer during that time of struggle between good and evil, and to free them from the snares and temptations of the devil. Every dying person is fearful, and they feel comforted merely by our taking their hand and talking to them, talking about the love of God and the wonder that awaits them in Heaven, close to Jesus and Mary, close to their departed ones.

The hour that we live does not allow us to side with the indifferent. We must be an extension of the hands of our priests and go where they cannot reach. But in order to afford ourselves the courage to do it, we must receive Jesus, live with Jesus and nourish ourselves with Jesus.

We are afraid to commit a little further. And yet, when the Lord says, "Seek first the Kingdom of God and the rest will be added onto you," it is about the whole thing, brothers and sisters. It means to seek the Kingdom of God in all possible ways and through all available means, and… to open our hands in order to receive EVERYTHING additionally! This is because He is the Boss, Who pays the best; the only One Who is attentive to the least of your needs!

Brothers, sisters, thank you for allowing me to carry out the mission that has been entrusted to me of having these pages reach you.

The next time you go to Holy Mass, live it. I know that the Lord will fulfill for you His promise that "Your Mass will never again be the same as before," and when you receive Him, love Him! Experience the sweetness of feeling yourself resting against the folds of His side, pierced for you to leave you His Church and His Mother; in order to open for you the doors to His Father's House, so that you can feel for yourself His Merciful Love through this testimony, and try to reciprocate with your small, little love.

May God bless you on this Easter.
Your sister in the Living Jesus,

Catalina

IMPRIMATUR

This publication "IN ADORATION" is a new contribution to meditation about our faith and the Eucharist.

In everything that is written here, I find nothing contrary to Sacred Scripture or the teachings of theMagisterium or the Tradition of the Church. It is my sincere belief that it is a testimony of sublime teaching on the love in the Eucharist and the Mercy of the Lord.

I recommend the reading of it to every child of God for whom this marvelous Gift was explicitly created.

Mons. Cristóbal Biaiasik
Bishop of the Dioceses of ORURO, BOLIVIA
Given in the city of Oruro, the 21st of November, 2007, the day of the Presentation of the Most Holy Virgin Mary

Chapter 2

In Adoration

This chapter gathers further personal testimony of Catalina Rivas, published and shared now for a duel purpose: that of transmitting to the reader a deep perspective with regard to the Adoration of the Eucharistic Christ – the Living Mystery of our Redemption; and that of inviting you to meditate on the infinite amount of graces which the soul receives when in the unique presence of the Sacramental Jesus.

We were told by John Paul II in his encyclical, Ecclesia de Eucharistía: "The worship of the Eucharist outside of the Mass is of inestimable value in the life of the Church." Further on, in his deeply moving and highly personal tone, he adds:

> "It is beautiful to be with Him, and leaning back on His bosom, like His favorite disciple (Cf. Jn. 13:25), and to feel the infinite love of His heart.
>
> "If Christianity is to be visible in our times, above all for the 'art of prayer', how is it possible not to feel a renewed need to spend long periods of time in spiritual conversation, in silent adoration, and in an attitude of love, before Christ present in the Most Blessed Sacrament? How often, my sisters and brothers, have I experienced this, and while doing it, have I found strength, consolation and support!" (John Paul II: Ecclesia de Eucharistia)

Which one of us could possibly say that they do not need strength and support... and often the consolation of God...? And yet how difficult it might seem to get ourselves to go directly to Him when problems overwhelm us! And how even more difficult it is for us to approach Him to simply say to Him, "thank you", when everything is going well...!

In the following pages, we will find a great many spiritual riches offered lovingly through the dialogues, locutions, visions and meditations of this writer herself. Through these writings, Jesus tells us, "When all of you contemplate Me in the Eucharist, your eyes touch Me and with even just a single glance from you filled with love and faith, you enter into Communion with Me immediately." And then He adds: "It is in the Tabernacle and in the holy Monstrance where I await you, in order to have you participate in the celebration of the Glory of My Father, in order for you to receive the flames of the Holy Spirit, in order to speak in loving words about the Heaven that awaits you, about the Love that is in store for you, and about the happiness that I promise you and that I give you."

His Holiness Benedict XVI expresses these words to us: "The prime reality of Eucharistic faith is the very mystery of God, Trinitarian love. In the Eucharist, Jesus does not give us "something" but gives us His very self. He offers His body and sheds His blood. Thus He gives up His whole life, by manifesting the original source of this divine love. It is a question of a gift which is absolutely free, which owes itself only to the promises of God, fulfilled beyond measure [...] The "mystery of faith" is the mystery of Trinitarian love, in which through grace, we are called to participate. Therefore, we also have to exclaim with Saint Augustine: 'You see the Trinity if you see love.'" (Benedict XVI: Apostolic Exhortation Sacramentum Caritas Nos. 7 and 8)

We know that faith is an ineffable gift from God, but we have also managed to understand, particularly those of us who did not have that gift for a long time in the course of our lives, that it is a question of a gift which the Lord is anxious to distribute among all His children. You only have to know how to ask for it!

We Catholics believe that Christ is the Bread come down from Heaven, and with deep and authentic ecumenical love, we lament its sacramental absence among Christian churches of different denominations, but we scarcely understand that that Bread remained among us only "for it to be eaten."

Saint Augustine said, "No one eats of this flesh without adoring it first [...] we would sin if we did not adore it." [Cf. Enarrationes in Psalmos (Narrations in Psalms) 98.9 CCLXXXIX 1385].

In the same chapter where the Sovereign Pontiff uses this quotation in his Apostolic Exhortation, he concludes by telling us: "Adoration outside of the Holy Mass prolongs and intensifies all that takes place during the liturgical celebration itself [...] 'only in adoration can a profound and genuine reception mature. And it is precisely this personal encounter with the Lord that then strengthens the social mission contained in the Eucharist which seeks to break down not only the walls that separate the Lord from ourselves but also and especially the walls that separate us from one another.'" (S.C., No. 66).

We hope, dear reader, that through the reading of this book, you may be able to find sufficient motivation for you to break those barriers, through frequent adoration of the Eucharistic Christ who awaits us every day, overflowing with tenderness, in all the Tabernacles of the world.

With gratitude to God for the infinite gift of the Body and Blood of Christ, we who now have the pleasure of editing this little book, ask the Lord of Life, with faith and hope, that your reading will help you to follow Him more closely, so that like the Apostle John and John Paul II, you may joyfully "touch the infinite love of His heart" while you contemplate Him in the Sacred Host, made captive by His own love for you and for humankind.

—Apostolate of the New Evangelization

In Adoration

Lord Jesus, When I started on this path at Your side, I remained in Your Presence for a long time, repeating interiorly, inside myself a hymn which is sung at the time of the Offertory of the Mass: "A child approached You that afternoon, gave You his five loaves of bread to help You, and you both made the hungry satisfied. I also wish to place on Your table, my five loaves of bread which are a promise to give you all my love and my poverty."

Today, I find no better way today to tell you "Thank you, Lord", for Your infinite Love and Your gift, in allowing me to hand my five loaves of bread to You.

November 25, 2007
Feast of Christ the King of the Universe

Introduction – Jesus, The Good Shepherd

A few years ago, we were invited to a Marian Conference in Pittsburgh, Pennsylvania, USA. These conferences takes place every year and many personalities from different Marian groups the whole world over are invited.

It was not too long after we had begun to preach abroad, so when I saw so many people in a huge auditorium, I felt quite nervous.

Whatever little of the presentations that I managed to hear in passing [this conference was not in Catalina's native language, Spanish], demonstrated to me the personal experiences or the knowledge of the participants, as well as their expertise in this field. All this was very intimidating for me since I did not have any particular subject [to speak on through a translator] except my testimony of conversion which I felt was not appropriate for that audience because of its humble nature. So I began praying and beseeching the Holy Spirit for help.

My team was made up of a group of people who were all well prepared in their fields: scientists, priests, some other people in the group and of course, me.

During the Holy Mass which was celebrated precisely before the final talk that our group was to make, I asked the Lord what it was that He wanted to say to the people through me and that He should let me know what was the purpose of my being there.

Practically all three thousand people attending the Mass received Holy Communion. We were the first to do so because we were seated closest to where we had to go up for Communion. I received the Holy Eucharist and kneeled down near my seat. At that moment I beheld something like a screen inside myself, a huge screen in which I saw an enormous field. There were green places, small hills with plants, wooded areas, and a very large lake... It was a very lovely place.

But in the middle of that whole field, there was a large uncultivated plot which looked very ugly, all full of thorns and dirt, something which was not in keeping with that magic scene.

There, in the middle of all those thorns was a little white sheep and you could not see much of its skin because it was covered with blood. There were many wounds on its little paws and its body, and it was weeping painfully and unceasingly. It was trying to escape from there, but was unable to do so. It would take two steps and the thorns would begin to grow and wound it even more.

The sky was dark and there were many large storm clouds in that place. There was thunder and lightning and a foul wind blowing made the scene uglier and frightened the little animal even more.

Suddenly I saw a woman with Her back to me, dressed in blue and with a white veil. I knew immediately that it was the Most Holy Virgin. She was extending Her hands and calling the little sheep to approach Her, but the frightened little sheep was trying to find its way out by another path, receding further and further in the distance because the thorns were growing quickly. It was trying to escape from the thorns and at the same time, from the hands that were calling it. It was so desperately afraid that it did not know in which direction to run. It was slipping and falling; fresh bleeding wounds were opening up on its flesh.

For a moment, the Virgin turned around and I managed to see Her profile which was so beautiful and so sweet. She gazed at a point in the distance, as if She were searching for someone with Her glance and then She disappeared.

At that moment there appeared before my eyes a man who was tall and strong, dressed in a bright pearl white colored tunic. He was wearing sandals and was holding a tall staff. His dark chestnut colored hair fell somewhat to his shoulders. His arms and the part of his neck that became visible when the wind stirred His hair, revealed his bronze colored skin. His arms were strong like those of a worker.

My heart was bursting with emotion: it was Jesus who without even thinking, got in among the thorns. Three or four times He beat back the tall thorns with His staff and made the plants break. Yet what was left of the thorns lacerated His skin too, tearing His tunic which got caught on them, but it did not seem to matter to Him that His garments were getting torn or that the thorns were lacerating His skin.

He hastened to enter and I saw how the blood was dripping from His feet, ankles and legs, splattering the ground wherever He went. The little sheep was getting deeper and deeper into more thickets of thorns and was already nothing but a single blood-stained mass when Jesus stooped down, took it in His arms and began to move out of the field. He was no longer even noticing the thorns which seemed to be attacking Him, lacerating His skin. His attention was focused solely on the little animal He was carrying in His arms.

He emerged from that field walking towards a spot where I could see Him facing me. He was weeping together with the little sheep. It was trembling in His arms which were getting stained with blood and it was looking at Him as if seeking consolation from Him. Jesus pressed it to His breast.

Suddenly He glanced toward Heaven. His expression hardened a trifle in seconds, enough time for all the dark clouds to rapidly disappear and for the sun to begin to come out. His eyes were filled with tears which were running down His cheeks.

Jesus began to kiss the little lamb and there where each one of His tears was falling or where He was kissing it, suddenly the wounds of the little animal were closing and white wool was appearing.

The tenderness and Love of Jesus were so great that it seemed as if that little animal were everything He possessed. The moment arrived when He was kissing the lamb's little head and it was licking His hand while the tears of both intermingled and they wept together, that Jesus smiled and the little lamb bleated faintly.

A moment later, I saw Jesus walking slowly as if He were waiting for His little companion. His bearing was noble. In spite of His simple garments, He was majestic like a King and the happy little lamb, her head held very high, now healed, was running after Him, bleating now even more strongly and occasionally licking the tips of the fingers of His hand. For a moment He patted her little head, responding to her tenderness.

Like in a series of images, I then saw Jesus seated on a rock. He was talking and the little sheep was sitting on her haunches, like dogs sit, listening attentively to Him. From time to time, He took her head in His hands and laughingly kissed her. Then she licked Jesus' feet and the wounds of the Lord were healing.

You could see all His wounds closed that way, and even Jesus' tunic looked new.

There was no longer any trace of so much blood and pain. It was a very beautiful scene. There were no more clouds, and the sun was shedding its golden rays upon the Shepherd's head. There was a fresh breeze that stirred His hair and He was smiling.

Another pitiful bleat was heard and I saw Jesus hurriedly walking again in the direction of the field of thorns. There was an expression of sadness and worry on His face. Once again, He was headed in search of another sheep, but this time the sheep that was already healed got ahead of the Lord and ran in search of the one that was now moaning.

As if it was an expert, it entered by the steepest paths. It was certainly hurting itself, but it was as if it mattered not to it, or else it was not causing it much pain because it was running along looking for its companion and guiding it towards the strong, safe arms of the Lord where He was standing.

At that moment, I was brought back to the celebration of the Mass when the Priest said, "Let us pray…" Greatly pained by the fact that such a beautiful vision had come to an end, I looked around me at all those people. My face was bathed in tears and even a sigh escaped me. Then Jesus spoke to me sweetly saying the words: "There is your subject. Tell the story of your conversion, because that first little sheep was you."

While the other people who came before me were talking, I no longer felt any fear about speaking. I hardly heard what each one was saying or any of the applause. It was as if I were listening from far away. I closed my eyes and I could see the beautiful Face of Jesus, now weeping, now smiling, and that completely filled my heart.

I know that was one of my best talks because I put my whole heart into describing to the people what the Lord had permitted me to experience a moment before. When the lights went on and I could see the audience, many people were weeping, perhaps identifying with the little lamb that had been rescued from the thorny field of the world, and had been healed with the tears and the blood of the Infinite Love of Jesus.

Several years have gone by, maybe eight or nine since that day, and while I am recording that experience in writing, the Lord has permitted me to live it again incredibly clearly and sharply.

Since that time I have had an image of the Good Shepherd at home opposite my bed, so that I may never forget the place from where I was rescued, and so as to always keep in mind the mission that God has assigned me, one of His flock. In that way, I am able to overcome the fear or discomfort that might prevent me from going out in search of other souls in need of Jesus… In order to be able to look to the future with hope and complete confidence in His Divine Will: all in a hymn of gratitude which each day and night I place, with a heart full of love, at the feet of my Good Shepherd.

Why that whole story for an introduction? Perhaps because those who have not read any of the other testimonies or who know nothing of the character of the woman who today is sharing with them the wonders worked by the Almighty in each one of us, might think that this is about some very pious person who spent her life before the Tabernacle, adoring Jesus in the Sacrament.

Nothing could be further from the truth. I am a woman who experienced conversion, touched by the Mercy of God when I was already mature. Conscious of my wretchedness and my many sins, I try to make up for that in the eyes of Jesus, with just my love.

One day, the Lord said that there were too many teachers and not enough witnesses in the world. That statement was the reason why our Apostolate assumed the New Evangelization as its main charism, seeking for its members to take on the duty of forming themselves IN the Lord, through a life in Grace and frequent reception of the Sacraments, to be witnesses for the world with the very testimony of their lives, of the Infinite Love and Mercy of God and of His transforming power.

Every good step that I have been able to take during these years, I have taken, impelled by the Lord and His Most Holy Mother, who has not failed to protect this Work with Her motherly tenderness.

It is They who are truly the authors of all these books, and who have charitably made use of this "hollow reed" in order to pour Their infinite Graces on today's men and women.

The Throne of God

One day in the month of April, 2006, I was once again favored by the Grace of the Lord, Who willed that the teachings about what I will share with you today should begin. They have to do with a Holy Hour to which I was invited by Jesus, "so that we can regale the world the gift of a new testimony... a few lessons more on your favorite subject, within the School of Love, which this Teacher wishes to impart to them," said the Lord gently to me.

At the hour agreed upon, I made my way to a very pretty Church near home where there is a tiny little chapel which has Perpetual Adoration of the Blessed Sacrament.

For those who do not know what this is about – possibly because of living in places far removed or because of having gotten away from pious Catholic devotions - Perpetual Adoration is the permanent exposition of the Most Blessed Sacrament, both night and day, in such a way that people take turns at the Adoration of the Eucharist at those Tabernacles so that Jesus is never left alone. It is a marvelous devotion which should be established in every Parish.

As I approached the Chapel, I saw that there was much more light than usual and I even thought, stupidly, that it might have been better for the place to have less light, or a less intense light, to create a more intimate atmosphere for the adoration of the Lord.

There was also music, because before I arrived at the Church, I heard first from very far away and then as I came nearer, more loudly, the voices of a great many people, like a polyphonic choir - composed of children, women and men – who were intoning hymns in a melody that I seemed to have heard before.

That music was very special to me and my whole body trembled for a fraction of a second, at the memory of another moment previously experienced.

The voices were intermingled with sounds like water cascading over a waterfall, with violins, organs or pianos, harps and flutes and from time to time when the voices were silent for a few seconds, some little bells ringing in harmony that seemed to me like a summons to Mass, perhaps because of memories of my childhood, in the small cities and little towns of my native land, where at different hours of the day and from different places, the call to Holy Mass could be heard.

Immediately I thought that it must be a recording from a CD that someone must have brought to accompany their Adoration with hymns of praise.

When I was almost at the entrance door to the Chapel, I saw that the light was diminishing, but at the same time, the place was becoming inexplicably brighter… At this moment, it is difficult to explain, but I think that soon I will be able to make myself understood.

When I went in, I saw a middle-aged man kneeling on a kneeler opposite the Monstrance containing the Divine Host. The Light that was coming from the Monstrance bathed the whole place, as if rays of Light were coming from it which were spreading and covering every place in that Holy enclosure.

I kneeled down to greet the Lord, but almost immediately, He instructed me to be seated so as to silently contemplate what was occurring. I knew that that day would also be another special one.

I had hardly kneeled when the Altar and the walls behind it vanished and before my eyes, Heaven opened up, so to speak, although perhaps this is using speech that is too earthly…

In place of the altar there was a huge throne. I cannot say now for sure whether it was covered with gold or silver, but I do know that it was filled with light, and on it the beautiful Monstrance was resting. The throne was inlaid in many places with what looked like precious stones that were enormous. They were shining and glittering as if they possessed a light of their own, that is, as if the light was emerging from inside of them.

I lowered my head for a second and then I raised my eyes. Thus, I managed to see that there were three seats connected, forming the same throne. There was a figure of Jesus sitting on each seat, or let us say, the same Lord but in triplicate – if I may use that term to make myself understood – but there were three perfectly identical persons…

There was no difference at all between the three of them, apart from their clothing. One was wearing a beautiful white tunic; another was dressed in one that was all in gold, and the third in red. It is hard to describe it, but those were the colors that predominated in their clothing, although a radiant light emanated from the three garments.

I heard the voice of the Lord saying to me:

> "Where will you find help on earth to describe Me, the Indescribable? Now that you are conveyors, where will you find your support to scale to My Height? No one and nothing will ever be capable of attaining and explaining completely My sweet Essence of God Triune and One. No one will comprehend the infinite Life that animates My whole Being.
>
> "Raise your hearts and your minds on high, because I wish to correct your impaired vision and to delight you with the brilliant appearance of even a single one of Us. Oh, glorious bond, sweet Son, You who leave the Father and deliver Love to human beings gone astray who walk the earth filled with grief.
>
> "Children, My Creatures, poor humans who cannot go further, and since their research into the knowledge of Me is never ending, they will always be happy to discover infinite and dazzling aspects of Me… Come to the bosom of My Divinity and stay with Us as eternal guests.
>
> "Learn more about Divine Love and stop putting up any inner and outer resistance in yourselves, so that Our Infinite Peace may enter your hearts and confirm to you that I want you with Me, and with that, I want to reveal Myself to you and give you My Love, eternal life and the unending holiness of My Being."

I remained overcome because even now it is hard for me to bring myself to think that it was the Father, through the Word in the Holy Spirit who spoke to me…

To the right of the throne stood the Most Blessed Virgin, more beautiful than ever. Her hands were joined in prayer and Her serene Face was very radiant. She was wearing a crown with many-colored precious stones that seemed more like colored lights, like those from the throne.

Beside the Virgin there was a very elegant and manly person with a small beard and a stance which showed humility and serenity at the same time and also exuded authority. A dignity never seen before radiated from all this… I knew it was Saint Joseph.

Immediately behind the Throne there were some men. I could not count them and the truth is that it did not even occur to me to do so. Then much further back in a kind of recessed area you could see hundreds of people like those whom I describe in chapter one on [my] Testimony about "The Holy Mass." Once again I saw the whole of Heaven before my eyes, thousands and thousands of Angels. It was they who intoned the hymns that I had been hearing when I approached the Chapel!

It was music praising God and of course, I know it will remain in my hearing and in my mind as long as I live, but I would be unable to repeat it today. Yet, since that day every time I begin praising the Lord, I hear those voices accompanying me as long as my humble prayer of praise lasts.

For Whom to Pray

I do not know exactly when I closed my eyes, but when I opened them again, I was lying prostrate on the ground, in adoration, before that magnificent vision which had even made me think that I might be dead… although I understood then that unfortunately, it was not so.

In a second, almost everything disappeared. Only Jesus remained with His splendid golden garments. He was wearing a lovely crown, and was holding a golden scepter in His left hand. He was standing on something that looked like a cloud, green in color…

"Be seated, little daughter," He told me very gently. I obeyed and then I realized that the man who was kneeling there had neither seen nor heard anything of what was happening.

The Lord said to me, "First of all, I want you to pray for the priest who made this meeting between you and Me possible, for the one who consecrated this Host." I did as He said.

Then He said to me, "Pray for the people who worked together to build this place set aside for these meetings. Yes, pray for them because there are many people who do so with the greatest devotion, and they are the first to receive My blessings from this place. There are those who labor and work together in building My House, but who do not do so for My sake, but for themselves, and not so that I will shine, but for them to shine.

"There are so many others who certainly do so out of love for Me, but who are not capable of coming to visit Me. They are the ones who honor Me with their lips but not with their hearts.

"Pray for the Parishes and Chapels where responsible persons and the community have undertaken to perform the hours of Eucharistic Adoration.

"Pray for those who close their hearts when I call them… For those who oppose the people that come to Me… For those who sully and offend My Presence by their lack of respect, their lack of reverence or lack of modesty in the way they dress. Observe…"

At that moment, I turned my head to look where Jesus was looking and I managed to see the Main Altar of the Church (not the altar of the small chapel where I was then). The Most Blessed Sacrament was exposed and there were quite a few people in the place. Many people were kneeling in prayer, but there were others who from behind the pews were passing before His Throne, chatting amongst themselves, eating something or chewing candy and gum as if there was no one there.

Some of them were making just a superficial gesture for the Sign of the Cross, and others, not even that. There followed a series of images (I understand they were of different occasions) of people whom I could observe, seated to one side of where I was. Some were whispering to each other while others were sitting with their legs crossed, both men and women, talking to each other or incessantly swinging one foot back and forth as if they were at an informal gathering…

They disappeared from my sight and immediately some couples came in and seated themselves very close to each other, but away from the other couples. I was embarrassed to see how they were openly exchanging gestures of affection with each other, in front of the Most Blessed Sacrament which was exposed. That was truly shameful, as if they were in some place reserved just for them.

Those people vanished before my eyes and something even worse followed. Some young and not so young women came in, dressed so inappropriately that they looked more like they were going to the beach, to a discotheque or who knows where. Parts of their bodies were uncovered like all those young little girls who did not seem to have any parents and who walk around wearing clothes that look two sizes smaller than they should be, and who call that "being in style"… How ashamed I was and how sorrowful I felt in the presence of the Lord who was looking at all those people with such a great deal of sadness!

Yes, I felt sorrow, but at the same time I felt like pushing them out of there like I have felt other times when by chance, I attend some wedding celebration, graduation Mass or a Mass for little girls celebrating their Fifteenth Birthday [a Latin American custom called "Quinceanos"].

On many of those occasions, I have felt ashamed for others when I saw the way some of the female guests at those events came into the Church. As if it were such a big deal throwing a stole around their shoulders to conceal a low-cut neckline and their bare arms and shoulders just for the few minutes they will be in Church!

And finally, while they are waiting for the celebration to begin, they all begin to chat as if they were already at the reception. The silence that they should observe in the House of the Lord is lost and with it, every trace of the spiritual preparation that each one of those ceremonies entails.

I want to make use of this occasion: to ask my lay brothers and sisters not to be afraid to take the microphone to ask those present to keep silent out of respect for the place where they are; and to ask ladies to cover themselves up when they go into Church, out of respect for the Lord, the priest, those attending and their own selves, because anyone seeing a woman dressed in a suggestive way in the House of God, immediately thinks that she is someone who has no respect for herself.

How fine it would be for anyone who is brave enough to take the microphone, to invite the faithful to say a prayer for the future bride and groom, or those graduating from high school, as the case may be, or to utter a prayer of intercession for the young girl for whom the celebration is to take place. In that way, we would help our brothers and sisters, by teaching them the respect due to the Church, and at the same time, we would fulfill what the Church asks us to do: to pray for each other.

We are called to build and yet we do our utmost to squander the good things from God, the dynamism of Grace, the fruitfulness of the Spirit, because we are afraid to proclaim a living God, and even more, to ask for due respect for His House.

I turned my eyes towards Jesus and tearfully begged His pardon, for those people who caused Him pain, and for us who are supposedly "conscious" of the place where we are, but who demonstrate cowardliness when it comes to instructing our neighbors. I felt ashamed for those feelings of anger that also crossed my mind.

Then Jesus said to me:

"Little daughter, it is so difficult for human beings today to change their patterns of comfort. Yet I assure you that through these testimonies, many simple people are learning to know Me, and to know about Me in words that are also simple. Do not become discouraged when we are just beginning.

"Look, I brought to the world a revolution of ideas that should amaze a weak humanity, so easily inclined to comfort itself, getting bogged down in old habits, not giving up a comfortable way of life because it does not go against its self love, which is the main counselor of its evil.

"Do not feel badly [referring back to Catalina's last comment]. I was direct and did not use neutral terms, precisely to clearly eliminate sensitivities and misrepresentations.

"Human beings are ungrateful. I provide for all and all live in Me. According to their dispositions, I endow some of them with a greater capacity to imitate Me and others with a lesser capacity. Yet, it would seem that I do not give them any guarantee of being interested in their sufferings, decisions, trials and much more than would a loving father."

The Communion of Saints

The Lord allowed images of political campaigns to pass quickly through my mind. Illuminated scenes with large numbers of people all worked up and shouting. Some were at a ball game, some at a concert of some fashionable artist or singer, some at a political rally, paying tribute to earthen vessels. And the King of Kings, the Lord of all humanity was seated on a gorgeous Throne illuminated by His own Light and abandoned, waiting for us. Only very few people were pausing there before Him.

When I observed them, I realized that they could not see Him as I was gazing at Him, surrounded by all the beautiful, radiant beings that dwell in Heaven. But they saw His earthly throne, that is, the place where He was, in an immaculate Host, inside of a beautiful Monstrance.

Among the people who entered and knelt before Jesus, there was respect and desire to adore Him. A great deal of sorrow and sadness was written on some of their faces, and some displayed fear and fright, while a few showed a great deal of love.

When one person entered, Jesus looked at her and extended His hand. The person knelt or sat down and suddenly the other people disappeared. It was as if only Jesus and that person were there. Then He embraced her and kissed the person's cheek, but doing everything with great tenderness, like someone who is in love receives his beloved, or like a father with a happy and joyful Welcome.

The person began to speak to Him and at first, Jesus listened to her intently, but then, He whispered some Words into the person's ear, and finally, raising His eyes, almost half-closing them, He raised His arms to Heaven.

Finally He blessed the person and remained gazing at her with a look of love, as if she were the only human being in the world…

There was so much Light coming from Jesus and illuminating the whole place! There was so much reverence and respect, adoration and love around Him, from a great many Saints and Angels and an enormous amount of people who seemed to possess their own light too, because of the happiness that was reflected in their faces…! This image, like that of the Most Holy Mother and Saint Joseph, appeared and disappeared from my sight from time to time.

The Lord was teaching me that we all need to open our eyes in order to be able to better contemplate the things of God, because frequently, our eyes are either closed or become dull when it comes to observing the things of the Spirit.

The Lord said to me:

> "Remember that in Psalm 24: 4-6, you are warned that in order to see the things of God, you need to have a clean heart, that is, purity of vision, purity of heart, uprightness of

conscience, and purity of intention, to be able some day to arrive at the knowledge of My Divine secrets...

"Learn from other human beings who came before you and who are Saints today! For them, the best resting place was in My hands, the best medicine and the most gentle relief was in having recourse to My Body in the Sacrament, seeking My company and conversation with Me.

"For that reason, they spent time in prolonged prayer, and from that period of time spent in adoration, they derived a renewed strength and greater energy to face life and all its sufferings, sorrows and humiliations, particular to their own situation, which would serve later for their crown of glory.

"It is essential that human beings be taught that it is not enough to confess their sins and come and receive Me, and then commit the same sins again and confess them again. They must be united to Me in thought, feeling, and will, that is, in body and soul,with the heart.

"That is how your human life succeeds in sharing My Divine Life, so that I myself will be the one who guides your being, along the journey that leads towards Eternal Delights.

"Do not forget that the greater your surrender to My Will, the greater are the Graces you will receive in the course of your visit to My Eucharistic Presence."

How deprived are those souls that remain far from the places where the Most Blessed Sacrament is Adored! There is so much ignorance and spiritual blindness that hinder us from believing in this absolute truth...

Humanity, what are we doing when we allow and even encourage immoral entertainment, depravity among our young people and the destruction of the planet, and do not run towards the Living God to beg His Mercy?

That night, I could hardly sleep. I felt guilty for staying there in my bed, so far and yet so near to Jesus. Far because I was no longer contemplating that which He had permitted me to experience, and near because it seemed that my pulse, my own heartbeat, was not mine, but His, that is, I felt Jesus' Heart upon my heart.

Then I promised Jesus that from that moment on, that every time that I should awake in the night, I would utter a Praise to Jesus in the Sacrament, to greet Him... And thanks to God, I awake several times and so I can say something like this: "In Heaven, on earth and everywhere, may the Divine Heart of Jesus in the Sacrament be blessed and praised forever" or "Blessed be Jesus Christ in the Most Holy Sacrament of the Altar and the Virgin conceived without original sin."

On other occasions, I place myself mentally and spiritually before a Tabernacle in some Church that I have known, and there, from my bed, I utter a prayer as if I were prostrate before His Divine Presence and I ask Him to allow me to accompany Him in thought and in heart.

How many sick people, to whom I have taught this type of adoration and keeping our Lord company from their places of confinement, have said that they have felt Jesus' loving Presence at their bedside! It is that the generous response of the Love of God never allows itself to be outdone..!

Almost when I woke up, Jesus allowed me to be present in spirit in a Church in my city which has a lovely Altar with an imposing Tabernacle.

There I prostrated myself to adore Him. At a certain moment, I heard...

> "When you contemplate Me in the Eucharist, your eyes already touch Me, with a single glance, full of love and faith, and you enter immediately into communion with Me.

"But if you feed yourselves with My Body and Blood, you experience the very life of God; you dwell in a foretaste of life in Heaven…! Because you gaze at Me with the eyes of faith while you wait to see Me, face to face, in the light of Glory.

"Those who truly feed themselves with My Body with a living faith, and are moved to practice charity towards their brothers and sisters, will enjoy eternal life since they will have arrived at the end of their lives, by yielding to a different way of life on earth…

"How much greater perfection will those achieve who give up all worldly things in order to possess everything. That is, those who give up everything that was created, in order to possess Me, the uncreated.

"An object of My delight is the one who is prepared to lose everything in order to gain God; to die so as to live then With and In everything…

"I do not tire of inviting all you whom I love to the fountain to refresh yourselves from the immense thirst that you experience, thirst for the love that I have placed in you for your own good.

"Can you possibly believe that I am in the Tabernacles or the Monstrances, just quiet and inactive, without providing you with the knowledge that I am the Life that is holy and everlasting? I am here in order to make Myself desired by you, so that when you come to receive My Body and My Blood as food at Communion, you hear Me say to you, 'Carry Me away in your heart because it is warmth that I seek, and I am not satisfied if I remain forgotten by you.'

"I remain on earth in order to provide easy access to Myself as food for those who do not forget Me, who know what I delight in, and who provide Me with those delights by receiving Me with holy love, joyfully, humbly and fervently.

"Tell My beloved to come to the One Who truly loves

them, to come to feed themselves, not only with My Body and Blood, but with My Presence, because the hunger that they experience is a Gift of Mine, a hunger for Me, although it is hidden and disguised by so many confused yearnings.

"Here, together with the Mother that I have given them, and with all their brothers and sisters in Heaven, I await those who do not reject Me but who seek Me and can so easily find Me, hidden and alive, in order to offer them the sweet Trinity that I Myself carry. I await them blazing with hope to see them near Me in order to cast upon them many rays of flaming light; to hold them close to Me so as to share with them doses of My own Holiness.

"It is in the Tabernacle and in the holy Monstrance that I await them so as to have them share in the celebration of the Glory of My Father so that they may receive the flames of the Holy Spirit, and to speak with loving words about the Heaven and the Love that awaits them, about the happiness that I promise and will give them."

Offenses Against Our Redeemer

Several days went by after that communication when at daybreak, the Lord awoke me sometime between 5:00 and 6:00 o'clock in the early morning. He asked me to engage in prayer for those people who had profaned the Tabernacles, committing sacrileges and stealing His Precious Presence in the Consecrated Hosts.

I began to weep from merely thinking about it and then I was filled with terror. There began to pass before my eyes scenes of people who were destroying the Tabernacles. They were breaking into them and removing the Consecrated Hosts with their filthy hands; they were throwing them into some boxes or bags, destroying them and stepping on them.

They were human beings but emanating a nauseating odor, their bodies and hands covered with hair, like dark wool and they walked grimly like four-footed animals when they walk on their hind legs, half bow-legged.

I am unable to describe the evil that I felt at that moment, but it was horrible, physically and spiritually. I thought I was going to die of sorrow. The powerlessness and futility of asking forgiveness of the Lord, to make reparation in some way for those horrible sins, overwhelmed me and I truly felt my heart leaping from my breast. I felt my pulse beating in my whole head. I was suffocating and I was gasping for oxygen.

I leaped out of bed and threw myself down on my knees begging forgiveness of God for such dreadful crimes and I realized that this could only be the work of Satan, through his followers, ignorant and stupid people who let themselves get involved in Satanic groups. Only the devil can inspire committing such vile sacrilege.

The only thing that occurred to me while praying, was to ask the Lord, "Please, Jesus, remove Your adorable presence from those Hosts; please, Lord, do not permit them to hurt You again. I beg You with all the love of my heart.

"I know it is little, but it is everything I can offer You: this poor love which wishes to make reparation for everything those savages are doing. Take me and put me in that place so that they may do to me everything they intend to do to Your Most Sacred Body. You can do everything. Please, Lord, depart from there and lift Yourself up to Your Glorious Throne. Do not remain in those Hosts…"

In a moment I felt that I was not the only one sobbing. Someone else was weeping with me, and then it was not only the deep sobbing of one human being but also of several persons which was gradually becoming louder and louder. I realized that it was Jesus Himself who was sobbing for sorrow when He saw the sin of His children, and near Him, the Most Holy Virgin and all the Saints… I ran to put something on and went to the little chapel of the Most Blessed Sacrament to be with my beloved.

He was there in the Consecrated Host and I could see His Face as if imprinted on the Wafer, like the head with the Divine Face sorrowing, with the Crown of Thorns, clearly outlined on His adorable head. I thought of Judas, of the sorrow of Jesus and of the

Father when His Son was going to be handed over, and at that moment the voice of Jesus reached me:

"Never forget, My daughter, that charity, the Love of Agape, is confirmed with works. The charity of the Father materialized in a gift: 'For God so loved the world that He gave His only Son' (Jn 3:16). And in turn, I, the Son, surrender My Life to show My Love.

"Do not forget this moment or this teaching. When I came into the world, I changed in form from God to Man and then to slave when I washed the feet of My Apostles.

"Know that the Word incarnate from then on, never strayed from that attitude of service. I told you, 'I am among you as the One who serves', and My program of humble abandon was to bring that about even to the shedding of blood.

"Today I am also among you as the One who serves, but yet in a more exalted form, because I surrender My Body, My Blood and Divinity to you, to feed you, to strengthen you and to heal you.

"I struggled so much against the spirit of the Jews of My own time, against the Ministers of the Temple of Israel, and I ended up as you know. And even today, there are many who should be ashamed, knowing that My most cruel enemies purchase or steal the consecrated Hosts in order to perform infernal things with them.

"In this way, My enemies believe in My Eucharistic Presence while My friends deny as usual by their words and deeds, the continuance, this Presence of Mine in the Host duly Transubstantiated... Oh, what an enormous piece of cruelty! Tell Me, what have I done to them...? Tell Me, why do they align themselves with My enemy?

"You, who rebel and yet belong to My Church, why do you not return to My Altars the dignity that you have stolen?

"I urge you to engage in fewer digressions, in more faithfulness, in more prayer and in less talk, more obedience, less critical spirit, more discipline and less evasiveness.

"Daughter, pray also for those bad children who come and ask Me for things that are inappropriate for another person, for the works of God and for their own souls. They selfishly think of themselves, of their possessions or of their comfort, and sometimes they do not know the good that person is bringing to their lives…

"Yes, pray for them, because at the hour they least expect, Divine justice will be turned against them, acting on their own beloved. What they wished for another is what they sowed and they will reap the consequences."

Kneeling before Him, I allowed a stream of tears to flow from my eyes. I did not restrain myself as on other occasions.

It was like a profound need to cleanse my sorrow, my guilt… Yes, I felt guilty for being part of the Church and keeping silent about all that, for not going out courageously to the streets, the high schools, everywhere, to tell the world that Jesus is there in that Consecrated Host, waiting for all of us.

I felt anguish over my guilt, over allowing prejudices and "the prudence" not to upset some persons with my testimonies, for having kept silent on so many occasions.

I experienced guilt as a lay person, because if the world were truly educated, if we taught what the Presence of the Living Jesus means in the Glory of each Consecrated Host, a great many lay persons would be keeping vigil at the Churches and Chapels, and preventing evil demons from profaning the greatest Sacrament of Love.

I prayed with all my strength to Jesus for Him to permit with His Grace, the testimony in the little book of "The Holy Mass" to circulate throughout the world, in order to educate lay people, to touch all the persons that He wanted and that He should truly make me a Missionary of His Eucharistic Heart through that little testimony.

That His Power should carry the little book to all the countries which I could not reach, and to all the persons that He wished to touch with His Grace. After a few months, that testimony had gone around the world and today, for the greater Glory of the One who is All powerful, it is translated into more than 12 languages without us having to lift a finger.

When I went into my room later, lying on my bed, I was gazing at the image that I have on the opposite wall that represents Jesus as the Good Shepherd, looking and smiling at the little black sheep in His arms.

Then Jesus' very gentle voice reached me:

> "You know that sheep are marked so that changes are not introduced into the different flocks. You too, like little sheep, are marked by My Father who wishes to offer you to Me.
>
> "If you could see that Divine sign My Father has imprinted on your foreheads, you would have no doubts about definitively entering through My gateway.
>
> "You are My little sheep, because besides dying for you, I am always showing you that I take care of you, purify you, feed you and protect you. I block the disturbing actions that My enemy, who hates you and Me, scatters among you. Be careful, for that wolf is always attempting to repeat his destructive works, and I am the One who blocks them.
>
> "Because of all that, I ask you to follow Me obediently and without giving up; to come to Me in order to know the gentleness of this your Shepherd who has been made to shed His blood for the purpose of saving you from death..."

Then I remembered the talk I had given at that Marian conference, and the Lord said to me,

"One day you are going to have to transcribe that talk, to be able to insert it in a book."

Today I have finished transcribing it, and out of obedience to Jesus and to a priest, who for the past three months has been helping me through his letters and whom I truly and greatly esteem, I have inserted it at the beginning of this book by way of an introduction, always seeking the greater glory of God and the good of other little sheep.

The Mysteries of the Kingdom

A few weeks after the first vision, one evening when it was raining a great deal and I was keeping the Lord company, the Altar displaying the Monstrance became much brighter, as if rays of the sun were shining through some window. It could not have been a flash of lightning, because if it were, it would have lasted only briefly, and this light kept on shining. I had just sat back, but when I saw the light, I knelt down again on the kneeler.

Then I saw two huge Angels with large wings. With hands clasped [in prayer], they were kneeling on either side of the Monstrance where Jesus was in the Eucharist. Their garments, very light silver colored, seemed to be of some velvet material.

They were so majestic and beautiful that their presence made me realize that those Creatures are in Heaven in the Presence of God, like so many other mirrors where the infinite purity of the Lord is reflected. That God of Love enjoys the fact that the Angels have a likeness similar to His, because their likeness is a reflection of the most pure Light of His Spirit.

I realized that from earth, we admire in the Angels, not exactly themselves, but God, at the same time as we reach out to Him by means of them. And just like the Angels, everything that is from God, attracts us.

As on other occasions, I did not know what was happening to me. It was as if I had read some book very quickly, as if a light had penetrated my mind. To express it another way, I "discovered" that angelic light is the purity of the eternal God, given to the heavenly spirits for His delight and for the immense delight of those creatures.

In the case of guardian angels, their work is pleasing to God because through it, they lead us in a delightful manner to the light of heavenly Love, possessed by them in different degrees, but in absolute and total purity.

Yet we do not follow their work, but instead, we often hinder it with plenty of burdens and enormous and diverse dark things.

At that moment, the Angels disappeared and I felt the need to give thanks to Jesus for my Guardian Angel whom I truly love and whose powerful help and intercession I feel every moment.

Then there began once again that music intermingled with little bells and the sound of water falling. Yet instead of distracting me, that melody was penetrating my being, during the contemplation of my prayer and dialogue with the Lord. That lasted the whole time of my encounter with Jesus and I know that the message was: "The choirs of Angels accompany us when we are at adoration."

That evening Jesus gently taught me about the benefits of receiving Him in our Holy Communion when properly disposed, and while He was speaking, I again felt that blaze of gratitude within me.

He was saying:

> "When you ask Me for something, while meditating on My Passion or during Holy Mass, you move My Heart, because you ask Me for it while keeping My Mother and John company at the foot of the Cross, for there are few whose prayer is steadfast. For that reason, the petitions vary in accordance with the way you pray and the hope you place in your petitions.
>
> "Your prayer at the foot of the Cross should be humble but firm, peaceful but fervent, filled with compassion for

My sufferings and gratitude for My Resurrection.

"Pause to meditate and to better experience the Martyrdom and renewal that I offer you in the Eucharist, by inviting you to be united with the Celebrant, and by removing your distractions. Be attentive to the one who renews My sufferings and prays with Me to the Father.

"I submit Myself. I am at the will of the Priest during his time and prayer, and you are so often distracted, absent and yet physically present at the Celebration. How hard it is for you to keep your minds continuously on the prayers and the spirit that moves My Church...!

"When you receive Communion, I Myself grant to your soul the elements which it requires to transform it and lead it to a path of greater holiness. Thus, you resemble Me more and more in your manner of thinking, feeling, reacting, and living...

"It is the Sacrament of union with Me and with your brothers and sisters. Therefore, the fewer obstacles I find in a soul for this union to be more perfect, the greater will be the Graces that you will receive from this encounter."

In a second I understood, though I myself could not fathom how, that when the priest says the words "The Body of Christ" to us, he is telling us, "Here is the food that will nourish you during your life and will save you at the hour of death". And our answer, "Amen" is the "Yes, I wish to save myself", or "May it be done to me according to Your word." Yes, that "Amen" is our "Fiat", and certainly this will not attract the attention of any priests because they are aware of it and they know it. But for us ordinary lay persons, all this is something new and an important part of the "Good News."

That surrender of the soul to the Lord and to His Divine Will is the disposition that makes it possible for Him to work wonders in it, with all His power and with all His Graces, to help us correct the course of our lives, to strengthen us and to love us.

I heard the voice of my Jesus:

> "How much love will the One Who formed you, have for you, the One who must remain hidden in order to save you! And I do it that way in order to prevent you from being blinded by My Majesty, in order that My Glory may not drown your desire of Me, and I do that with everyone. You do not know what it is to love this way without My Love being understood, accepted, and responded to.
>
> "You do not know how holy, how misunderstood and how maltreated is that unique Sacrament in which I give Myself to you.
>
> "That is the reason for this book with these Testimonies of Catalina, because a large part of the laity in My Church, are ignorant of so many things that for the other part are common and even ordinary.
>
> "In a simple and loving encounter through this book, I wish to make lay persons into beings who, by possessing knowledge of the Mysteries of the Kingdom and of things that by their nature they have had no education about or access to, may raise their hearts towards the encounter with Heaven.
>
> "Tell people to come to Me here, for I AM, the Almighty, the Infinite. Tell them to allow My Angels to bring them before My Presence and that one puff of air is enough for Me to blow away the dust harboring within you."

At that moment I managed to make out in the distance a person approaching the Chapel of the Most Blessed Sacrament, but not walking alone. There were four Angels, one in front, one behind and one on each side of the person. Those on either side of him and the one behind him were surrounded by a silvery light and the one that was walking (or rather gliding) in front of the person was enveloped in golden lights. "That is the Guardian Angel", the voice of Jesus explained to me.

At that moment, I understood why He was saying "we should allow ourselves to be lead before His Presence by the Angels". It is they who are permanently inviting us to visit Jesus in the Sacrament, and when we listen to their invitations, they themselves accompany us. The reason for the other three angels, I still do not know.

Often when I have just received Jesus in Holy Communion, I think about the fact that I do not know how it is that I am still alive, and how it is that I have not died in the face of the wonder of possessing the certainty that I am united in that way to my Lord and my God, to the Being whom I love above all things, to that Being who loves me with a Love without boundaries, to the point of forgiving me from time to time for every offence and omission of my daily life.

Then a wave of love surges up and envelopes me, causing me to emerge in some way like an eddy of fresh, golden water, embraced by Him, or dancing for Him up to the surface where everything is filled with that feeling that emanates from the heart and penetrates it at the same time. They are the moments of "I love You with all my being; thank you Jesus, thank you my Lord."

It is that wish that no one should speak to you, draw near, or say anything, that desire to remain united to Jesus waiting for a word from Him, a new gesture, a sigh, or a silence that speaks volumes…

On several occasions, during adoration I have only repeated the prayer that the Angel of Fatima gave to the three little shepherd children: "Oh Most Holy Trinity, Father, Son and Holy Spirit, I adore You profoundly. I offer You the most precious Body, and Blood, Soul and Divinity of Jesus Christ, present in all the Tabernacles of the world, in reparation for the outrages, sacrileges and indifference with which He is offended. And through the infinite merits of His Most Sacred Heart and through the Immaculate Heart of Mary, I beg You for the conversion of poor sinners. Amen."

On other occasions, when I feel so inhibited by the loving Presence of Jesus, I can only repeat to Him that I love Him, that I want to love Him more, that I want to be the way He wants me to be and then I keep silent, while noting that I am blushing like an adolescent girl in front of the boy who is looking affectionately at her.

How great it is to note that it is for Him, for the beloved, for our Jesus, that everything survives, and that going to Him, being at His side, uniting ourselves to Him, signifies meeting, earning, possessing the Love of that One for Whom we as well as the entire Universe exist. Like the saints, we should desire to be in the place of the Angels, because the Angels remain surrounding the Tabernacles.

God Desires to Dwell in Us

One morning at daybreak the Lord asked me to remain completely silent after speaking to me about the deep and silent encounter with God. He told me that to reach that state when the soul is inhabited by its Creator, is the greatest thing that souls seeking union with Him aspire to.

He explained to me that many things have been written about this, but that even those who have written about these capacities of the soul, have not been able to go beyond the point where their natural reason has led them.

There was absolute silence and within moments I became so tense trying to hear any sound that I could hear even the sound of my own breathing while trying to breathe more softly. Then in an instant, I do not know if I was inside my body or not, my eyes were closed and I no longer felt or heard anything. I do not know how much time I passed in this way.

When I opened my eyes, there was an immense light in front of me which made me blink two or three times. It was not a dazzling light, but it powerfully attracted me. It penetrated me through my eyes, my nose, my mouth, and through every pore of my skin, leaving me submerged in an indescribable peace...

For a few seconds, a silence even much more profound than the previous one that invaded me, and then, inside me I felt something like the beginning of a murmur, then like a wind and immediately a voice said: "My own, I love you"... Then the light and the voice vanished inside me.

Once again I was in front of my Jesus in the Eucharist, in the Monstrance, in the immaculate white Host, but I experienced such great peace and joy that I felt like laughing and crying at the same time... and I think I did so. It was a timid smile and then a broad smile mixed with my sobbing which was gentle, joyful and grateful.

There was a book on top of the kneeler and Jesus told me to take it and read where it was marked. It was the Prayer after Communion in the Liturgy of the Church for a Sunday in Ordinary Time, and it read like this:

> "May the grace of this communion, Lord, penetrate our body and spirit in order that it should be your strength, not our feeling, that moves our life."

I discovered that what Jesus was asking me to do at that moment, was to meditate on the conditions necessary for receiving His Most Holy Body, not only on the normal dispositions requested by our Church, but on the interior dispositions of the soul, to receive the greatest amount of Graces possible from this marvelous gift of God.

I know nothing about theology, but as a simple housewife, I think that if we are sure that Jesus is Present in the Consecrated Host, the very least we can bring to Him is our gratitude, our trust, our will, our love, and the desire for intimacy to know Him and to remain united to Him.

Why? So that He can make use of us as His instruments. God does not deposit some certain amount of power in human beings. He retains the power in Himself. Infinite resources are found only in Him.

It is only when we are united to Him, when we are accessible to Him and permit Him to work within us and through us, that we can succeed in seeing the great and powerful things that He does. It is only in that way that "His strength and not our feelings, is what moves our life."

"Come to Me All You Who Are Burdened..."

How often do we deprive ourselves of walking in that marvelous Company, because we do not know first of all, how to fill ourselves with Him and allow ourselves "to be gilded" by the Sun of His Eucharistic Presence.

We deprive ourselves of His continuous protection, of being able to see the abundance of fruits in our lives, in good moments and especially in bad, because it is in critical moments that it is possible to see if the fruits that we bear are permanent.

What a pity for those persons who receive the Lord in a humdrum routine manner, without the wonder of telling Jesus something new, but always using the same tiresome words, or even worse, not saying anything to Him, or feeling anything, as if they were actually receiving just a piece of bread.

Jesus said:

> "How can you possibly be surprised at the laity if the majority of them are scarcely aware of My Presence in the Eucharist, and are just beginning to believe that I am here alive...
>
> "How can you possibly be surprised if on multiple occasions I prove in My own brothers and sisters, that the lessons I have tried to give them through so many Eucharistic Miracles have rolled right off their souls without penetrating them.
>
> "How sad it is to see that so many of My own, from the moment of their ordination have still not acquired My Spirit, My feelings, and My plan for life: to rescue human beings through My absolute surrender, to lower Myself to the point of making Myself into bread and to raise them from their lowliness to My Divinity so as to confer on them My own inheritance.
>
> "My children, a person would be deceived who only saw in this plan a spectacular and fleeting gesture, nothing more than an ingenious lesson by an incomparable educator.

"On earth, I played a role in which I surrendered Myself entirely. The will to serve sprang from My very core, because the decision made by God to annihilate Himself, to humble Himself and to sacrifice Himself has always been alive for all of eternity, in the very depths of Me, the Word.

"It is difficult to understand the scope of My gesture, if I am not placed in the perspective of the redemptive Incarnation.

"Understand why you must carry your cross every day. Just as it was impossible to share in My society beyond, if I did not humble Myself and did not pay My ransom of pain, in the same way it is impossible to collaborate here below in the work of salvation if those who follow Me do not conform themselves to the Will of God. The two ideas are bound together.

"For you are not attracted to the metamorphosis that I demand of My Apostles even now. Authority implies service. I, the Son of God, assumed the nature of a slave. Yet, I did not divest Myself of My Divine personality, while still serving My own servants. I lowered Myself without losing My rank. I did not give up My privileges.

"My mission, par excellence, has always been to expose the void in mankind, the moral vacuum that My Divine Love came to fill in the hearts of Creatures.

"My Divine task is to produce in the hardened and insensitive hearts of human beings the impression of their misery, and to make them turn to the God of every Grace, to the God that many of them reject, in order to be saved from their ruin and to be forgiven and justified.

"That is the marvelous work that I have fulfilled in this world, and that I still fulfill through My Words and the working of the Holy Spirit. If the Light uncovers their sins, Love is also there, ready to cover them.

"Bring human beings to My Altars. They do not know the things that are lost by not coming before My Presence to

> learn how to ask for them. They have financial concerns and they turn to Banks or lenders; they have health problems and they go to one doctor or another in search of the remedy for healing; they have problems with their children and they seek institutions and professional people to help them to contend with them. Almost all of them have spiritual problems, yet look at this Chapel, built so that My children may come and tell Me their sorrows, their joys and no one hardly ever comes."

(The Lord was referring to a chapel in a South American country where I was at that time and which was built for the purpose of holding many hours of monthly Eucharistic Adoration.)

I began to weep, while telling Jesus that He knew how often and in what ways I had insisted that this should be carried out. Apart from one day per week when a Holy Bishop goes to celebrate Holy Mass and after Mass he exposes the Most Blessed Sacrament for Adoration, rare are the persons who come in order to accompany the Lord during the day.

With His usual gentleness, He consoled me by telling me that those persons who came there were heard with special attention, since they did so with love, without wishing to be seen by any other persons except Jesus Himself, and that this compensated for the lack of love of those who only attended large Churches when they were filled with people, to get the attention of priests or to take the pulpit and direct the prayers which were recited more for the purpose of being heard by human beings than by God.

He went on to say:

> "That is how things are nowadays, little daughter. Everyone will tell you that they have no time, but they all have problems. There are so many who wait for "an opportune moment" to concern themselves with the things of God and the needs of their souls, a moment that never comes. Then

there are those who entrust those concerns to other human beings established for carrying out that duty; and there is no shortage of those who have had to betray religion and their moral principles, like those who sell any article for which the market has more than enough.

"And when people are in need or are ill, they willingly accept a little religion to appease their consciences when it comes to their responsibility as creatures before God, yet not enough to silence the petition that their heart is requesting.

"How I should like for all to be like Nicodemus, in the sense that he was not saved by knowledge or by his religion, but by his simple faith in My works, for even if he did not fully understand them, he trusted in them, knowing that his salvation did not come from him, but only from God.

"How I should like for all to respond to that powerful Grace that is offered to them with Love. Those who are wise and famous among their peers, succeed in understanding that the work of salvation is something impossible for them to carry out by themselves. But they also learn that God has intervened to free them from their state of ruin and perdition.

"It was in the presence of his Savior that the doctor of Israel discovered the desperate state of his soul. In no other place would he have been able to discover that the Light and the Divine Love had carried out their work of salvation."

The Proofs of His Presence

On one occasion, we had gone to preach in a maximum security prison, and when we came out, the guard accompanying us said to me, "Thank you for coming, madam. I hope your words have reached the prisoners because they need them." I asked him what he had thought of my words. He said, "Well, but you were preaching to the inmates of the prison, not to us." I told him that I had preached about the Love of Jesus to all those who heard me and that he and all the guards needed that Love as much as the prisoners, and that everyone of us needs the Gospel and the Love of God because those benefits cannot be found anywhere else or in any other person.

It was Holy Thursday and Jesus had poured Himself out, full of Mercy that afternoon, at the pavilion of "the punished" where many were afraid to enter. We felt that Jesus Himself had opened the prison bars for us when we arrived there, and that He was our Host.

It was so, because there were a great many who went to confession. My spiritual director was hearing confessions while a choir sang between my preaching and prayers. From five to ten o'clock at night, tough men filed through the confessional box enjoying in an unforgettable way, the brokenness that is experienced when one has returned to life after twenty or even fifty years. They had a new label on their chests: instead of a number, now they had the word "Forgiven."

In the presence of Jesus, at the beautiful Monstrance of the little chapel, I was thinking that day about those people, and about how Jesus must feel every year on Holy Thursdays, and what He must have felt when He washed the feet of His disciples.

Jesus said to me:

> "Little daughter, I want there to remain engraved in your memory and carved on your heart, all the details of the scene that I relive before your eyes.
>
> "On that Thursday, everyone was full of enthusiasm. I was thoroughly acquainted with those men whose feet I was kneeling before, and I read their hearts without any need of being informed by them about the secrets of their souls.
>
> "I was not unaware, in particular, that one of them, like a rabid animal that bites the hand of the master that feeds it, was plotting and preparing a satanic plan against Me."

I buried my face in my hands, sobbing because of the sadness that I felt in the voice of my Lord. When I looked again, I saw Jesus and some men (His Apostles) reclining around a table. Jesus arose from the table and removing His cloak, dressed only in His white tunic, took a piece of cloth and tied it around His waist.

Already on other occasions, the Lord had granted me the immense gift of allowing me to contemplate scenes like this one. But they always acquire a different shade, something different for me to dwell upon.

On this occasion, my attention was attracted by the sight of Him clad so poorly without His beautiful cloak.

Jesus went on with His story:

> "They were the garments of a slave, of any servant at all who was not from the tribe of Israel, because they were exempt from that service.
>
> "In My hands, I held sovereign power, that universal authority that the Father in His goodness had communicated to Me.
>
> "At that precise moment, My gaze penetrated them and I tried to forestall the crisis that would shake the unselfishness of My Apostles. They were all on fire, like a flame and promised to follow Me to the death, but the enthusiasm of the spirit does not remove the weakness of the flesh, and I was looking into the future.
>
> "A mystery surrounds My whole human life: I spent My existence loving those who were Mine. As a Man and for mankind, the Son, the exegete of God offered thus, the definition of the Father: 'God is Love.'
>
> "That is why it is in My Heart that you should seek the sense and the importance of that supreme hour: I, who had consumed My Life in Loving, was reserving for them a supreme testimony of My charity. The height of Love at the end of My life!
>
> "I experienced then, with extraordinary strength, the feeling that your beloved mother and all those who pass

away in Grace acknowledged, knowing that life is scarcely a passage to the House of the Father, and that the prospect of separation enlivens the affection for those who pass away on the part of those who remain.

"My children, ask Me to instruct you and clothe you in My natural grandeur and My voluntary acts of abasement, so that at least in your natural littleness, you will have no difficulty in stepping down from your lowly pedestal and in serving your brothers and sisters.

"It is not the Tabernacles that are closed, but your hearts. For very few succeed in understanding how I, who am hidden and enclosed, have the freedom to reveal Myself, to make My presence felt, there in the Host which every one of those Tabernacles encloses.

"My Presence can be noticed if you have open minds, hearts and souls. Whoever comes to Me receives the proofs of My Eucharistic Presence, since I cause that marvelous miracle, precisely in order to approach you, welcome you, and console you who suffer from the life that is passing."

How stupid are we men and women, not to think about all of this. At the moment when Jesus goes to surrender Himself to the Will of the Father in order to save us, knowing everything that He had been for eternity, in the Present and what He was going to be forever and ever, after His Resurrection and Ascension into Heaven, His Love has reached the peak and He expresses it, not by embracing them but instead, He began to wash the feet of His disciples and to dry them with the towel He had around His waist.

The Lord went on to say:

"And you will tell My People to pray for their authorities, especially for the authorities of the Church, because of the fact that the powerful with the greatest of ambition seek honor and glory, that humans run after external titles to have themselves called 'Benefactors' or 'Saviors', and that monarchs impose their power on their subordinates, which is what humans normally expect, because they are glories that come from humans.

"But within My Church, among the ecclesiastic communities, this should never, never happen. The Church authorities have the strict duty of bowing in devotion to carrying out the exclusive wish of the Glory of God.

"Transubstantiation is not some fanciful miracle; it is a lasting miracle. It is to summon Me, to announce Myself to you, and it is not just some bread that has been blessed. Transubstantiation does not take place by leaving the bread as mere bread, because in that way there would be no change of substance.

"I have said: 'This is My Body.' This statement carries the force of My Omnipotence, if it is proclaimed by My authentic Ministers.

"Poor and unfortunate are the Ministers who place My Words in doubt and they do so much damage to souls…

"I allow Myself to bleed in many Hosts, before your eyes, so that you will be certain that Miracles keep on occurring before your unbelief, today like yesterday or before yesterday. Will the donkey have to humble human beings again, by kneeling before My Eucharistic Presence? [Note: the donkey reference is explained below.]

"Convey to them that I try through every means, to snatch from the clutches of My adversary, any soul already compromised.

"That I struggle indefatigably right until the end, that I show it (the soul) the greatest tactfulness and limitless patience. Internally and externally, I make it aware of the fact that nothing escapes Me of the drama developing in its heart or mind, in its soul or senses. I put everything into it and I only request that which they are least disposed, to give Me: their will."

In view of the fact that Jesus spoke to me about a donkey, and that I did not know what He was referring to, I consulted a Theologian and he explained to me that He is referring to a passage from the life of Saint Anthony of Padua which must be well known to every priest and nun, but not to the majority of lay persons, or at least to those lay persons whom the Lord wishes to reach with this little book. Therefore, I consider it important to transcribe the text that this Father made available to me:

> "In the life of Saint Anthony of Padua, a surprising event occurred which is known by all. There was a heretic called Guillardo who did not believe in the real Presence of Jesus in the Eucharist in spite of the numerous conversions that took place through the preaching of Saint Anthony. This heretic went around confusing people with his errors.
>
> "One day, Saint Anthony engaged in a public discussion with Guillardo and the latter was humiliated, not knowing what to reply to the masterful defense made by the Saint. So in order to get out of the matter, he asked the Saint to perform a miracle for the purpose of belief in the Real Presence of the Eucharist, proposing the following to him: 'I have a mule which I will deprive of food for three days, and if after those days he refuses the food that I will offer him to adore instead the consecrated Host that you present to him and in which you say the substance of Christ truly and really exists, then I will fully embrace the doctrine of the Catholic Church.'
>
> "Saint Anthony, moved by God, accepted the proposal and spent those three days in devout prayer and penance. At the end of the third day, Anthony celebrated Holy Mass and then without removing his sacred vestments, he took the Consecrated Host, and accompanied by a crowd of the faithful, he went to the middle of the square. Guillardo took the hungry mule from the stable and placed fodder before it. Then the Saint addressing the mule, said to him: 'In the

name of your Creator, whom I hold in my hands, I order you to prostrate yourself immediately before Him so that heretics will know that the whole of creation is subject to the Lamb that sacrifices Himself on our altars.'

"Before the admiration of all those present, the mule who was hungry, completely ignoring his food offered to him by Guillardo, went to the Most Blessed Sacrament held by the Saint and bending his hind legs, remained prostrate and motionless, in an attitude of profound reverence. This event caused the conversion not only of Guillardo but of many heretics who were present at the challenge.

"Because news of this event spread rapidly throughout the whole world, Saint Anthony received the title of 'Hammer of the Heretics.' This is a true historic testimony publicly acknowledged."

Know Yourself In Order to Change

How could we possibly live eternal life if we do not rise from the dead with Jesus? The Lord said, "those who eat My flesh and drink My blood have life everlasting." Today, this carries the same meaning: Those who eat the Bread of life today "live eternal life" and are risen from the dead in body and soul. This is a Mystery of Faith.

And that faith when it is genuine and solid, urges us to give up everything in order to have EVERYTHING, as the Lord said previously. And we can be sure that we have to experience hardship and troubles, but those things are needed for our own purification. To attain the resurrection, suffering, sorrow or the passion is necessary. This and only this is the true path of the Christian.

One day, during Communion, Jesus told me:

> "I will cleanse you with My Blood and I Myself will completely satisfy you, because I desire you to be so united to

> Me that it will be very easy to love Me on earth, in Heaven and wherever I am hidden, covering Myself completely with the Bread and the Wine. Always come to My flame; I am the Love that is eternal and invincible; I am your God."

That day I learned something else: that when He gives Himself in Communion, Jesus bestows His Spirit on us, and He does so by transmitting that evangelical Love that He desires us to keep enkindled in our hearts.

That Love is not earthly or limited, but it is universal like that of the Father, who no matter what we do, "makes the rain fall and the sun shine on all of us, on the good as well as the bad" according to the words of Sacred Scripture.

It is a Love that does not live by hoping for something from others, because it always takes the initiative, and because it is the first to love. It is a feeling that it becomes one with all in order to suffer and to rejoice with each one of us. It is a Love that is concerned for all, and that waits for all; the kind of Love that is not just sentimental, but a Love made obvious not just in word but in deed.

We all need for Jesus to bestow His Spirit on us. There are so many people, especially at this time, who perhaps because of their little faith or knowledge of God, suffer from illnesses that wither their spirit and prevent them from carrying out positive spiritual works.

We are in need of the Holy Spirit. Those who receive the Spirit of God enter into a process of conversion, since His mission is to transform "believers" into disciples and disciples into witnesses of Jesus Christ.

How pitiful to see so many people who come punctually to Sunday Mass and are spiritually inactive, as if too lethargic from all their worry to grow spiritually, and from getting to know their faith a little better.

You see them there, sunken in an alarming state of passivity, not only with no concern for improving their spiritual life, but also unable to do any good works, as if their spirit were ill and on the point of listlessness. It is as if they did not know or believe that Jesus came precisely to bring about the ability of human beings to rise up against themselves, by penetrating their innermost being in order to destroy that which is old and ugly within themselves.

It is as if they did not understand that Jesus is still here among us to make each one of us flourish in whatever qualities we possess that are admirable and beautiful. He is among us so that humans may be capable of separating from themselves the chains of their selfishness that transform them into people around whom the planet revolves, and so that men and women may be capable of feeling that they are not only children of the Most High but also brothers and sisters of the rest of humankind.

Yet I am not saying that those people are not in the state of grace. No. Certainly Grace is there, but it is inactive and purposeless.

I believe that true knowledge of the Presence of Jesus in the Eucharist should encourage us to lean completely on that Christ who wishes to extract us from that state of spiritual listlessness, because He has promised to be with us until the end of our days. We need to warm our hearts with the fire of the Holy Spirit in order to heal our despondency.

If our faith is weak, the Eucharist is that source which we need in order to nourish it. In the Person of Christ we encounter relief for our ills. It is His contact in Communion and dialogue during the hours of Eucharistic Adoration that free our lives from the effects of dangerous spiritual illnesses.

Where there is one of the Persons of the Most Holy Trinity, there are the other Two. It is there that we should adore and give thanks to the Father and receive the Holy Spirit. Many of us have filled ourselves not with the flame, but with artificial lights, but we need the light, the warmth and the flame of God in order to exist, to grow, to receive, to understand, to transform ourselves and to help others travel this same path. We need to pray to Him, who speaks in the silence of the soul, to give us a spirit of recollection, in order to understand what God desires of us, and to give us the strength, to encourage us to carry it out.

Jesus said:

> "Ask the Holy Spirit to dwell in you so that you will always recognize the footprints of God, so that He will unveil to you the magnificent plan that the Father has for each one of you… so that He will work in your hearts by shielding them from every lowly ambition, from appearances, from superficiality, and from cowardliness…
>
> "Every person should know how to develop their capabilities. So instead of focusing on the defects of others, disciples are those who learn to focus on their own defects and they should ask the Holy Spirit to teach them to be fruitful in their personal and family lives, and as members of the Church."

The Mercy of the Lord

One day, I asked the Lord, that if it was His Will, He should meet me no matter where I was, at exactly three o'clock in the afternoon, on a day when the Church celebrates the feast of Divine Mercy. I have lived before through some experiences on that day and at that hour, but today I want to tell what happened this year.

As I have done through all these years, I try to make a good confession, prepare my documents and arrange my belongings, closets and everything before that day. This time it was no different, except for the great consolation of having our [ANE] founding father with us for reasons of health. While yet convalescing, he celebrated Holy Mass at two thirty in the afternoon.

When we got to the Offertory, I closed my eyes, handing My offering to my Angel, for him to take to the Altar, but a light illuminated my eyes and my mind. I opened my eyes again and saw Jesus, or that is, the outline of Jesus, the silhouette of the Lord of Divine Mercy and the rays that radiated from His breast, which were shedding a strong light on me. I gave a start which Father Renzo noticed and mentioned to me later.

Jesus spoke to my heart asking me to surrender myself to Him.

I closed my eyes and immediately saw myself before the Throne that I have been allowed to see so many times. I saw someone, a being filled with silvery light and I realized that it was God the Father. I thought, "I have died" and I saw Jesus before me, dressed as the Merciful Jesus.

Suddenly I saw myself enveloped in some hoops like red and white rings, but they were loose, as if I were covered with a barrel, but I was aware that I was naked below and I began to feel badly, and ashamed because I was afraid that God the Father would realize this. I raised my eyes, seeking Jesus on my left, but in front of me on the other side of Jesus, on my right, there was a being clothed in a flame, but a flame that was reddish gold. I was not frightened but on the contrary, it made me feel very well.

It was at that moment that I realized... I was presenting myself before God the Father, before the Most Blessed Trinity, and I was clothed only in the colors of Divine Mercy... I understood that the only thing that can possibly make us worthy to present ourselves before the Throne of God is the Mercy of Jesus and that we must have recourse to It.

I gazed at that Being filled with light and I was able to make out His eyes, enormous eyes like those of my Jesus, but with a look of tenderness in them: wise, mature, and loving, as if they were inviting me to trust and not fear him. There was a "smile" in that gaze and I could see nothing more. Everything was light, but those eyes, or rather that gaze I saw clearly. Joining many voices, I repeated: "Holy God, Holy Mighty One, Holy Immortal One, have mercy on us and on the whole world." We repeated it three times.

A very sweet voice which I immediately recognized as the voice of my dear Holy Mother, said, "Holy God"... and my eyes looked towards God the Father. Then the Virgin said, "Holy Mighty One" and my eyes looked towards the Being clothed in a flame. When the Virgin said, "Holy Immortal One" my eyes searched for Jesus. That was it! God the Father is the Holy One; the Almighty One is the Holy Spirit, and the Immortal One, the one who has conquered death, is Jesus...!

My mind was being opened up to things that undoubtedly may be well known during the formation of a priest, a nun, and a lay person doing religious studies, but for us ordinary lay persons, for me, it was a revelation. The Voice of Jesus said – but I knew it was the Father who was speaking to me: "With the knowledge that you have received now, tell the world to repeat this prayer."

At that moment I realized that I was not dead, that the Lord was giving me more time, and that He was assigning me a new mission: to prepare human beings so that their encounter with God at the hour of their death, would be clothed in His Mercy, in the Infinite Merits of Jesus, since it is the only "clothing" that we can wear to present ourselves before the Throne of God in order to be judged…

I was pulled from there by a force that absorbed me, and I saw myself, as if I were floating in the sky (surely like what a parachutist sees). It was a place with mountains, but I was slowly descending, passing through the clouds above a plain.

I thought, "this is certainly a cold place because there are mountains." As I descended lower, I could make out some men and women, more men than women, dressed in black and holding hands, one beside the other. As I was descending, I felt a force requesting me to say the prayer, and I began: "Holy God, Holy Mighty One, Holy Immortal One, have mercy on us and on the whole world." Suddenly, some persons among them vanished and I ascended a little. Again I repeated the prayer and the same thing happened. Then, I began to repeat it over and over again. I ascended, I ascended, I ascended and the people were vanishing until I lost them from sight and I heard the voice of the priest continuing with the Celebration.

I began to cry; I could not help it. On the one hand, I felt sorrow and pain for having left that majestic place and that vision, but I was happy, too, because the Lord had entrusted another mission to me.

The celebration was hardly over when I requested that we should pray the Chaplet of Divine Mercy before Jesus in the Sacrament, and when I repeated the prayer of "Holy God, Holy Mighty One, Holy Immortal One, have mercy on us and on the whole world," I heard and felt within myself many voices were joining ours in accompaniment.

Then I realized that the vision I had had, suspended in the air with all those beings below, as if they were waiting for something, was a vision of the souls that were going to die and were waiting for a prayer on their behalf.

I have related this because I want to ask all those who may kindly accompany me in this apostolate for the dying, to repeat this prayer every time they remember, presenting to the Lord all those who are going to die in the course of that day, so that the Grace and the Mercy of God will reach them at the moment of their death, and so that they may unite themselves to our prayers through their guardian angels and ours, whom we will ask to whisper the words [of the prayer] into the ears of those who are dying, so that they may repeat the prayer, even if only once, and thus be saved.

A Balsom and Twelve Promises

There are many ways to encounter God, but there is a unique, privileged moment like no other, when we can nourish ourselves with His Presence. It is when we are before the Most Blessed Sacrament. Without perceiving anything else but that white Host, we can pray and go deeply in search of that direct relationship with Jesus.

To accomplish this, it is enough to collect ourselves and silently search first for the Holy Spirit of God, that source that is inside of us and from which there begins to spring forth, little by little, the Heavenly water: Jesus. He who is before us but is entering through His Love, His Tenderness, His Words or His whispering, until the flow of water from the spring becomes heavier, as if the abundance of water is increasing in order to quench our thirst, to water the dryness of our thoughts and feelings, until we can reach the point of sensing Jesus in complete union with us, (in true Communion), so that we are no longer He and I, but "You in me and I in You."

One afternoon the images of "the three figures of Jesus" or the Most Blessed Trinity with three identical persons came to my mind.

Being reminded of that vision which I have previously related, Jesus spoke to my Heart from the Monstrance:

> "When I said: 'I am the Way and the Truth and the Life'; 'No one comes to the Father except through Me'; 'If you know Me, My Father will know you also'; 'From now on you do know Him and have seen Him'... I did so in order for you to know that it is not possible to know Me without also knowing the Father, to see the one without [seeing] the other, to hear My words and to contemplate My works without becoming aware of the words and the works of the Father.
>
> "This dialogue with Saint Thomas should lead you into a lengthy meditation. Under the guidance of My Holy Spirit, it should lead you to examine the depths that one day also caused many saints to be transported to heights inaccessible to the natural intelligence, that is, towards the dizzying peaks of the Gospel that contains so many pinnacles!
>
> "My children, never has human language enunciated more sublime realities. In flowing and concise language, I proclaimed decisive rulings; yet human language is ignorant of the fullness of them.
>
> "I desire that you know Me, not like My Apostles knew Me one day, according to the flesh. It is an incentive for you to penetrate beyond appearances so that you acquire a loving contemplation, superior to the abstract and speculative knowledge of many philosophers.
>
> "You who visit Me at My Altars, should know that you are already treading the soil of the gardens of Paradise because even if it is true that Heaven is at the end, you are now more certain that it is your inheritance because through your faith, you are assured of real victory during your trials, tribulations and doubts."

One day during my meditation, I thought of how disconcerting it is to see the resistance of the world to the Good News, and their harsh opposition to the message of life and joy. It might seem as if a bitter resentment were mounting against Love…

Then I thought, how can I defend myself against the aggressor?

How often we clash with ignorance and indifference which often seem worse than aggressor.

Many times it upsets us to think that when we seek to bring the world close to the Love of God, instead of success, we receive persecution and so often we feel, like a heavy burden, the sensation of having failed in the undertaking…

I was startled to hear Jesus addressing my worries:

> "Through this union, I want to teach you not to give way to setbacks and fruitless lamenting, but rather to face the hatred of the world in an atmosphere of calm and joy, with the soul of a conqueror.
>
> "And do not be afraid. It was and always will be that way. Rather, rejoice the more you are persecuted because each time that the world abuses its victims, the latter penetrate further in their knowledge of Me and in their understanding of the cross.
>
> "I want to strengthen you in the faith, that you may learn to Love Me even more, through your visits, the secrets you confide, and your dialogues with Me, even though often you do not perceive them as such.
>
> "The soul that tends to be righteous, that is obedient to interior grace, opens itself fully to the light of the Spirit. It does not happen that way with souls that are selfish and unfaithful, because steeped in their knowledge and obstinate about being right, their glances become darkened, fleeing from the light of faith. It is the sin of darkness against the light.
>
> "Those words that I uttered: 'Come to Me' were and are directed to all souls without exception; to all those who suffer and carry burdens or traumas very difficult for them to

> shoulder. They are the words that promise them the most genuine consolation for their sufferings, and the most efficacious relief for their trials.
>
> "But you should know, My little children, that trials and sufferings accepted as having come from the hand of God and looked upon with supernatural judgment, open to you the doors of Heaven.
>
> "You understand all this when you spend moments in prayer before Me, and that is because I speak to your soul. Yet even though most of the time you are not aware of it, you leave those encounters with renewed energy and increased strength to face life with all its sufferings and humiliations."

On several occasions, Jesus made known that the path to Heaven was difficult and filled with self- sacrifices, that the life of human beings is a continual struggle, and that the gate to Heaven is narrow. On the other hand, from His Eucharistic Presence He now informs us that all that can be changed into something easy and smooth, "provided that we do so with Him, and assisted by Him."

On one occasion, while I was witnessing one of our brothers of the Apostolate visiting Jesus in the Sacrament, the Lord explained to me that the prime benefit of those visits is the granting of His peace to us, so that every difficult moment of our days may be faced with serenity. He said that He rewards the soul that responds to His invitation with countless earthly and spiritual benefits.

I recognized that indeed that person had changed a great deal since his visits to the Most Blessed Sacrament. Effectively, I confirmed how it was that the person, only by going to visit Jesus, goes on transforming his life.

Suddenly I saw that person as if in a globe of light, and I saw that while he was praying, the globe of light was growing, extending and reaching his wife and family. Suddenly I saw a car traveling at high speed. I saw it colliding and being destroyed. But the person who got out of the car was uninjured and surrounded by a halo a little brighter than the one enveloping the man who was praying before the Lord.

I realized that the Lord wanted to show me that God protects those beings that one loves. Prayer has so much value for Jesus, as well as the company that human beings willingly keep with Him at the tabernacle, that as a reward, He takes charge of their loved ones and of everything pertaining to them.

Late one Thursday afternoon, in another chapel, a priest was directing Eucharistic Adoration with his faithful. There were plenty of people in the Church. I was watching from outside and I saw a globe emerge, similar to the one previously described, but with red and white lights surrounding the entire periphery of the chapel. The people were praying with the priest, and those lights, like shock waves, were extending out to one or two city blocks, and then, to yet another and another block…

I looked in a different direction and managed to see two chapels relatively close to each other. From each of them those red and white waves were emerging and extending to the point where the rays from each chapel joined each other.

"My God," I thought. "that is the way a city and all its people are protected."

Jesus came to my help and said to me:

> "Write down these promises that I am telling you today:
>
> "I promise to the soul that visits Me frequently in this Sacrament of Love, that I will receive it affectionately together with all the Blessed and the Angels in Heaven, and that each of its visits will be written down in the *Book of Its Life* and I will grant to it:

1. Every petition that is presented before the Altar of God in favor of the Church, the Pope and consecrated souls.

2. The annulment of Satan's power over its person and its loved ones.
3. Special protection in case of earthquakes, hurricanes and other natural disasters which otherwise would affect it.
4. It will be lovingly withdrawn from the world and its attractions, which are the cause of perdition.
5. The elevation of its soul, desiring to attain sanctification, in virtuous eternal contemplation of My Face.
6. Relief of its loved ones from the pains of Purgatory.
7. My blessing on every material and spiritual project it undertakes, if they are for the good of its own soul.
8. Mother at the moment of its death.
9. To listen to and to look after the needs of the persons for whom it prays.
10. The intercession of the Saints and Angels at the hour of its death, in order to diminish temporal punishment.
11. That My Love will cause holy vocations consecrated to God among its loved ones and friends.
12. That the soul which preserves a genuine devotion to My Presence in the Eucharist will not be condemned or die without the Sacraments of the Church.

"To the priests and nuns that propagate the devotion of Adoration, I will grant many special graces, the complete recognition of their sins and the Grace to amend them. I will help them to form communities of devout and holy faithful, and they will attain many privileges.

"I promise these things to all persons, under only two conditions which are the fruit of genuine love towards My Real Presence in the Eucharist, and which are absolutely indispensable for My promises to become a reality in their lives:

- † That they strive to preserve the dignity of My Altars.
- † That they be merciful towards their neighbor."

John Paul Near the Throne

A long time before the visions inserted in this book began, the Lord permitted me to experience something very beautiful, made known to very few people previously. He wishes that I should be the one to record that experience in writing, here and now. I am only obeying because I know Jesus has a special reason for asking me to do so.

Early in the morning of the third of April, 2005, a short while after the death of His Holiness John Paul II had been announced, it is very difficult for me to describe the emotions that overcame my heart. I was in front of the Most Blessed Sacrament, praying all the decades of the Rosary.

When I got to the moment of praying for the intentions of the Holy Father, I broke down right there. I felt the bereavement that millions of Catholics would be experiencing, a feeling that was with me during the following days, until His Holiness Benedict XVI was nominated. Every time I prayed the Rosary, I said: "My God, we have no one to pray for! And I know that there will probably be many responses, but that was how I felt."

I wept a great deal. In less than two months time, my spiritual director had to leave my side in order to comply with his new obedience [i.e., a new assignment in his religious order], after having guided me for more than eight years, and now our spiritual Father whom I deeply loved, had just died.

I gazed at Jesus, begging compassion for that feeling of loneliness, for that sensation of dangling on a rope that was swinging dangerously, because the devil was stirring up a great deal of wind and filth.

Several hours went by and it was already morning when, almost finished with my prayers, I saw the wall at the back of the chapel disappear and the left side was greatly illuminated, attracting my eyes towards it. It was the Most Holy Virgin, clothed in white, wearing a long very light heavenly-blue veil, and a golden crown with many lights like diamonds in it. She looked beautiful and majestic, with that characteristic dignity of hers…

She was smiling and while gazing to one side, she spoke these words gently to me: "Daughter, do not weep. My beloved son is already with Me". A few steps behind Her, the place was also illuminated and I saw the Holy Father, John Paul II, very erect and a great deal younger, like he looked fifteen or twenty years before his death. He was smiling and clothed in a white tunic with a cape and something that appeared below his cape, at the height of his waist, like a golden cord. His face was filled with light, and he was smiling and very happy.

The vision vanished and I was left with a feeling of very great happiness and immense peace. When I looked again at Jesus in the Eucharist in front of me, I thanked Him with all my heart for that enormous gift.

I am convinced that if we still have brothers and sisters who are forsaking our Church, it is obviously because we are not witnessing in their presence. And we cannot be witnesses if we do not know the meaning of the deep Love of Jesus who wants to lower Himself to our miserable humanity, to give Himself as spiritual food and to live with us in the Holy Eucharist.

It is not necessary to read great treatises, although that would be the ideal thing for every Christian to do, but the Eucharistic legacy left to us by John Paul II is of enormous value. And now we even have the gift that Jesus has permitted: that of his successor, our present Pope Benedict XVI, being a man whose heart and thought are deeply rooted in the Eucharist.

To read something about what they have written and have said about this marvelous and unique Sacrament, to study the Word of God and to remain for a few minutes periodically, in meditating before His Divine Presence is enough to get to know what it is to live near a God who gazes at you from close by, listens to you, speaks to you, kisses you, wipes your tears away and smiles during your happy moments.

Let us know how to react and run to Him, before it is too late. We have only one life and it is not a rehearsal. It is the only performance of the play that continues with eternal life.

Beloved brothers and sisters, the moment has arrived for us to say "farewell." I want you to know that there is a Eucharistic community that will pray for you, for each one of you, the readers of this writing. Thanks only to these encounters with the Lord, there has there come to birth an Institute of consecrated life which makes intercession for all these testimonies to join many other testimonies of holy lives, for the Glory of God and the good of our Church.

I want to say "farewell" to you with a prayer of the one who endured every suffering and emerged from it strengthened and victorious. His strength came to birth in front of the Tabernacle, and with the loving hand of Mary; he walked to the cross, while guiding like the Good Shepherd, all the people of God.

For God and Heaven, there is no time or distance. For that reason, I invite you join me at this moment in placing yourself in the Presence of Jesus and of John Paul II, in order for us to raise this prayer together. God knows that it will be in full communion…

Prayers of the Servant of God: His Holiness John Paul II

Lord Jesus:

We come before you knowing that you call us and that you love us just as we are.

You have the words of eternal life and we have believed and acknowledged that you are the Son of God." (Jn. 6:69). Your presence in the Eucharist has begun with the sacrifice at the Last Supper, and it continues as communion and the giving of all that you are.

Increase our FAITH.

Through you and in the Holy Spirit who communicates to us, we want to reach the Father to say our YES to Him united to yours.

With you, we can now say: Our Father.

By following you, "the way, the truth and the life", we want to penetrate the apparent "silence" and "absence" of God, by tearing the cloud at Tabor in order to hear the voice of the Father who tells us: "This is my beloved Son, with whom I am pleased: Listen to him." (Mt. 17:5)

With this FAITH, born of contemplative listening, we will know how to shed light on our personal situations, as well as the different areas of our family and social life.

You are our HOPE, our peace, our mediator, friend and brother. Our heart is filled with hope and joy knowing that you live "forever interceding for us." (Heb. 7:5).

Our hope translates into trust, the joy of Easter and a quick path with you towards the Father. We want to feel as you do and value things as you value them. For you are the center, the beginning and the end of everything.

Supported in this HOPE, we want to infuse in the world this scale of evangelical values through which God and His salvific gifts occupy the prime place in the heart and in the activities of real life.

We want to LOVE LIKE YOU, who give life and make known everything that you are. We would like to say like Saint Paul: "My life is Christ" (Phil. 1:21).

Our lives make no sense without you. We want to learn to "be with the One whom we know loves us" because "with such a good friend present, every suffering can be endured." In you, we will learn to unite ourselves to the will of the Father, because during prayer "it is love that speaks" (St. Teresa).

Entering into intimacy with you, we want to adopt basic resolutions and attitudes, make hard decisions, and fundamental choices according to our very own Christian vocation.

BELIEVING, HOPING AND LOVING, WE ADORE YOU with an attitude of simple presence, silence and hope that will also be reparation, in response to your words: "Stay here and watch with Me" (Mt. 26:38).

You overcome the poverty of our thoughts, words and feelings;

for that reason, we want to learn to adore by admiring the mystery, loving it just as it is, and maintaining a friendly silence, with a generous presence.

The Holy Spirit that you have instilled in our hearts, helps us to utter those "inexpressible groanings" (Rom. 8:26) which translate into a simple and thankful attitude, and into the filial gesture of one who is now content with just your presence, your love and your word.

During our nights, physically and morally, if you are present and you love us and speak to us, that is already enough for us although often, we will not experience your consolation.

By learning this further dimension of ADORATION, we will be intimately in you, or in the "mystery" of you. Then our prayer will be translated into respect towards the "mystery" of every brother and sister, and of every event, in order to insert ourselves in our family and social atmosphere and to build history with this active and fruitful silence which is born of contemplation.

Thanks to you, our capacity for silence and adoration will change into a capacity to LOVE and to SERVE.

You have given us your Mother as ours, for Her to teach us to meditate and adore in our hearts. By receiving the Word and putting it into practice, She became the most perfect Mother.

Help us to be your missionary Church which knows how to meditate by adoring and loving your Word, in order to transform it into life and convey it to all brothers and sisters.

Amen.
John Paul II

Chapter 3

Holy Hour

IMPRIMATUR

As given to Catalina Rivas by the Blessed Virgin Mary, including traditional prayers and verses from Holy Scripture. Of this Devotion, the Archbishop of Cochabamba, Monsignor René Fernández Apaza, wrote in March 1998:

> May our Lord allow, in His infinite Mercy, that each prayer be pronounced from the heart, as our Blessed Virgin Mary has requested. That today's man, from whatever place our Lord has put him, may understand that Jesus must be the center of his life. That humanity rediscovers the value of the Holy Eucharist, the bread of life, to which Mary takes us.
>
> We are certain that the Most Blessed Virgin Mary will protect all the faithful, who unite themselves to her in this Holy Hour in petitioning the conversion of the world and in asking particularly for the longed, Ecclesiastical Renewal in order that our Church may truly be a communion of faith and fraternity.
>
> It is with pleasure that we authorize this publication, which was the initiative of the Apostolate of the New Evangelization, with the desire that it be put to practice with fervor, in order to attract Our Lord's blessings to His people on the vigil of the third Christian millennium.
>
> Monsignor René Fernández Apaza
> ARCHBISHOP OF COCHABAMBA
> Cochabamba, Bolivia - March 1, 1998

Adoration

Eternal Father, I thank You because Your infinite Love has saved me, even against my own will. Thank You, my Father, for Your immense patience, which has waited for me. Thank You, my God, for Your incommensurate compassion, which has had pity on me. The only return I can make to you in payment for all that You have given me is my weakness, my pain and my misery.

I am before You, Spirit of Love, you who are an ever-burning fire, and I want to remain in Your adorable presence. I want to make reparation for my faults, renew myself in the fervor of my consecration, and render to You my homage of praise and adoration.

Blessed Jesus, I am before You and I want to draw from Your Divine Heart countless graces for me and for all souls, for the Holy Church, and for your priests and religious. Grant, Oh Jesus, that these hours be truly hours of intimacy, hours of love in which I will be granted to receive all the graces that Your Divine Heart has reserved for me.

Virgin Mary, Mother of God and my Mother, I unite myself to you, and beg of you to have me share in the feelings of Your Immaculate Heart.

My God, I believe, I adore, I trust and I love You. I ask pardon for those who do not believe, do not adore, do not trust and do not love You.

Most Holy Trinity, Father, Son and Holy Spirit, I adore You profoundly and I offer You the Body, Blood, Soul and Divinity of Jesus Christ, present in all the tabernacles of the world, in reparation for the outrages, sacrileges and indifferences whereby He is offended. And through the infinite merits of His Most Sacred Heart and the Immaculate Heart of Mary, I beg of You the conversion of poor sinners.

Act of Faith and Adoration

I believe, O Jesus, with my liveliest faith that You are present, here, in front of me, under the Eucharistic Species. You, the Eternal

Word of the Father, are begotten from all eternity and incarnate in the womb of the Virgin Mother. Jesus Christ, Redeemer and King, I truly believe that You are present in the ineffable truth of Your Divinity and Your Humanity.

Jesus, You are the same Jesus of Bethlehem, the Divine Child, who for my sake will accept banishment, poverty and persecution. You are the Jesus of Nazareth, who for my love, embraced concealment, hardships and obedience. You are the Divine Teacher, who came to teach me the sweet truths of the Faith, to bring the great commandment of love: Your Commandment. You are the Merciful Savior, the One who bends over all my miseries with infinite understanding and moving kindness, always ready to forgive, to heal, to renew. You are the Holy Victim immolated for the glory of the Father and the good of all souls. You are the Jesus, who sweated blood for me in the Garden of Gethsemane; who suffered for me the condemnation of human tribunals, the most painful flagellation, the cruel and humiliating crowning of thorns, the cruel martyrdom of the crucifixion. You are He, who wanted to agonize and to die for me. You are the Risen Jesus, the vanquisher of death, of sin and of hell, who longs to communicate the treasures of Divine Life, which You possess in all its fullness.

My Jesus, You are here, present in the Consecrated Holy Host, with a Heart overflowing with tenderness, a Heart, which loves infinitely. In Your Heart, Jesus, I find the infinite Love, the Divine Charity - God, the beginning of Life - existent and alive. How sweet it is for me, My God, Trinity most blessed, to worship You in this Tabernacle where You are now!

Therefore, I join the angels and the saints, who invisible but present and vigilant around Your Tabernacle, adore You incessantly. I join, above all, Your most holy Mother, and her feelings of profound adoration and intense love, that sprang from her soul from the first instant of Your Incarnation, when she carried You in her immaculate womb.

And while I worship You in this Tabernacle, I do so in all the Tabernacles of the world and especially in those where You are most abandoned and forgotten. I adore you in each Consecrated Host that exists between Heaven and Earth.

I worship You, God the Father, because through Christ, You have descended to my humanity, and because through His adorable Heart, You have united Yourself so closely to man, to me, a poor ingrate creature. I adore You in this church sanctified by the ever current Presence of Your Divine Being. I prostrate myself in profound adoration before Your Sovereign Majesty. Yet, at the same time, love draws me up to You.

I worship You, God the Father, and I love You. My love and my adoration are totally mixed and combined in my soul, so much that I could not tell whether I love more than I adore or adore more than I love. I adore You because I find in You: all power, all holiness, justice and wisdom. You are My Creator and My God. I love You because I find in You all beauty, all kindness, all tenderness and all mercy. I love You because You have given me, as a present, an invaluable treasure.

Jesus is my Treasure. He is mine and at any moment I can draw graces from Him with full hands, since I find this Treasure always abundant. I take all I need from Him, in order to pay my debts, to meet my needs, to find delight, to earn a crown. What an ineffable gift is this Jesus, whose Heart overflows with all tenderness! A treasure, which is never depleted, the more I take, the more He gives.

O God the Father, You have loved your creatures so much, that You gave them Your only Son. In order that the majesty of Your Word would imbue us with fear and our souls could address Him with confidence, You clothed Him with flesh like ours. You adorned Him with the most attractive graces. Above all, You gave Him an infinitely perfect Heart, such, that It had to be the abode of Your delights, because in this Heart lives Your Divine Fullness, and in It the most humble of creatures has a place of privilege.

That adored Heart is as immense as Yourself, My God, because It contains You. It is also my dwelling place, since It loves me. In It I meet Your Divinity, and upon seeing me in this sacred refuge, Your just wrath is placated and Your Justice is disarmed.

I adore You, God the Father, through Jesus and in Jesus. I worship Jesus, Your Son, who by His Humanity is My Brother and by His Divinity is My God. I love You through Jesus and with Jesus. I love You through the Heart of Jesus, made mine by love. I love You in Jesus. Through Him my love reaches You. Through Him I can reach You and embrace You.

Response (R/): My God, I acknowledge that You are infinite kindness and I believe in Your Love for me.

† In the sublime mystery of the unity of Your Nature and the Trinity of Your Persons, R/.

† In the harmony of Your innumerable Perfections, R/.

† In the inexhaustible wealth, with which you make beings out of nothing, R/.

† In the peaceful possession of Your eternal Happiness, R/.

† In the infinite Wisdom, with which You govern all things, R/.

† In the unfathomable kindness, with which You elevate man to the dignity of being Your child, R/.

† In the infinite Mercy, with which You tolerate and conserve the sinner, R/.

† In the mysterious decree by which Redemption was established, R/.

† In the infinite debasing of Your Incarnation, R/.

† In the humiliations, the concealment and the labors of Your earthly life, R/.

† In the ignominy of Your Passion and Death, R/.

- † In the glory of Your Resurrection, of Your Ascension and of Your triumph in the heavens, R/.
- † In Your Divine Heart opened by a lance on Calvary, R/.
- † In Your Divine Heart revealed to Your saints in the course of the centuries, R/.
- † In Your Divine Heart, beating with Love for us in Your adorable Chest, present in our Tabernacles, R/.
- † In Your Divine Heart, overflowing with Mercy for poor sinners, especially in the Sacrament of Penance, R/.
- † In Your priesthood, which in the course of the centuries continues Your work of Love and Salvation, R/.
- † In Your Vicar, Your visible representative on earth, R/.
- † In the Church, which conserves and dispenses the treasures of Your Divine Grace to souls, R/.
- † In its infallible Magisterium, its wise ruling, and its unfathomable power to sanctify, R/.
- † In Most Holy Mary, Your Mother, enriched with so many privileges and also established as our Mother, Coredemptrix and Advocate, R/.
- † In the exuberant fruitfulness with which You produce saints, R/.
- † In the moving generosity with which You dispense Your gifts, R/.
- † In the mysterious work of grace in the intimacy of the soul, R/.
- † In the purifying gift of Your Cross, R/.
- † In the marvelous Providence, with which You follow each creature through the course of his life, R/.
- † In Your infinite Glory, which You communicate to Your elect, making them eternally happy in Heaven, R/.

Lord, in the recitation of the Gloria at Holy Mass, the Church invites me to give You thanks for Your infinite glory. She invites me to thank You, to glorify You and to praise You for all that You are, My God. For this reason I take pleasure in repeating: I give You thanks for You Are Infinite Love.

After having prostrated myself to worship You in the Heart of Jesus, I want to give You thanks. I thank You, my God, because You are Love, and I thank You for all the gifts of Your Love. And since it is through Jesus that You have given us the most precious gifts, the gifts of supernatural life, it is also through Him, with Him and in Him, that I want to lift up to You this hymn of thanksgiving.

In union with Jesus I thank You, God the Father, for all the personal graces You have bestowed upon me. You gave me life, bringing me out of the void. You have conserved my life, day after day up to this moment. But You have given me another more valuable life, the life of grace, which makes me share in Your own Divine Life. And after the first grace, with which You sanctified me on the day of my Baptism, I have received from You so many more graces that have conserved, increased and, perhaps, regained my supernatural life!

I think of the gifts of Your Love, which I have enjoyed so abundantly:

- † In the Church You have given me as my teacher and guide towards eternity.
- † In the priests who have conferred on me the gifts of Your Love.
- † In the forgiveness, continually renewed.
- † In the Eucharist, which has been my nourishment, strength and consolation.
- † In the Virgin Mary, who is my good Mother, my consoler, my help and my special protector during every instant of my life.

- † In the Paradise You have prepared for me, which with Your grace, I hope to reach.

I look at my life, sown with joys and sorrows, and I understand that all in it has been Love. All of it, O My God, because from Your Loving Heart nothing but Grace and Love can flow:

- † **For all these things,** R/: I thank You, my God.
- † For all the gladness You have allowed me to enjoy; as well as for all the sorrows and trials You have scattered on my path, R/.
- † For the known, as well as for the unknown graces, R/.
- † For the favors of the past and for those in the future, R/.
- † For all You have done in me and for me and for all that You will still want to do in the future, R/.
- † Above all for calling me to the knowledge of Your Love and to consecrate myself to It, R/.
- † For Your Light and Joy, of which I am far from being worthy, R/.
- † For the light and joy that the knowledge of Your Love has brought to my life, R/.
- † For the possession of Your Love, which makes You mine, and makes me Yours, R/.

But I do not want and ought not to give thanks for myself only. I give You thanks also for all the gifts which Your Love has poured out on the Church. I give You thanks for all the benefits granted to the angels and to the saints, perpetual praises of Your Love. And I thank You above all, for the innumerable benefits granted to Most Holy Mary, our sweet Mother. I thank You for having made Her so great, so holy, so beautiful. I thank You for the privileges that You have given Her and for the throne of glory, on which You have placed Her.

I give You thanks for having made of this creature of Your predilection, a Mother in whom I can and should place all my hopes.

In order to offer a more efficacious thanksgiving, I permit myself, O Lord, to liven it with my love. Therefore, I tell You again and again that I love You with all my heart, with all my soul, with all my mind and with all my strength:

† You, who are infinite Love, R/: I love You, my God.

† You, who have saved me by Your Love, R/.

† You, who command me to love You, R/.

† With all my heart, R/.

† With all my soul, R/.

† With all my spirit, R/.

† With all my strength, R/.

† Above all possessions and honors, R/.

† Above all pleasures and joys, R/.

† More than myself and all that belongs to me, R/.

† More than my parents and friends, R/.

† More than all men and angels, R/.

† Above all created things in Heaven and on earth, R/.

† Only for Yourself, R/.

† Because You are the utmost Goodness, R/.

† Because You are infinitely worthy of being loved, R/.

† Because You are infinitely Perfect, R/.

† Even if You had not promised me Paradise, R/.

† Even if You did not threaten me with hell, R/.

- † Even if You tried me with misery and misfortune, R/.
- † In abundance and in poverty, R/.
- † In prosperity and in misfortune, R/.
- † In honors and in scorns, R/.
- † In joys and in pain, R/.
- † In health and in sickness, R/.
- † In life and in death, R/.
- † In time and in eternity, R/.
- † In union with the love, with which all the saints and angels love You in Heaven, R/.
- † In union with the love, with which the Blessed Virgin Mary loves You, R/.
- † In union with the infinite Love, with which You eternally love us, R/.

O My God, You who possesses in an unfathomable abundance all that is perfect and worthy of love, extinguish in me all culpable, sensual and inordinate love towards creatures. Ignite in my heart the most pure fire of Your Love so that I may love only You, for You, to the point of being consumed in Your Most Holy Love, so that I may go, together with the chosen, to love You eternally in Heaven. Amen.

Lord, now I want to make atonement before You. O Jesus, Divine Victim of our altars, great and only Atoner, I also unite myself to You in order to perform with You and through You, the role of a small atoning soul.

And I also call upon You, O my Mother, that just as You offered Your Jesus to the Father at the same time that He immolated Himself for His Glory and for the salvation of souls at Calvary, may You renew at this moment, that mystical offering in my place.

Offer in the chalice of Your Immaculate Heart, O sweet Virgin, the sorrows of Jesus together with Yours in order to invoke Divine Mercy on me and on the whole world. After having thanked You for your endless gifts, how could I not be troubled at the sight of my many faults and infidelities? How ungrateful and cold I have been in response to Your benefits!

Prostrated before You [Jesus], who has loved me so much, filled with confusion and regret, I beseech Your Pardon and Your Mercy:

- † For the misuse I made of the natural gifts I received from You: my life, my energy, my time, my senses, my intelligence, my tongue, R/. O Jesus, have mercy on me!
- † For the great and small acts of disobedience to Your law, R/.
- † For the duties, disregarded or carelessly completed, R/.
- † For the good I could have done and have not done, R/.
- † For allowing many times the triumph of bad inclinations in me; of pride, vanity and egoism, R/.
- † For not having practiced Your commandment of charity as You ordained it, R/.
- † For having left barren in me so many graces, R/.
- † For the lukewarmness with which I practiced my life of piety, R/.
- † For the indifference and coldness with which I responded to Your gifts of Love, R/.
- † For having many times preferred the creatures and human satisfactions to You and Your consolations, R/.
- † For the little fidelity and generosity with which I have lived my consecration, R/.
- † For the lack of faith in Your Love and the abandonment of It, R/.

✝ For the lack of dedication to souls and to the Church, R/.

✝ For my rebelliousness and lack of love for Your Will, and Your Cross, R/.

I lose myself in Your Presence, O my God.
I kneel at Your Feet.

I prostrate myself in front of You, O Jesus, Divine Host, My Redeemer and Savior, as did Mary Magdalene. And even though it is true that I am unworthy of Your Love, I am certain that You will have for me the same merciful tenderness.

Psalm 51 (50) - The Miserere

Have mercy on me, God, in your kindness.
In your compassion blot out my offenses.
O wash me more and more from my guilt
And cleanse me from my sin.

My offenses truly I know them;
My sin is always before me.
Against you, you alone, have I sinned;
What is evil in your sight I have done.
That you may be justified when you give sentence
And be without reproach when you judge.
O see, in guilt I was born,
A sinner was I conceived.

Indeed you love truth in the heart;
Then in the secret of my heart teach me wisdom.
O purify me, then I shall be clean;
O wash me, I shall be whiter than snow.
Make me hear rejoicing and gladness,
That the bones you have crushed may revive.
From my sins turn away your face
And blot out all my guilt.
A pure heart create for me, O God,

Put a steadfast spirit within me.
Do not cast me away from your presence,
Nor deprive me of your Holy Spirit.

Give me again the joy of your help;
With a spirit of fervor sustain me,
That I may teach transgressors your ways
And sinners may return to you.

O rescue me, God my helper,
And my tongue shall ring out your goodness.
O Lord, open my lips
And my mouth shall declare your praise.

For in sacrifice you take no delight,
Burnt offerings from me you would refuse,
My sacrifice, a contrite spirit.
A humbled, contrite heart you will not spurn.

In your goodness, show favor to Zion:
Rebuild the walls of Jerusalem.
Then you would be pleased with lawful sacrifice,
Holocausts offered on your altar.

Glory be to the Father, and to the Son, and to the Holy Spirit, as it was in the beginning, is now, and ever shall be, world without end. Amen.

Being confident that in Your infinite Mercy You have granted me pardon for my countless faults, offenses and acts of negligence, I dare, O Jesus, to also ask pardon for my brothers and sisters.

I think of the untold number of sins being committed in the world, day after day, by individuals and by nations: sins committed by rulers and by subjects; sins of pride, sensuality and covetousness; and sins of thought, word, deed and omission.

For all these sins and for all the poor wretches who commit

them, I dare to ask You, O Jesus, for the outpouring of Your infinite Mercy. It is our sins that caused You to agonize in the Garden of Olives, and to submerge Your most Holy Soul in a sea of sadness.

Do not forget, O Jesus, that You freely wanted to take up our burden, that You wanted to become sin in order to erase ours. Do not forget, O Jesus, that You offered Yourself to the wrath of the Father in order to rescue Your guilty brothers.

O Jesus, I beg You to renew Your offering to the Father by again presenting Your wounds to Him. Show Him the thorns, the scourging and the nails that pierced Your Flesh, but especially let Him see Your wounded Heart, overflowing with Love for Him and for us, and ask His forgiveness.

Remember, O Jesus, that greater than all our faults is Your Mercy. Pour It, O Jesus, over this guilty world. Seek out the sheep that have strayed away from the herd, and show them the great power of Your saving Love.

And since Your Heart is wounded by the faults of those nearest to You, I beseech Your Forgiveness, O Jesus, for those who renew the kiss of Judas or the denial of Peter. May none carry out Judas's desperate action, but may Your Grace prompt them, as it did Peter, to a reparation of love.

The Litany of the Sacred Hearts of Jesus

† Lord, have mercy. R/: Lord, have mercy.

† Christ, have mercy. R/: Christ, have mercy.

† Lord, have mercy. R/: Lord, have mercy.

† Christ, hear us. R/: Christ, hear us.

† Christ, graciously hear us. R/: Christ graciously hear us.

† God, the Father of Heaven, R/: Have mercy on us.

† God the Son, Redeemer of the world, R/: Have mercy on us.

† God the Holy Spirit, R/: Have mercy on us.

† Holy Trinity, one God, R/: Have mercy on us.

† Heart of Jesus, Son of the Eternal Father, R/: Have mercy on us.

† Heart of Jesus, formed by the Holy Spirit in the womb of the Virgin Mother, R/: Have mercy on us.

† Heart of Jesus, substantially united to the Word of God, R/: Have mercy on us.

† Heart of Jesus, of Infinite Majesty, R/: Have mercy on us.

† Heart of Jesus, Sacred Temple of God, R/: Have mercy on us.

† Heart of Jesus, Tabernacle of the Most High, R/: Have mercy on us.

† Heart of Jesus, House of God and Gate of Heaven, R/: Have mercy on us.

† Heart of Jesus, burning furnace of charity, R/: Have mercy on us.

† Heart of Jesus, abode of justice and love, R/: Have mercy on us.

† Heart of Jesus, full of goodness and love, R/: Have mercy on us.

† Heart of Jesus, abyss of all virtues, R/: Have mercy on us.

† Heart of Jesus, most worthy of all praise, R/: Have mercy on us.

† Heart of Jesus, king and center of all hearts, R/: Have mercy on us.

† Heart of Jesus, in whom are all treasures of wisdom and knowledge, R/: Have mercy on us.

- † Heart of Jesus, in whom dwells the fullness of divinity, R/: Have mercy on us.
- † Heart of Jesus, in whom the Father was well pleased, R/: Have mercy on us.
- † Heart of Jesus, of whose fullness we have all received, R/: Have mercy on us.
- † Heart of Jesus, desire of the everlasting hills, R/: Have mercy on us.
- † Heart of Jesus, patient and most merciful, R/: Have mercy on us.
- † Heart of Jesus, enriching all who invoke Thee, R/: Have mercy on us.
- † Heart of Jesus, fountain of life and holiness, R/: Have mercy on us.
- † Heart of Jesus, propitiation for our sins, R/: Have mercy on us.
- † Heart of Jesus, loaded down with opprobrium, R/: Have mercy on us.
- † Heart of Jesus, bruised for our offenses, R/: Have mercy on us.
- † Heart of Jesus, obedient to death, R/: Have mercy on us.
- † Heart of Jesus, pierced with a lance, R/: Have mercy on us.
- † Heart of Jesus, source of all consolation, R/: Have mercy on us.
- † Heart of Jesus, our life and resurrection, R/: Have mercy on us.
- † Heart of Jesus, our peace and reconciliation, R/: Have mercy on us.

- † Heart of Jesus, victim for our sins, R/: Have mercy on us.
- † Heart of Jesus, salvation of those who trust in Thee, R/: Have mercy on us.
- † Heart of Jesus, hope of those who die in Thee, R/: Have mercy on us.
- † Heart of Jesus, delight of all the Saints, R/: Have mercy on us.
- † Lamb of God, who takes away the sins of the world, R/: spare us, O Lord.
- † Lamb of God, who takes away the sins of the world, R/: graciously hear us, O Lord.
- † Lamb of God, who takes away the sins of the world, R/: have mercy on us, O Lord.
- † Jesus meek and humble of heart, R/: Make our hearts like to Thine.
- † Sacred Heart of Jesus, R/: I trust in You.
- † Holy Heart of Mary, R/: rescue my soul.
- † Jesus and Mary, I love You with all my soul, save souls, and save my soul.

Supplication

Before leaving this Holy Tabernacle I want, O my Jesus, to have recourse to Your Divine Heart's infinite wealth.

Consecrated to Your Love, I believe that I can ask for nothing better than the fulfillment of Your own desires. It is Your Divine Desires that I want to present to the Father, before the conclusion of this time of graces, and beg Him in Your Name, to answer them.

The first desire of Jesus is the salvation of souls: to redeem the world by means of love, to establish the Kingdom of infinite Love throughout the earth.

Allow me then, O Jesus, to express my ardent wish that the Kingdom of Your Love be established all over the earth. O infinite Love, living in the Divine Heart of Jesus, make Yourself known to men so that men may love You, as You want to be loved.

The second desire of Jesus is to make use of priests for this great work, to make of them active laborers, and by means of them, to work in souls and in the world.

O Jesus, eternal Priest and Savior of the world, in order to realize this burning desire of Your Heart, multiply vocations, and send many holy workers to Your harvest.

O Jesus, make every priest an authentic sower of Your Love.

I beg You for the Holy Father, for the bishops, for all the priests who have helped me, for all priests.

I ask You, O Jesus, to sustain them during battle, to comfort them in loneliness, to encourage them in their failures, to make their hardships fruitful, and to pour into their hearts your Divine Heart's Love.

† Lord, to watch over Your honor and glory, R/: Give us holy priests.

† Lord, to increase our faith, R/.

† Lord, to sustain Your Church, R/.

† Lord, to preach Your doctrine, R/.

† Lord, to defend Your cause, R/.

† Lord, to counteract error, R/.

† Lord, to annihilate the sects, R/.

† Lord, to uphold the truth, R/.

† Lord, to guide our souls, R/.

† Lord, to improve habits, R/.

- † Lord, to vanish vices, R/.
- † Lord, to illuminate the world, R/.
- † Lord, to teach the riches of Your Heart, R/.
- † Lord, to teach us to love the Holy Spirit, R/.
- † Lord, to have all Your ministers become the light of the world and the salt of the earth, R/.

O Jesus, Holy Priest, we ask You with the greatest humility in our souls to increase priestly vocations and to form them according to the designs of Your loving Heart. Only then will we obtain holy priests, and there will soon be in the world only one flock and only one Shepherd. Amen.

Concluding Prayer

O Jesus, Eternal Priest, Divine Victim, who moved by an impulse of incomparable Love for men, Your brothers, You made Your Heart bring forth the Christian priesthood. Deem worthy to continue pouring over Your ministers the life-giving torrents of Your infinite Love.

Live in Your priests. Transform them into You. Make them, by Your Grace, instruments of Your Mercy. Work in them and through them. Grant that after having clothed themselves completely in You, by the faithful imitation of Your Divine Virtues, they may accomplish the same works that You Yourself accomplished for the salvation of the world, in Your Name and by the power of Your Spirit.

Divine Redeemer of souls, look how great is the multitude of those who still sleep in the darkness of error. Count the number of the straying sheep, who walk amidst steep cliffs. Consider the throngs of the poor, the hungry, the ignorant and the feeble, who groan in the neglect.

Come back to us, Lord, through Your priests. Truly live again in them. Work through them, and walk again in the world, teaching, forgiving, consoling, sacrificing and renewing the sacred links of love, between the Heart of God and the heart of man. Amen.

Grant, O Jesus, that the labor of Your Love may always be in complete accordance with the purposes, for which You intended. Grant that it expands and consolidates itself, and that it conquers all souls for the sweetest Kingdom of Your Love.

O Jesus, I have asked for Your Kingdom. I do not need to ask for myself, for everything will be given to me. You know what I need. Look, and do what Your Heart suggests. I put my trust in Your Heart. I abandon myself to Your sweet Providence, and I give You thanks for the gift of these hours of intimacy with You. I thank You in union with Mary, for all the benefits that Your Love has yet reserved for me, in time, and in eternity.

The Blessed Mother's Canticle "The Magnificat"

My soul proclaims the greatness of the Lord, and my spirit rejoices in God, my savior; for He has looked upon the lowliness of His handmaid.

From now on all generations shall call me Blessed, for the Almighty has done great things for me.

Holy is His Name, and His mercy is on His faithful from generation to generation.

He shows mighty deeds with His Arm: He scatters the proud of heart, He throws down the mighty from their thrones, and raises the lowly to high places.

He fills the hungry with good things, while the rich he sends away empty.

He helps Israel, His servant, ever mindful of His Mercy, as He had promised our fathers, in favor of Abraham and his descendants forever.

Glory be to the Father, and to the Son, and to the Holy Spirit, as it was in the beginning, is now, and ever shall be, world without end. Amen.

IMPRIMATUR:

We have read Catalina's books and we are sure that their only objective is to guide us all on a journey of authentic spirituality, founded on the Gospel of Christ. The books likewise highlight the special place occupied by the Blessed Virgin Mary, our role model in loving and following Jesus Christ, our Mother to whom we should offer our complete trust and love.

In renewing the love and devotion to the Holy Catholic Church, the books enlighten us on the actions that should characterize a truly committed Christian.

For all this, I authorize their edition and distribution, and recommend them as texts of meditation and spiritual orientation, with the purpose of answering Our Lord's calling to save many souls, showing them that He is a living God, full of love and mercy.

Mons. René Fernández Apaza
Archbishop of Cochabamba
April 2, 1998
The Passion
"Love Him totally, He who totally surrendered
Himself for your love." - Clare of Assisi

Chapter 4

The Passion

Reflections that Jesus makes on the mystery of His suffering and the value it has on Redemption.

Jesus Dictates to Catalina

My little daughter, let yourself be embraced by My most ardent desire that all souls come and purify themselves in the water of penance, and that the feelings of trust, and not fear, may penetrate them, because I am a God of Mercy and I am always ready to receive them in My Heart.

Thus, day by day, we shall be uniting ourselves in our secret of love. A tiny spark and then a great flame... Only real Love is not loved today! Make Love be loved! But before that, pray, little daughter, much for the consecrated souls who have lost their enthusiasm and joy in doing service. Pray also for those priests who accomplish that miracle of miracles on the altar and whose faith is weak.

Lose yourself in Me like a drop of water in the ocean... When I created you, I kissed your forehead, marking you with the sign of My predilection. Seek souls because there are few who love Me; seek souls and impress on their minds the vision of the pain that consumed. Mankind, without knowing it, is about to receive great gifts.

When you do what I ask, I am near you; it is as if you quenched that burning thirst which dried even My lips when I was on the Cross.

I will make Myself present each time that you invoke My Passion with love. I will permit you to live united to Me in the sorrow that I experienced in Gethsemane when I knew the sins of all mankind.

Be conscious of that because I call few creatures to this kind of Passion, but none of them understand the predilection I have placed upon them by joining them to Me in the most painful hour of My earthly life.

Jesus Prepares Himself

There are souls who consider about My Passion, but very few who think about My preparation for My public life: My loneliness!

The forty days that I spent on the mountainside were the most distressing days of My life because I spent them completely alone, preparing My Spirit for what would come. I suffered hunger, thirst, discouragement, and bitterness. I knew that for those people, My sacrifice would be useless since they would deny Me. In that solitude, I perceived that neither My new doctrine nor My sacrifices and miracles could save the Jewish people who would become God-slayers.

Nevertheless, I had to carry out My duty, the Divine Mission. I had to first leave My seed and die later. How sad this is, looking at it from the human point of view!

I was also a man and felt sadness and anguish. I found Myself very alone! I mortified My Body by fasting and My Spirit by prayer. I prayed for all humanity who would deny Me, who would sacrifice Me so many times…

I was tempted as any other mortal, and Satan was never more curious to know who the man was that remained so alone and so abandoned.

Think about everything that I had to suffer to save man, to be able to reign in his heart, to make possible his entrance into My Father's Kingdom.

The Last Supper

Now let us go to the story of My Passion... The story that will give glory to the Father and holiness to other chosen souls...

The night before I was handed over was a night full of joy because of the Paschal Supper, the inauguration of the Eternal Banquet at which human beings must sit to feed themselves of Me.

If I were to ask Christians, "What do you think of this Supper," surely many would say that it is the place of their delight, but few would say that it is My delight... There are souls who take Communion, not for the joy that they experience but for the joy that I feel; they are few because the rest of them only come to Me to ask for gifts and favors.

I embrace all the souls that come to Me because I came to Earth to make the love with which I embrace them grow. And since love does not grow without sorrows, little by little, I withdraw the sweetness to leave the souls in dryness. And this is so that they fast from their own joy to make them understand that they must keep their light focused on another desire: Mine.

Why do you talk about dryness as if it were a sign of diminishment of My Love? Have you forgotten that if I do not give happiness, you must taste your dryness and other sorrows?

Come to Me, souls, but think only that I am who wills everything and who incites you to look for Me. If you only knew how much I value unselfish love and how it will be acknowledged in Heaven! O, how greatly the soul who possesses it shall rejoice!

Learn from Me, dear souls, to love only to give joy to the One who loves you... You will have sweetness and much more than what you leave behind; you shall enjoy so much of everything that I have made you capable of. It is I who prepared the Banquet for you. I am the food! How, then, can I let you sit at My table and leave you fasting? I promised you that whoever feeds on Me will no longer hunger... I serve Myself of things in order to reveal My Love to you. Follow those called to act as My priests to you, who take the occasion of this Paschal feast to lead you to Me, but do not linger over what is human; otherwise, you will nullify the other purpose of this feast.

Nobody can say that My Supper has become their nourishment when they only experience sweetness... For Me, love grows with denial of self.

Many are priests because I wished to make them My ministers, not because they truly follow Me... Pray for them! They should offer My Father the sorrow that I felt when in the Temple I overturned the benches of the merchants and I reproached the ministers of that time for having turned the house of God into opportunists.

When they asked Me under what authority had I done that, I felt an even greater sorrow upon confirming that the worst denial of My Mission came precisely from My ministers.

For that reason, pray for the priests that treat My Body with a sense of habit and, therefore, with very little love.

You will soon know that I had to tell you this because I love you and because I promise anyone who prays for My priests, the remission of all due temporal punishment. There will be no Purgatory for those who grieve because of lukewarm priests, but rather Paradise immediately after their last breath.

And now, let Me embrace you again in order for you to receive the life that I, with infinite joy, made you part of.

That night with infinite Love, I washed the feet of My Apostles because it was the culminating moment in which to present My Church to the world.

I wanted My souls to know that even when they may be burdened with the greatest sins, they are not excluded from graces. They are close to My most faithful souls; they are in My Heart, receiving the graces that they need.

What anguish I experienced at that moment knowing that in My Apostle Judas was represented so many souls who gathered at My feet and cleansed so many times with My Blood, were yet to be lost! At that moment, I wanted to teach sinners that because they have sinned, they should not distance themselves from Me thinking that they no longer have recourse and that they will never be loved as before they sinned. Poor souls! These are not the feelings of a God who has shed all His Blood for you. Come to Me all of you and fear not because I love you. I will cleanse you with My Blood and you will be as white as snow. I will drown your sins in the water of My Mercy and nothing will be able to snatch from My Heart the Love that I have for you.

My beloved, I have not chosen you in vain, respond to My election with generosity. Be faithful and firm in the faith. Be meek and humble so that others may know the greatness of My humility.

The Depth of Jesus' Love

Nobody really believes that I sweat blood that night at Gethsemane, and few believe that I suffered much more in those hours than in the Crucifixion. It was more sorrowful because it was clearly revealed to Me that the sins of everyone were made Mine and that I should answer for each one. Thus I, being innocent, answered to the Father as if I were really guilty of dishonesty and I, being pure, answered to the Father as if I were stained of all the impurities committed by you, My brothers and sisters. You dishonor God who created you to be instruments of the greatness of Creation and not to stray from the nature given you with the purpose of having it gradually behold the sight of the purity Me, your Creator.

Therefore, I was made a thief, a murderer, an adulterer, a liar, a sacrilegious person, a blasphemer, slanderer and a rebel to the Father whom I have always loved.

It was precisely this contrast between My Love for the Father and His Will that caused My sweating blood. But I obeyed until the end and for love of everyone, I covered Myself with the stain so that I could do My Father's Will and save you from eternal damnation.

Consider how many agonies more than human I had that night and, believe Me, nobody could alleviate such anguish because, on the contrary, I was seeing how each one of you devoted yourself to making cruel at every moment the death given to Me because of the offenses whose ransom I have paid in full. I want it to be known once again how I loved all mankind at that hour of abandonment and indescribable sadness…

Jesus Institutes the Holy Eucharist

The desire that souls be clean when they receive Me in the Sacrament of Love led Me to wash the feet of My Apostles. I also did it to represent the Sacrament of Penance, in which the souls that have had the misfortune of falling into sin, can wash themselves and regain their lost purity.

When washing their feet, I wanted to teach the souls that have apostolic tasks, to humble themselves and treat with tenderness the sinners and all souls entrusted to them.

I wrapped Myself in linen to teach them that, in order to achieve success with souls, one has to gird oneself with mortification and self-denial. I wanted them to learn mutual charity and how the faults they observed in their neighbor should be cleansed, concealing them and always forgiving them without ever disclosing their faults. The water that I poured over My Apostles' feet was a reflection of the zeal that consumed My Heart in desires for the salvation of mankind.

At that moment, the love that I felt for mankind was infinite, and I did not want to leave them orphans… In order to live with you until the consummation of time and to show you, My Love, I wanted to be your breath, your life, your support, your everything! Then I saw all the souls that, in the course of time, would be nourished by My Body and Blood, and I saw all the divine effects that this nourishment would produce in many souls…

That immaculate Blood would engender purity and virginity in many souls; in others, it would light the fire of love and zeal. Many martyrs of love gathered at that hour before My eyes and in My Heart! Many other souls, after having committed many, and serious sins and weakened by the force of passions, would come to Me to renew their strength with the Bread of the strong!

How I would like to make known the feelings of My Heart to all souls! How much I desire that they know the Love I felt for them at the Cenacle when I instituted the Holy Eucharist. Nobody could penetrate the feelings in My Heart during those moments - feelings of love, joy, tenderness... But also immense was the bitterness that invaded My Heart.

Are you perhaps good ground for the construction of a magnificent building? Yes and no... Yes, because of the gifts that I have made for you since birth; no, because of the use that you have made of them. Do you think that your ground is adequate in proportion to the structure of the building that I raise? Oh, it is paltry! Then, in spite of all the opposing elements that exist in you, My calculations will not fail because it is My skill to choose that which is poor for the purpose that I intend. I never make a mistake because I use skill and love. I construct actively without your realizing it. Your own desire to know what I am doing serves Me for proving to you that you can do nothing and know nothing without My desiring it...

It is time to work; do not ask Me for anything because there is someone who is thinking about you.

I want to tell My souls the bitterness, the tremendous sorrow that filled My Heart that night. Although My joy was great at accompanying mankind until the end of time and in becoming the Divine Nourishment of souls, and of seeing how many would render Me homage of adoration, love, and reparation, great was the sadness that caused Me to contemplate all those souls that were to abandon Me at the Tabernacle and how many would doubt My presence in the Eucharist.

In how many hearts stained, impure and completely torn by sin I would have to enter! And how My profaned Flesh and Blood, would become the reason for the damnation of so many souls! You cannot understand the way in which I contemplated all the sacrileges, offenses, and tremendous abominations that would be committed against Me... the many hours that I would spend alone in the Tabernacles. How many long nights! How many human beings would reject the loving calls that I would address to them.

For love of souls, I remain a prisoner in the Holy Eucharist, so that in their sorrow and grief they are being consoled by the most tender of Hearts, by the best of Fathers, by the most loyal friend. But that Love, which is consumed for the good of mankind, is not going to be returned.

I live amongst sinners to be their salvation and their life, their doctor and medicine; yet they, in return, in spite of their sick nature, distance themselves from Me. They offend Me and scorn Me.

My children, poor sinners! Do not distance yourselves from Me. I wait for you night and day at the Tabernacle. I will not reproach you for your crimes; I will not throw your sins in your face. What I will do is to wash you with the Blood of My wounds. Do not be afraid; come to Me. You do not know how much I love you.

And you, dear souls, why are you cold and indifferent to My love? I know you have to attend to the needs of your family, your home, and of the world that constantly demands of you. But, can it be that you do not have a moment to come and give Me proof of your love and gratitude? Do not allow yourselves to be carried away by so many useless worries; reserve a moment of your time to visit the Prisoner of Love. If your body is sick, can you not find a few minutes to seek the Doctor who must cure you? Come to He who can restore strength and health of the soul. Give alms of love to this Divine Beggar, who calls you, wants you, and waits for you.

These words will produce the effect of a great truth in souls. They will penetrate families, schools, religious congregations, hospitals, and prisons, and many souls will surrender to My Love. My greatest sorrows come from the souls of priests and nuns.

At the moment that I instituted the Eucharist, I saw all the privileged souls that would be nourished with My Body and My Blood and the effects produced in them.

To some, My Body would be a remedy to their weakness. To others, a fire that would succeed in consuming their miseries, inflaming them with love. Ah!... Those souls gathered before Me will be an enormous garden in which every plant produces a different flower, but all delight Me with their scent. My Body will be the sun that revives them. I will come close to some to be consoled, to others to hide, and in others, I will rest. If you only knew, beloved souls, how easy it is to console, to hide, and to give rest to the one God.

This God, who loves you with infinite Love after freeing you from the bondage of sin, has sown in you the incomparable grace of the religious vocation. He has brought you in a mysterious way to the garden of His delights. This God, your Redeemer, has become your Spouse. He Himself nourishes you with His Body so pure, and with His Blood, He quenches your thirst. In Me you shall find rest and happiness.

O, little daughter! Why is it that so many souls, after having been filled with so many blessings and caresses, have to be the cause of such sadness in My Heart? Am I not always the same? Can it be that I have changed for you? ... No! I will never change, and I will love you with predilection and tenderness until the end of time.

I know you are full of miseries, but this will not keep from you My most tender looks and I wait for you anxiously, not only to ease your miseries, but also to fill you with My blessings.

If I ask for your love, do not deny it to Me. It is very easy to love the One who is Love itself. If I ask for something dear to your nature, I give you both the grace and the strength necessary so you can be My comfort. Allow Me to come into your souls and, if you do not find in them anything that is worthy of Me, tell Me with humility and trust: "Lord, You already see the fruit that this tree produces. Come and tell me what I must do, so that from now on it may bear the fruit that You desire."

If the soul tells Me this with a sincere desire of proving its love to Me, I shall answer: "Dear soul, allow Me to cultivate your love Myself ..."

Do you know the fruits that you will obtain? The victory over your character will make amends for offenses; it will atone for faults. If you do not get upset when you are corrected and you accept it gladly, you will make it possible for souls blinded by pride to humble themselves and ask for forgiveness.

This is what I will do in your soul if you allow Me to work freely. The garden will not flourish immediately, but you will give great comfort to My Heart.

All this passed before Me when I instituted the Eucharist and I was enkindled with longing to nourish souls. I was not going to stay on Earth to live with perfect beings, but rather to support the weak and nourish the children… I would make them grow, strengthen their souls, and rest in their miseries, and their good desires would console Me.

But among My elected ones, there are souls that cause Me sorrow. Will they all persevere? This is the cry of pain that escapes from My Heart; this is the moan that I want souls to hear.

The Eternal Love is looking for souls who may say new things about old truths already known. The Infinite Love wants to create in the bosom of humanity a tribunal of pure Mercy, not of Justice. That is why the messages are multiplying in the world. Whoever understands them admires their work, takes advantage of them, and causes others to profit from them as well. Whoever does not understand keeps on being a slave of the spirit that dies and condemns.

To the latter, I direct My word of condemnation because they hinder My Divine Work, and they become accomplices of the devil.

What cunning produces pressure on their childish minds when they condemn and repress what proceeds not from miserable creatures but from the Creator? To those whom I have called little ones, I reveal My knowledge, which on the other hand, I hide from the proud.

Soul, allow Me to pour Myself in you. Become a valve of My Heart because there is no shortage of those who stifle My Love…

Jesus Does the Will of the Father

Of My Passion. I want you to consider, above all, the bitterness I experienced caused by My knowledge of the sins that darken the minds of men and women and lead them to commit aberrations. Most of the time, these sins are accepted as the outcome of natural inclinations that, it is said, cannot be opposed, as they say, by one's own will. Today, many live in grave sin, blaming others or fate without the possibility of getting rid of them. I saw this in Gethsemane and knew the great evil that My soul would absorb. So many are lost like that, and how I suffered for them!

Thus, by My example of washing their feet and becoming their Food, I taught My Apostles to give each other mutual support. The hour was approaching for which the Son of God had been made man and Redeemer of the human race, for which He would shed His Blood and give His Life for the world.

At that moment, I wanted to be in prayer and surrender Myself to the Will of My Father… It was then that My Will as a man conquered My natural resistance to the great suffering prepared for Me by Our Father, who you see was more aggrieved than I Myself. Then, among those lost souls, I surrendered My Own Soul in order to make reparation for that which had already become corrupt. My Omnipotence can accomplish everything, but it requires that a minimum be met on which to add the rest. And I offer that minimum requirement with infinite love.

My Passion… What an abyss of bitterness enclosed in itself!

How mistakenly afar from understanding are those who think only about the terrible sufferings of My Body.

My daughter, I have reserved for you other scenes of the intimate tragedies that I lived through and wish to share with you because you are one of those whom the Father gave Me in the Garden.

Beloved souls, learn from your Model that the only necessary thing, even if your nature rebels, is to humbly submit and surrender yourselves to fulfill the Will of God.

I also wanted to teach souls that every important act must be prepared for and given life through prayer. In prayer, the soul is fortified for the most difficult things, and God communicates with it, advises it, and inspires it even if the soul does not feel it.

I withdrew to the Garden with three of My Disciples in order to teach them that the three Powers of the soul should accompany them and help them in prayer.

Let your memory recall the divine benefits, the perfections of God: His Kindness, His Power, His Mercy, and the Love that He has for you. Seek afterward, with understanding, how you will be able to respond to the marvels that He has done for you… Through prayer, in your retreat and silence, allow your will to be moved to do the most and the best for God, and to be consecrated to the salvation of souls, whether by means of your apostolic works or by your humble and hidden life.

Humbly prostrate yourselves as creatures in the presence of your Creator, and adore His designs over you, whatever they may be by submitting your will to the will of the Divine.

In this way I offered Myself to carry out the work of redeeming the world. Ah! What a moment that was when I felt come over Me all the torments that I was to suffer during My Passion: the slander, the insults, the scourging, the kicks, the Crown of Thorns, the thirst, the Cross…

All that passed before My eyes at the same time that an intense pain hurt My Heart; the offenses, the sins, and the abominations that would be committed during the passing of time. And I not only saw them, but I felt covered with all those horrors, and in this way, I presented Myself to My Heavenly Father to implore Mercy.

My little daughter, I offered Myself as a lily to calm His anger and appease His wrath. Nevertheless, with so many crimes and so many sins, My human nature experienced mortal agony to the point of sweating blood.

Can it be possible that this anguish and this Blood are useless for so many souls? … My Passion was the origin of My love. If I had not wanted it, who would have been able to touch Me? I wanted it, and to accomplish this, I made use of the cruelest amongst men.

Before suffering, I knew, in Myself, all suffering, and I could evaluate it entirely. Yet when I wanted to suffer, in addition to full knowledge and appraisal, I had the human sensation of all suffering. I took all of them.

Speaking of My Passion, I cannot go into so much detail. Other times, I have done so, and you cannot understand it. Because of your human nature, you could not grasp the enormous extent of the pain that I have suffered.

Yes, I enlighten you, but I stay within a limit beyond which you cannot advance. I made everything to do with Me known only to my mother, and that is why she suffered them more than anyone.

Jesus' Suffering in the Garden of Gethsemane

But today, the world will know more than I have granted it up to now because My Father so desires it. For that reason, in My Church, there flourishes a ray of love for all the changing circumstances that carried Me from the Garden to Calvary. More than anyone else, I manifest my passion to the loved ones I had in the Garden. They are able to mention something that adapts to the mind of those who journey today. And if they can, they should do so. Therefore, write everything I tell you, little one, for yourself and for many others, for the comfort of souls and for the Glory of the Holy Trinity who desires that My suffering in Gethsemane be known.

My soul is sad unto death. While the sadness of physical illness could become the cause of death, the sadness of the spirit that I wanted to experience, consisted of the complete absence of the influence of the Divinity and the heartbreaking presence of the causes of My Passion.

In My Spirit, which was in death agony were present all the reasons that impelled Me to bring love to earth. Foremost were the offenses committed against My suffering Divinity as a man, yet with the very knowledge of God. You cannot find anything like this type of suffering because the man who sins understands, with My light, the part that corresponds to him and many times, imperfectly, he does not see what sin is like before Me. For that reason, it is clear that only God can know what is an offense committed against Him.

Nevertheless, Humanity should be able to offer to the Divinity, full knowledge and true sorrow and repentance and I can do so as often as it wishes. I do this in fact by offering My knowledge that has worked within Me, a Man, through the process of making human the offense against God.

This was My wish: that the sinner having repented through Me should have the way of presenting to his God the knowledge of the offense committed, and that I, in My Divinity, could also receive from the human person the full understanding of what has been committed against Me.

Enough for today; you do not know how much you console Me when you surrender to Me in complete abandonment. Not every day can I talk to souls… Let Me tell you My secrets for them! Let Me make use of your days and nights!

I was sad unto death because I could see everywhere the enormous accumulation of offenses committed. And if for one I experienced a death beyond compare, what do you suppose I have experienced for all the accumulated offenses? "Sad is My Soul unto death…" with a sadness that produced in Me the abandonment of all strength; with a sadness which was centered in the divinity towards which were converging in Me, the flood of faults and the stench of souls consumed by all types of vices. For that reason, I was at the same time target and arrow - as God, the target, and as man, the arrow. As soon as I had absorbed all sin, I appeared before My Father as the only offender. There could be no greater sadness than this and I wanted to take in all sin for the Love of the Father, and for Mercy to all of you.

If he does not pay attention to this matter, man ponders in vain over the meaning of these words, which include My entire being as God and as Man. Look at Me thus in this gigantic spiritual prison. Do I not deserve love if I struggled and suffered so much? Do I not deserve creatures making use of Me as their own property, knowing that I give Myself entirely to them without reserve? Drink all of you from My inexhaustible fountain of goodness. Drink! I offer you My sadness in the Garden; give Me your sadness, all your sadness. I want to make of your sadness a bouquet of violets, whose perfume is constantly directed toward My Divinity.

"Father, if it is possible, take this Cup away from Me, but let not My Will but Yours be done." I said this at the height of bitterness, when the burden weighing down on Me had become so bloody that

My Soul found itself in the most unbelievable darkness. I said so to the Father because, when I assumed all guilt, I presented Myself before Him as the only sinner against whom all His Divine Justice was discharged. And feeling deprived of My Divinity, only humanity appeared before Me.

Take from Me, O Father, this extremely bitter Cup that You present to Me, and which, nevertheless, I accepted out of love for You when I came into this world. I have reached a point where I do not even recognize Myself. You, O Father, have made of sin My inheritance and this makes unbearable My presence before You who love Me. The ingratitude of human beings is already known to Me but how will I endure seeing Myself alone? My God, have pity on the great solitude in which I find Myself. Why do even You want to leave Me so abandoned? What help will I find then in such great desolation? Why do You also strike Me this way? And if You deprive Me of Yourself, I feel like I am descending into such an abyss that I do not succeed in recognizing your hand in such a tragic situation. The Blood that oozes from My whole Body gives You testimony of My annihilation under Your powerful hand.

Thus, I wept; thus, I fell downwards. But then I continued: It is just, Holy Father, that You do with Me all that You desire. My life is not Mine; it belongs totally to You. I do not want My Will but Yours to be done. I have accepted a death on the Cross; I also accept the apparent death of My Divinity.

It is just. All this I must give You and, before everything, I must offer You the holocaust of My Divinity, which, nonetheless, unites Me to You. Yes, Father, with the Blood that You see, I confirm My donation and My acceptance: Your Will be done, not Mine…

Jesus Looks for His Disciples, Who Are Asleep

In spite of everything, the enormous burden and the dreadful fatigue, together with the sweat of Blood, I had been overwhelmed in such a way that when I went to look for My Apostles, I felt tremendously exhausted.

Peter, John, James! Where are you that I do not see you alert? Wake up! Look at My face! See how My body trembles with this confusion I experience! Why do you sleep? Wake up and pray with Me, for I have sweated Blood for you!

Peter, My chosen disciple, do you not care about My Passion? James, to you, I have given so much preference; look at Me and remember Me! And you, John, why do you let yourself plunge into sleep with the others? You can bear more than they can… Do not sleep; keep watch and pray with Me!

This is what I obtained: seeking comfort, I found bitter affliction. Not even they are with Me. Where else will I go? It is true; My Father gives Me only what I knew to ask of Him so that the judgment of all humanity would fall upon Me. My Father, help Me! You can do all; help Me!

I prayed again like a human being in whom all hopes have sunk and who seeks understanding and comfort from on high. But what could My Father do if I had freely chosen to pay for everything? The choice I made had not changed. Yet, natural resistance had reached such an excessive degree that My humanity was overwhelmed.

Again, I fell to the ground flat on My face out of shame for all your sins; again, I asked My Father to take that Cup away from Me. But He answered that if I did not drink from it, it would be as if I had not come to this world and that I should console Myself because many creatures would take part in My agonies in the Garden.

I answered: Father, do not let My Will be done, but Yours. This Angel has assured Me of Your Love, and this brief joy that You have sent Me has worked well even on My natural resistance. Give Me My creatures, those whom I have redeemed. Take them Yourself because, for Your sake, I accept this. I desire to see You pleased. I offer You all My sufferings and My unchanging Will, that in truth is not in disagreement with Yours, because We have always been One… Father, I am destroyed, but it is thus that Our Love will be known. May Your Will be done, not Mine!

Again I returned to wake My Disciples, but the rays of the Divine Justice had left indelible scars within Me. They became filled with astonishment when they saw how distressed I had become and the one who suffered most was John. I, silent… they stunned… Only Peter had the courage to speak. Poor Peter! If he had known that part of My troubled state had been unleashed by him!

I had taken My three friends for them to help Me by sharing My anguish, for them to pray with Me, for Me to rest in them and in their love. How can I describe what I experienced when I saw them sleeping?

How My heart suffers even today, and wanting to find relief in my soul, I go to them and find them sleeping. More than once, when I wanted to wake them and bring them out of themselves, out of their worries, they answered Me, if not with words, with deeds: "Not now, I am too tired; I have too much to do; this is bad for My health; I need a little time; I want some peace."

I insist and gently tell that soul: Do not fear. If for Me you leave that rest, I will reward you. Come and pray with Me, just for one hour! Look, this is the moment when I need you! If you linger, will it already make you late? How many times have I heard that same answer?

Poor soul, you have not been able to keep watch for one hour with Me. Soon, I will come, and you will not hear Me because you are asleep. I will want to give you the Grace but since you are asleep, you will be unable to receive it. And who can assure you that later you will have the strength to wake up? It is likely that if you are deprived of food, your soul will be weakened, and you may not emerge from that lethargy.

Many souls have been surprised by death in the middle of deep sleep. Where and how have they awakened?

Beloved souls, I also want to teach you how useless and vain it is to try to find relief in creatures. How often they are asleep and, instead of finding the relief I seek in them, I depart with bitterness for they do not share Our desires or return Our love.

When I prayed to My Father and asked for help, My sad and abandoned soul was suffering the anguish of death. I felt overwhelmed by the weight of the most heinous ingratitude.

The Blood that issued from the pores of My Body and which soon would burst forth from all My wounds would be of no use to the great number of souls that would be lost. A great many would offend Me, and many would not know Me! Later, I would shed My Blood for all, and My merits would be applied to each one of them. Divine Blood! Infinite merits! And yet, useless for so many, many souls.

But by then, I was already going to encounter other things, and My Will was bent on the fulfillment of My Passion.

Mankind, if I suffered, it has certainly not been fruitless nor without reason. The fruit that I have obtained has been Glory and Love. It is now up to you, with My help, to show Me that you appreciate My work.

I never tire! Come to Me! Come to He who vibrates with Love for you and who only knows how to give you the true Love that reigns in Heaven, and that transforms you now on earth.

Souls that taste My thirst, drink from My bitter and glorious Chalice, for I tell you that the Father wants to reserve some of the drops of this Chalice precisely just for you. Think that these few drops were taken from Me and then, if you believe, tell Me that you do not want them. I have not set limits, and neither should you. I was destroyed without mercy. For love, you should allow Me to destroy your self-esteem.

I am He who works in you, just as My Father worked in Me when in the Garden.

I am He who gives you sufferings so that one day you may rejoice. Be docile for a time; be docile in imitation of Me because this helps you greatly and greatly pleases Me. Do not lose anything, but rather gain love. How could I actually allow My beloved ones to suffer real losses while they try to show Me love?

I'll wait for you. I am always waiting, and I will not tire. Come to Me; come as you are; it does not matter as long as you come. Then you will see that I will adorn your foreheads with jewels, with those drops of Blood that I shed at Gethsemane, because those drops are yours, if you want them. Come, soul, come to Jesus who calls you.

I said: My Father; I did not say: My God. And what I want to teach you when your heart suffers most is that you should say "My Father" and ask Him for comfort. Show Him your sufferings and your fears, and with moaning, remind Him that you are His children. Tell Him that your soul can bear no more! Ask trustingly like children and wait, for your Father will help you; He will give you and the souls entrusted to you the necessary strength to go through this tribulation.

This is the Chalice that I accepted and drained to its last drop. Everything to teach you, dear children, to never return to believing that suffering is useless. If you do not witness the results that you always aim for, yield your judgment and allow the Divine Will to be fulfilled within you.

I did not retreat. On the contrary, knowing that it was in the Garden where they had to apprehend Me, I stayed there. I did not want to flee from My enemies.

My daughter, tonight, allow My Blood to irrigate and strengthen the roots of your littleness.

Jesus is Handed Over by Judas

After having been comforted by My Father's messenger, I saw Judas approaching Me, followed by all those who were to seize Me. They had ropes, sticks, and stones. I stepped forward and said to them, "Whom do you seek?" While Judas, with his hand on My shoulder, kissed Me.

So many souls have sold Me and will sell Me for the wretched price of a delight, for a momentary and passing pleasure. Poor souls who seek Jesus, as did the soldiers.

Souls whom I love, you who come to Me and receive Me in your bosom, who tell Me so many times that you love Me—will you hand Me over when you leave after receiving Me? In the places that you frequent, there are stones that wound Me, there are conversations that offend Me, and you, who have received Me today, lose the beautiful whiteness of Grace there.

Why do the souls who know Me hand Me over that way when, on more than one occasion, they boast of being pious and practicing charity? All things that truly could help them acquire greater merits… What are they to you but a veil to cover your crime of accumulating goods on earth?

Be watchful and pray! Fight unceasingly, and do not let your wicked inclinations and shortcomings become habitual.

Look, it is necessary to mow the grass every year and possibly even during the four seasons. You have to work the land and clear it. You have to improve it and take care to uproot the weeds that sprout up in it.

The soul also needs diligent care, and the twisted tendencies need to be straightened.

Do not think that the soul that sells Me and surrenders to serious sin began with a serious fault. Usually, the great fall began with something insignificant—some pleasure, some weakness, an illicit consent, a pleasure not forbidden but inappropriate. In this way, the soul becomes blind, Grace is diminished, passion is strengthened, and lastly, the soul is overcome.

Understand this: if it is sad to receive an offense and an ungrateful act from any soul, it is much more so when it comes from My most beloved, chosen souls. However, others can make reparation and console Me.

Souls, you whom I have chosen to make My resting place, the garden of My delights, I expect from you much greater tenderness, much more gentleness, and much more love.

I expect you to be the balm that may heal My wounds, the one who may clean My face made ugly and dirty, and who may help Me give light to so many blind souls that in the darkness of night seize Me and bind Me to hand Me over to death.

Do not leave Me alone… Wake up and come, for My enemies already arrive!

When the soldiers approached, I said to them, "I Am." These same words I repeat now to the soul who is about to fall into temptation: "I Am." There is still time, and if you want, I will forgive you. Instead of your binding Me with the ropes of sin, I am He who will bind you with the bonds of Love.

Come, I am He who loves you, the One who has so much compassion for your weaknesses, the One who is anxiously waiting to receive you in His arms.

The episode of My capture, well examined, has much importance. If Peter had not struck Malchus that blow, I would not have had the opportunity to call to your attention the method I want you to use in fighting for Me.

Then I made use of a proverb to admonish Peter, and I restored Malchus' ear because I do not like violence, being that I am the Lord of liberty. But notice that apart from that, I expressed to Peter the firm desire that My Passion should be fulfilled, and I caused him to reflect on the fact that if I wanted, the Father could have Me defended by My angels.

Do you see how many things there are in just one episode? But the main thing is precisely the lesson that I had to give to all of you in the struggle against your enemies. Whoever is like Me acts in this way: he allows those who surround him to take him where they will because he will have his strength in the moments which are not those sought after by the world, by human experience, and by the shrewdness of self-love.

No, whoever is like Me will find and obtain unrecognizable and vigorous strength to dominate those who suppress him by remaining in the situation where he is placed. My true disciple does the most improbable things without interrupting in the least My designs for him. The world delights in uniqueness, in excelling, and demonstrating its own superiority. This is the spirit that I have fought and conquered. That is why I told all of you to take courage because as I have conquered it, that world can now do nothing to sever your union with Me, provided that you do not unite with it. If you do, you would have to suffer the consequences with the added difficulty that since I Myself oppose its victory with worldly weapons, many times you will have as adversaries the world and Me—the world because of its self-love, and Me for pure Love, out of genuine Love for your well-being.

Therefore, strike no blows like Peter's to the ears of your enemies without full acceptance of the Chalice that I offer you. A Chalice in which you should see My Will as I saw that of My Father when I asked the beloved Peter: "Do you not want Me to drink from this Chalice that My Father gives Me?"

Always meditate on My Passion, but penetrate intimately into My Spirit and obtain the impressions that are wholesome and incite you to imitate Me. Naturally, I am the One Who works these things in you, but you should take pains yourselves, and later, you will attain what I say.

Ah! If mankind could only understand this aspect of My Passion! How much easier it would be to yield and relive My Life!

Take courage, My children, everything is a question of love, not of anything else. Of love and My work that I want to accomplish in you, and of your always loving Me more. Stop reasoning in a human way; open your mind to My world, to the one that I have with you. This is important!

You are Mine for three reasons: because I created you from nothing; because I redeemed you; and because you will receive part of a share in My Crown of Glory. That is why you must remember that I care for you for these three reasons, and that I could never lose My interest in those whom I have created, in those whom I have saved, and in those who should be My Glory.

You are driven to this path, and you must traverse all of it. And like it was for Me, it will not only be good for you but also for many of your brothers and sisters who should receive from Me, through you, Grace and Life.

Advance, because I delight in it; learn, because Love wants to possess you completely.

I give you My Blessing, full of promise. I give it to all of you with the power that I enjoy as a man, power that is yours, and joy that I shall award with the prize, which will confirm My infinite Love for all of you.

My hour had come, the hour in which I had to consummate the sacrifice, and I surrendered Myself to the soldiers with the meekness of a lamb.

Jesus is Taken Before Caiaphas

I was taken before Caiaphas, where I was received with jeers and insults. One of his soldiers struck My cheek. It was the first blow I received, and in it, I saw the first mortal sin of many souls who, after living in grace, would commit that first sin. So many other sins followed that first sin, serving as an example so that other souls would also commit them.

My Apostles abandoned Me, and Peter remained hidden behind a fence, among the servants, spying, moved by curiosity.

With Me were men only trying to accumulate crimes against Me, accusations that could further incite the anger of such wicked judges. There I saw the faces of all the demons, of all the bad angels. They accused Me of disturbing the order, of being an instigator and a false prophet, of being blasphemous and profaning the Sabbath. And the soldiers, worked up by the lies, hurled their shouts and threats.

Then My silence cried out, shaking My whole Body. Where are you, Apostles and disciples who have been witnesses to My Life, My teachings, and My miracles? Of all those from whom I was expecting some proof of love, there is no one left to defend Me. I am alone and surrounded by soldiers who want to devour Me like wolves.

Contemplate how they mistreated Me: one deals Me a slap upon My face; another thrusts his dirty saliva at Me; another twists his face, mocking Me; another pulls My beard; another twists My arms with his fingers; another hits My genitals with his knee, and when I fall, two of them pull Me up by the hair.

Peter Denies Jesus

While My Heart offers to suffer all these ordeals, Peter, whom I had named "Leader and Head of the Church" and who hours before had promised to follow Me unto My death, denies Me in response to a simple question that is asked of him and which could have served him in giving testimony of Me. Gripped even more by fear, when the question is repeated, he swears that he has never known Me or been My disciple. Questioned for the third time, he answered with dreadful curses.

Little children, when the world cries out against Me and, turning towards My chosen souls, I see Myself abandoned and denied, do you know how great is the sadness and bitterness in My Heart?

I will tell them as I told Peter: Soul, whom I love so much, do you no longer remember proofs of love that I have given you? Have you forgotten that many times you have promised to be faithful to Me and defend Me?

You do not trust yourself because you are lost. But if you come to Me with humbleness and firm trust, fear nothing; you are well sustained.

Souls, you who live surrounded by so many dangers, do not enter into occasions of sin through vain curiosity. Be careful, for you will fall like Peter.

And you souls who labor in My vineyard, if you feel moved by curiosity or by some human satisfaction, I will tell you to take flight. But if you labor out of obedience and are driven by zeal for souls and for My Glory, be not afraid. I will defend you, and you shall depart victorious.

My beloved, I am educating you little by little and with much patience. I am consoled by the thought of having a pupil being able to learn. Thus, I forget your carelessness and mistakes. If I look in creation for the most beautiful names to call you, be not afraid. Why do you suppress them? Love has no boundaries.

Jesus is Taken to Prison

Let us go on with this painful story, which you will have to carry to as many people as you can. I will enlighten all of you in the way you will do it.

When the soldiers were taking Me prisoner, Peter was amid the crowd, half hidden in one of the courtyards. We exchanged glances; he was wide-eyed. It was only for a fraction of a second and yet, I told him so much. I saw him cry bitterly over his sin and with My Heart I told him: "The enemy has tried to possess you, but I do not abandon you. I know that your heart has not denied Me. Be ready for the battle of the new day, for the renewed struggles against spiritual darkness, and prepare yourself to carry the Good News. Farewell, Peter."

How often do I look toward the soul that has sinned, but does she also look? Not always do our eyes meet. How often do I look at the soul and she does not look at Me; she does not see Me; she is blind. I call her by her name, and she does not answer Me. I send her a sorrow, a suffering so that she can emerge from her sleep, but she does not want to wake up.

My beloved ones, if you do not look at Heaven, you will live like beings deprived of reason. All of you, raise your heads and contemplate the Homeland that awaits you. Search for your God and you will always find Him with His eyes fixed upon you, and in His look, you will find peace and life.

Contemplate Me in prison where I spend a great part of the night. The soldiers came to insult Me with words and deeds, pushing Me, hitting Me, mocking My condition as a man.

Close to dawn, having had their fill of Me, they left Me alone, tied up in a dark, damp, and foul-smelling room, full of rats. I was tied in such a way that I had to remain standing or sitting on a pointed stone, which was all they gave Me for a seat. My aching body was soon stiff with cold. I remembered the thousands of times that My Mother covered My Body, wrapping it up when I was cold, and I wept.

Now let us compare the Tabernacle with the prison and, above all, with the hearts of men. In prison, I spent one night. How many nights do I spend in the Tabernacle?

In prison, the soldiers, who were My enemies, insulted Me. But in the Tabernacle, souls who call Me Father mistreat and insult Me. In prison, I suffered cold, sleeplessness, hunger, shame, sadness, pains, loneliness, and abandonment. I could see over the course of time how, in so many Tabernacles, I would lack the covering of love. How many frozen hearts would be for Me like the stone in the prison.

How many times I would be thirsty for love, thirsty for souls! How many days do I wait for such a soul to visit Me, to receive Me in her heart, because I have spent the night alone and was thinking of her in order to quench My thirst. So many times, I hunger for My souls, for their fidelity, for their generosity.

Will they know how to calm these longings? When they have to undergo some suffering, will they know to tell Me, "This will help to ease Your sadness, to be with You in Your loneliness?" And, O! If at least united to Me and as long as you would console My Heart, you would endure everything peacefully and be strengthened.

In prison, I felt shame when I heard the horrible words that were hurled against Me, and that shame grew when I later saw that those same words would be repeated by beloved souls.

When those filthy and repugnant hands dealt Me blows and slaps, I saw how often I would be struck and slapped by so many souls who, without purifying themselves of their sins, without cleaning their house with a good confession, would receive Me in their hearts. Those habitual sins would deal Me blows repeatedly.

When they forced Me to get up by shoving Me, being without strength and because of the chains that bound Me, I would fall to the ground. I saw how so many souls, tying Me up with the chains of their ingratitude, would let Me fall upon the stones, renewing My shame and prolonging My loneliness.

Chosen souls, contemplate your Spouse in prison. Contemplate Me on this night of so much pain and consider that this pain is prolonged in the solitude in so many Tabernacles, in the coldness of so many hearts.

If you want to give Me proof of your love, open your heart so I can make it My prison. Tie Me up with the chains of your love. Cover Me with your gentleness. Feed Me with your kindness. Quench My thirst with your zeal. Console My sadness and abandonment with your faithful company. Make My shame disappear with your purity and righteous intentions.

If you want Me to rest in you, avoid tumultuous passions, and in the silence of your soul, I shall sleep peacefully. Now and then, you will hear My voice that softly tells you: My Spouse, you who are now My rest, I will be yours through eternity. To you, who provide Me the prison of your heart with so much dedication and love, I promise that My reward shall have no limits and the sacrifices that you have made for Me during your life will not weigh you down.

Jesus is Taken Before Herod

Pilate ordered that they take Me to the presence of Herod. He was a poor, corrupt man who sought only pleasure, allowing himself to be swept away by his disorderly passions. He was glad to see Me appear before his tribunal because he hoped to amuse himself with My words and miracles.

Consider, My children, the repulsion that I felt in the presence of the most repulsive of men, whose words, questions, gestures, and affected movements covered Me with confusion. Pure and virginal souls, come to surround and defend your Spouse.

Herod expected Me to answer his sarcastic questions, but I did not utter a word; I kept the most absolute silence before him. Not answering was the greatest proof of My dignity that I could give him. His obscene words were not worthy of an exchange with My pure ones. In the meantime, My Heart was infinitely united to My Heavenly Father. I was consumed with the desire to give even the last drop of My Blood for souls. The thought of all human beings who would later follow Me, conquered by My example and generosity, enflamed love in Me. Not only did I endure that terrible interrogation, but I also desired to run to the torture of the Cross.

Jesus is Taken Again Before Pilate

I allowed them to treat Me like a madman, and they covered Me with a white tunic as a sign of their ridicule and derision. Later, amid furious shouting, they took Me again before Pilate.

Look how this man, bewildered and filled with confusion, does not know what to do with Me. To appease the fury of the mob, he commands that they have Me scourged.

Represented in Pilate, I saw the souls who lack the courage and generosity to vigorously break away from the demands of the world and their own nature. Instead of uprooting what their conscience tells them is not of the world and not in the right spirit, they yield to a whim. They get pleasure out of superficial satisfaction and partially surrender to the demands of their passion. To ease remorse, they tell themselves, "I have already deprived myself of this or that, and that is enough."

I will only say to this soul: "You scourge Me as did Pilate." You have already taken one step, tomorrow another. Do you plan to satisfy your passion in this way? No! Soon it will demand more and more of you.

As you have not had the courage to fight your own nature in this minor thing, much less will you have it later when the occasion will be greater.

The Scourging of Jesus

Look at Me, My beloved ones. Letting Myself be led with the meekness of a lamb to the terrible torture of the scourging. On My Body, already covered with blows and overwhelmed with fatigue, the executioners cruelly discharged terrible lashes with braided rope and rods. They punished Me so violently that there was no part of Me which was not prey to the most terrible pain. The blows and the kicks caused Me countless wounds. The rods tore away pieces of My skin and flesh. Blood flowed from all My limbs. Time after time, I fell because of the pain caused by the blows. My Body was in such a state that I resembled a monster more than a man. The features of My face had lost their shape; it was all swollen.

The thought of so many souls who would later be inspired to follow My footsteps consumed Me with Love.

During My hours in prison, I saw the faithful imitators learning from My meekness, patience, and serenity. Not only accepting suffering and scorn but even loving those who persecute them and, if necessary, sacrificing themselves for them as I sacrificed Myself.

During those hours of solitude in the midst of so much pain, I became enflamed more and more with desires of fulfilling perfectly the Will of My Father. How I offered Myself in reparation for His deeply offended Glory! Thus, you, religious souls who find yourselves in the prison chosen out of love, who more than once pass before the eyes of creatures as useless and possibly harmful, do not be afraid. Let them shout against you and, during those hours of pain and solitude, unite your heart intimately with your God, the only object of your love. Make reparation for His Glory violated by so many sins.

Jesus is Sentenced to Death

At dawn, Caiaphas ordered them to take Me to Pilate so that he might pronounce the sentence of death. Pilate questioned Me, hoping to find a reason to condemn Me, but at the same time, his conscience tormented him, and he felt great fear at the injustice he was about to commit. Finally, he found a way to ignore Me and had Me taken to Herod.

In Pilate are faithfully represented the souls who feel the movement of grace and, at the same time, their own passions. Dominated by human respect and blinded by self-love, they allow that moment of grace to pass for fear of looking ridiculous.

I did not answer any of Pilate's questions. But when he asked, "Are You the King of the Jews?" I answered with seriousness and integrity, "You have said so; I am the King, but My kingdom is not of this world." With these words, I wanted to teach many souls that when they are presented with the opportunity to endure suffering or humiliation that could easily be avoided, they should answer with generosity: "My kingdom is not of this world." That is to say, I do not seek the praises of human beings. My Homeland is not this one. Soon, I will rest where it truly is. Take courage to fulfill My duty without taking into account the opinion of the world. What matters to Me is not their esteem but following the voice of grace that suffocates the inducements of nature. If I am not able to conquer alone, I will ask for strength and counsel since, on many occasions, passions and excessive self-love blind the soul and impel it to act wrongly.

Jesus is Crowned With Thornes

In the Will of the Father, I have lived days of intense sadness without complaining, accepting what the Father wanted to make Me feel. When I was seized in the Garden, My accusers were quick with every lie, and I, without the least resistance, allowed them to take Me wherever they wanted. When they encircled My Head with the crown of thorns, I bowed My Head without resistance because I took everything from the hands of the One who had sent Me into the world.

When the arms of those cruel men were exhausted by the violence of discharging blows against My Body, they placed upon My head a crown woven with branches of thorns. Parading before Me, they said: "So you are a King? We salute you!"

Some spat at Me; others insulted Me; still others dealt further blows to My head, each one adding a new pain to My Body, so battered and destroyed.

I am tired; with nowhere to rest. Lend Me your heart and your arms to cover Myself in your love. I am cold and feverish; embrace Me for an instant before they continue destroying this temple of Love.

The soldiers and executioners, with their filthy hands, shoved My Body. Others, with disgust for My Blood, pressed Me with their lances and reopened My flesh. With a shove, they placed Me on sharp stones. I silently wept because of the pain while they, in grotesque fashion, made fun of My tears. Finally, they tore My temples, forcing down the crown woven of thorny branches.

Consider how, with that crown, I wanted to make reparation for the sins of pride of so many souls who, wishing to be excessively praised, allow themselves to be mastered by the false opinions of the world. Above all, I allowed them to crown My Head with thorns so that, in this way, My head should suffer cruelly in order to make reparation through voluntary humility for the loathing and proud pretense of so many souls. Souls who, because they judge it unworthy of their condition and status, refuse to follow the path laid out by My Providence.

No path is humiliating when it is planned by the Will of God. It will be fruitless for you to try to deceive yourselves into thinking you are following the will of God and fully submitting to everything He asks of you.

There are people in the world who, when the moment of decision arrives (to undertake a new type of life), reflect and examine the desires of their hearts. Maybe they will find, in him or her with whom they plan to unite, the solid foundations for a Christian and pious life. Perhaps they will see that they will carry out their duties as a family in a way necessary to satisfy their wishes of happiness. But vanity and pride come to obscure their spirit, and they let themselves be swept along by the desire of being important and showing off. Then they do their best to seek out someone, who, being richer or of high class, satisfies their ambition. O! How foolishly they blind themselves. No, I will tell them, you will not find true happiness in this world, and I hope that you will find it in the next. Beware; you are putting yourselves in great danger!

I will also talk to the souls to whom I called to the path of perfection. How many illusions there are in those who tell Me that they are ready to do My Will and then drive the Crown of thorns onto My Head.

Respectively, there are souls whom I want for Myself. Knowing them and loving them, I want to place them where I live, in My infinite wisdom, where they will find all that is necessary to reach sanctity. It is there where I will make Myself known to them, and where they will give Me more comfort, more love, and more souls.

But, so many disappointments! How many souls are blinded by pride and arrogance or by miserable ambition. They fill their heads with vain and useless thoughts; they refuse to follow the path that My love lays out for them.

Souls whom I had chosen, do you think that you fulfill My Will by resisting the voice of grace that calls you and guides you along that path which your pride rejects?

My daughter, love of My sorrows, console Me. Make a throne in your little heart for your King and Savior, and crown Me with kisses.

Crowned with thorns and covered with a purple cloak, the soldiers presented Me again to Pilate. Not finding in Me a crime for which to punish Me, Pilate asked Me several questions, asking Me why I did not answer him, knowing that he had full power over Me.

Then, breaking My silence, I told him: "You would not have that power if you had not received it from above, but it is necessary that the Scriptures be carried out." And, abandoning Myself to My Heavenly Father, I fell silent again.

Barabbas is Set Free

Pilate was looking for ways to free Me. He was worried because of his wife's warning and confused between the feelings of remorse from his conscience and the fear that the people would initiate a riot against him. In the pitiful state I was in, he exposed Me to the sight of the mob, proposing to them that I be freed and Barabbas, a famous thief and criminal, be condemned in My place. The people answered in one voice: "Let him die and let Barabbas be set free!"

Souls who love Me, see how they have compared Me to a criminal. See how they have reduced Me to lower than the most perverse of men. Listen to the furious shouts hurled against Me. See with what rage they ask for My death. Did I refuse to endure such a painful insult? No, on the contrary, I embraced it for My Love of souls and to show them that this Love not only led Me to death but to the most ignominious death.

However, do not believe that My human nature did not feel revulsion or pain. On the contrary, I wanted to feel all its revulsion and be subject to its same condition, giving you an example that may strengthen you in every circumstance in life and teach you to overcome the aversions offered when fulfilling the Divine Will.

I return to the souls to whom I was speaking yesterday, those souls called to the state of perfection, who argue with grace and retreat when faced with the humility of the path I show them, fearing how they will be judged by the world or, as they assess their capabilities, convincing themselves that they will be more useful somewhere else for My service and My Glory.

I am going to respond to those souls: Tell Me, did I refuse or even hesitate when I saw Myself being born of poor and humble parents in a stable far from My home and country, in the harshest season of the year and at night?

Afterwards, I lived thirty years in obscurity doing rough labor in a workshop. I suffered humiliation and disdain at the hands of those who requested work done by Joseph, My father. I did not shrink from helping My Mother in the most menial household tasks. Yet, did I not have more talent than what is required to perform the rough trade of a carpenter? I, who at the age of twelve, taught the Doctors in the Temple? But it was the Will of My Heavenly Father, and I glorified Him in that way. When I left Nazareth and started My public life, I could have made Myself known as the Messiah and Son of God so that men and women would listen to My teachings with veneration. But I did not do so, because My only wish was to fulfill the Will of My Father.

When the time of My Passion came, through the cruelty of some and the insults of others, the abandonment of My own, and the ingratitude of the mob, through the unspeakable martyrdom of My Body and the revulsion of My soul, see how, with still greater love, I revealed and embraced the Will of My Heavenly Father.

Thus, when overcoming difficulties and revulsion, the soul generously submits itself to the Will of God. There comes a moment in which, intimately united to Him, the soul enjoys the most indescribable sweetness.

What I have said to souls who loathe the humble and hidden life, I repeat to those who are called to labor in constant contact with the world when, instead, they would be attracted to complete solitude and humble and hidden works.

Chosen souls, your happiness and perfection do not consist in following the tastes and inclinations of nature, in being known or unknown by creatures, in using or hiding the talent you have, but rather in uniting and conforming yourselves through love and with total submission to the Will of God to what is asked of you for His Glory and your own sanctification.

Enough for today, My little daughter; love and embrace My Will joyfully. You know that it is always designed by love.

Meditate for a moment upon the unspeakable martyrdom of My Heart, upon seeing it valued less than Barabbas. How I remembered the tenderness of My Mother when She was embracing Me close to Her Heart! And how vivid were the anxieties and fatigue that My adoptive father suffered to show Me his love. How I remembered the benefits I so freely poured over those ungrateful people, giving sight to the blind, restoring health to the sick, the use of their limbs to those who had lost them, feeding the crowds, and bringing the dead back to life. Now to see Myself reduced to the most despicable state! I am the most despised of men, and I am being condemned to death like an infamous thief.

Jesus Forgives Even the Greatest Sinners

Pilate has pronounced a sentence. My little children, consider attentively how My Heart suffered.

After Judas handed Me over in the Garden of Olives, he wandered off and took flight, unable to stifle the cries of his conscience, which accused him of the most horrible sacrilege. When the news of My death sentence reached his ears, he gave in to the most terrible despair and hanged himself.

Who can possibly understand the intense pain in My Heart when I saw that soul cast himself into eternal damnation? He who had spent three years in the school of My Love, learning My doctrine, receiving My teaching, and many times hearing My lips forgive the greatest sinners.

Judas! Why do you not come and throw yourself at My feet so that I may forgive you? If you do not dare to come near Me for fear of those who surround Me and so ardently abuse Me, at least look at Me, and you will see how soon My eyes will fix on you.

Souls who are entangled in the greatest sins—if at times you have lived wandering as fugitives because of your crimes, if the sins of which you are guilty have blinded you and hardened your hearts, if in the pursuit of some passion you have fallen into greater disorder, do not allow desperation to take possession of you when the accomplices to your sin abandon you and your soul realizes its guilt. As long as man has an instant of life, he still has time to appeal to My Mercy and implore forgiveness.

If you are young and the scandals of your past life have left you in a state of degradation before men, do not be afraid! Even though the world may despise you, treat you as wicked, insult, and abandon you, be certain that your God does not want your soul to be fodder for the flames of hell. He wants you to dare to speak to Him, to direct your gaze and the sighs of your heart to Him, and you will soon see that His kind and paternal hand will lead you to the source of forgiveness and life.

If out of malice you have perhaps spent a large part of your life in disorder and indifference, and now, near eternity, desperation wants to blindfold your eyes, do not allow yourself to be deceived. There is still time for forgiveness. Listen carefully: if you have but a second of life left, take advantage of it because you could gain eternal life during that second.

If your existence has passed in ignorance and in error, if you have been the cause of great harm to people, to society, and even to religion, and for any reason you recognize your mistake, do not allow yourself to be pulled down by the burden of your sins or by the harm for which you have been instrumental. Instead, allow your soul to be penetrated with the deepest sorrow, absorb yourself in trust, and turn to the One who is always waiting to forgive you.

The same happens for a soul who has spent the first years of its life in faithful observance of My Commandments but who has little by little fallen away from fervor into a lukewarm and comfortable life.

Do not hide anything that I tell you, for it is all for the benefit of the whole of humanity. Repeat it in broad daylight; preach it to those who truly want to hear it.

The soul who one day receives a strong jolt that awakens her suddenly sees her life fruitless, empty, and undeserving of eternity. The Evil One, with infernal jealousy, attacks her in a thousand ways, exaggerating her faults. He inspires sadness and discouragement, leading in the end to fear and desperation.

The souls that belong to Me do not pay attention to that cruel enemy. As soon as you feel the movement of grace at the beginning of your struggle, come to My Heart. Feel and watch how it sheds a drop of its Blood upon your soul. Come to Me. You know where I am, under the veil of faith. Lift it and, with complete trust, tell Me all your sorrows, your miseries, your falls. Listen to My words with respect, and do not fear for the past. My Heart has submerged it in the endless depths of My Mercy and My Love.

Your past life will give you the humility that will fill you. And if you want to give Me the best proof of love, trust Me and count on My forgiveness. Believe that your sins will never be greater than My infinite Mercy.

Jesus on His Way to Calvary

Let us continue, My little daughter. Follow Me on the way to Calvary, weighed down by the weight of the Cross.

While My Heart was bewildered with sadness for the eternal perdition of Judas, the cruel executioners, insensitive to My pain, loaded My wounded shoulders with the hard and heavy Cross on which I was to consummate the mystery of the Redemption of the world.

Contemplate Me, Angels from Heaven. See the Creator of every marvel; the God to whom all the heavenly spirits render adoration; the God walking towards Calvary and carrying on His shoulders the holy and blessed log that will receive His last sigh.

Also look at Me, you souls who wish to be My faithful imitators. My Body, destroyed by so much torture, walks without strength, bathed in sweat and Blood. I suffer, without anyone feeling sorry for My pain! The mob accompanies Me, and there is not a single person who feels pity for Me. They all surround Me like hungry wolves, wanting to devour their prey. All the demons came out of Hell to make My suffering worse.

The fatigue that I feel is so great, and the Cross so heavy, that halfway along the path, I fall from weakness. See how those inhuman men lift Me up in the most brutal manner. One grabs My arm; another pulls My clothes that are stuck to My wounds, tearing them open again. This one grabs Me by the neck, another by the hair. Others discharge dreadful blows to My whole Body, with their fists, and even with their feet. The Cross falls upon Me, and with its weight causes new wounds. My face is scraped by the stones in the road, and the blood which runs down My face sticks to My eyes that are almost closed because of the blows they have received. The dust and the mud mingle with the blood, and I am turned into the most repugnant of objects.

My Father sends Angels to help support Me so that My Body does not lose consciousness when it falls, so that the battle may not be won before its time and all My souls are lost.

I walk over the stones that destroy My feet. I stumble and fall time and time again. I look at both sides of the road, searching for the slightest look of love, of surrender, of union with My pain, but… I do not see anyone.

My children, you who follow in My footsteps, do not let go of your cross no matter how heavy it seems to you. Do it for Me because by carrying your cross, you will help Me carry Mine, and on the difficult path, you will find My Mother and the holy souls who will give you encouragement and comfort. Continue with Me for a few moments, and a few steps ahead you will see Me in the presence of My Most Holy Mother who, with Her Heart pierced by sorrow, comes out to meet Me for two reasons: to gain further strength to suffer at the sight of Her God and, with Her heroic attitude, to give Her Son encouragement to continue His work of Redemption.

Consider the martyrdom of these two Hearts. What My Mother loves most is Her Son. She cannot ease My pains, and She knows that the sight of Her will increase My sufferings even more, but it will also increase My strength to fulfill the Will of the Father.

For Me, My Mother is the most beloved being on earth, and not only am I unable to console Her, but the sad state in which She sees Me causes Her Heart to suffer similar to Mine. She allows a sob to escape. The death I suffer in My Body, My Mother receives in Her Heart. Oh, how Her eyes are fixed on Me and Mine on Her! We do not utter a single word, but Our Hearts express so many things during that painful look.

Yes, My Mother witnessed all the tortures of My Passion, which were presented to Her spirit by Divine revelation. Moreover, several disciples, even though they remained far away for fear of the Jews, tried to find out everything and would inform My Mother. When She found out that the death sentence had already been pronounced, She came to meet Me and did not abandon Me until they placed Me in the tomb.

Jesus is Helped to Carry the Cross

I am on My way to Calvary. Those wicked men, fearing to see Me die before reaching the end, arrange among themselves to find someone to help Me carry the Cross, and from the vicinity they requisitioned a man called Simon.

Look at him behind Me, helping Me carry the Cross, and above all, consider two things: this man lacks goodwill and is a mercenary because, if he comes and shares with Me the weight of the Cross, it is because he has been requisitioned. For that reason, when he feels too tired, he lets the weight fall more on Me, and thus, I fall to the ground twice.

This man helps Me carry part of the Cross but not My entire Cross.

There are souls that walk this way behind Me. They accept helping Me carry My Cross, but they still worry about comfort and rest. Many others agree to follow Me, and to that end, they have embraced the perfect life. But they do not abandon their self-interests, which keep on being, in many cases, their prime concern. That is why they waver and let My Cross fall when it weighs upon them too much. They look to suffer in the least possible way, measure their self-denial, and avoid humiliation and fatigue as much as possible. Remembering perhaps with sorrow those whom they left behind, they try to obtain for themselves certain comforts and pleasures.

In a word, there are souls who are so selfish and egotistical that they have come to follow Me more for themselves than for Me. They resign themselves only to contribute what bothers them and what they cannot avoid. They help Me carry only a very small portion of My Cross, and in such a manner that they can hardly acquire the merits indispensable for their salvation. But in eternity, they will see how much further remained the path that they should have traveled.

On the other hand, there are souls, and not few, who, moved by their desire for salvation but above all, by the love inspired in them by the vision of what I have suffered for them, decide to follow Me on the path to Calvary. They embrace the perfect life and give themselves to My service, not to help Me carry just a part of the Cross but all of it. Their only desire is to give Me rest and to console Me. For that purpose, they volunteer for everything that My Will asks of them, searching for how they can please Me. They do not think about the merits or the reward that awaits them, or the tiredness or the suffering that will result for them. The only thing they have in mind is the love that they can show Me and the comfort they give Me.

If My Cross is presented as an illness, if it is hidden under a job contrary to their inclinations and of little agreement with their abilities, if it comes accompanied by the thoughtlessness of people surrounding them, they accept it with total submission.

Oh! These are the souls that truly carry My Cross; they adore it. They make use of it for obtaining My Glory with no interest or payment other than My love. They are the ones that consider Me and glorify Me.

If you do not see the result of your sufferings or your self-denial, or if you see it later, be certain that they have not been in vain and fruitless. On the contrary, the fruit will be abundant.

The soul who truly loves does not keep count of how much it has suffered or labored, nor does it expect this or that reward. It seeks only that which it believes glorifies its God. For Him, it spares neither labors nor weariness. It does not become agitated or restless. Far from it, it does not lose its peace if it finds itself thwarted or humiliated because the only motive for its actions is love, and love abandons the consequences and the results. Therein lies the purpose of souls who do not seek rewards. The only thing they hope for is My Glory, My comfort, My rest, and, for that reason, they have taken My Cross and all the weight that My Will desires to place upon them.

My children, call Me by My name, for Jesus means everything. I will wash your feet, those feet that have trodden a slippery path and are now wounded by the blows against the rocks. I will wipe away your tears, cure you, kiss you, and you will remain healthy and know no other path but the one that leads you to Me.

We are now at Calvary! The mob is excited because the dreadful moment is near. Exhausted by fatigue, I can hardly walk. My feet bleed because of the stones on the way. Three times I have fallen along the way: once to give sinners used to sinning the strength to convert; another to give encouragement to souls who fall because of being frail and to souls who are blinded by sadness and restlessness, encouraging them to rise and embark with courage upon the path of virtue; and the third time, to help souls depart from sin at the hour of their death.

Jesus is Nailed to the Cross

Look with what cruelty these hardened men surround Me. Some pull the Cross and lay it on the ground; others tear off My clothes that adhere to the wounds that again open and blood again oozes out.

Look, beloved children, at how much shame and confusion I suffer seeing Myself this way before that immense crowd. What sorrow for My soul!

The executioners tear off My tunic and cast lots for it—the tunic with which My Mother so carefully clothed Me during My childhood and which She had been increasing in size as I grew. What would be My Mother's affliction as She contemplates this scene? How She must have desired to keep that tunic, now stained and soaked with My Blood.

The hour has arrived, and the executioners, stretching Me out upon the Cross, grab My arms and pull them until they reach the holes prepared in it. My whole Body is breaking; it swings from one side to the other, and the thorns of the crown penetrate even deeper into My head. Listen to the first blow of the hammer that nails My right hand. It resounds to the depths of the earth. Listen yet again. Now they are nailing My left hand, and, in the presence of such a spectacle, the heavens tremble, and the Angels prostrate themselves. I keep the most profound silence. Neither a complaint nor a moan escapes My lips, but My tears mingle with the blood that covers My face.

After they have nailed My hands, they cruelly pull My feet. My wounds open, the nerves in My hands and arms tear, and the bones are dislocated. The pain is intense!

My feet are pierced, and My Blood soaks the earth.

Contemplate for a moment these bloodstained hands and feet. This naked body, covered with wounds, with urine, and blood. Filthy. This head pierced by sharp thorns, soaked in sweat, full of dust, and covered in blood.

Admire the silence, the patience, and the conformity with which I accept this suffering. Who is the One who suffers like this, a victim of such ignominy? He is the Son of God! The One who has made the heavens, the earth, the seas, and all that exists. The One who has created man; the One who sustains everything with His infinite power. He is there motionless, despised, stripped, and followed by a multitude of souls who will abandon worldly possessions, family, country, honors, well-being, glory, and whatever may be necessary to give Him Glory and show Him the love owed Him.

Be attentive, Heavenly Angels, and you too, souls who love Me. The soldiers are going to turn over the Cross, to rivet the nails to prevent them from coming out due to the weight of My Body and allowing Me to fall. My Body is going to give the earth the kiss of peace. And while the blows from the hammering resonate throughout space, on the summit of Calvary the most admirable spectacle is carried out. In a plea, My Mother, who is contemplating all that was happening and, being unable to give Me relief, implores the Mercy of My Heavenly Father. Legions of Angels come down to adore My Body and to hold it up so as not to touch the earth and to prevent it from being crushed by the weight of the Cross.

Contemplate your Jesus, stretched out on the Cross, unable to make the slightest movement. Naked, without fame, without honor, without liberty. Everything has been snatched away from Him! There is no one who takes pity and sympathizes with His pain. He only receives torments, ridicule, and mockery.

If you truly love Me, will you be ready to do anything to be like Me? What will you refuse to obey Me, to please Me, to console Me? Prostrate yourself to the ground and let Me tell you a few words:

May My Will triumph in you.
May My Love destroy you.
May your misery glorify Me.

Jesus Pronounces His Last Words

My daughter, you have heard and seen My sufferings; accompany Me until the end and share My pain. My Cross is now raised. Here is the hour of the Redemption of the world!

To the crowd, I am the spectacle of jeers but also of admiration and love for souls. This Cross, which until now was an instrument of torture where criminals expired, will be from now on, the light and peace of the world. Sinners will find forgiveness and life in My Holy Scriptures. My Blood will wash and erase the stains of their sins. Souls who are pure will come to My Sacred Wounds to refresh themselves and to burn in My Love. In them, they will take refuge and make their dwelling forever.

"Father, forgive them, for they know not what they do." They have not known the One who is their life. They have unleashed against Him all the fury of their iniquities. But I beg of You, O My

Father, release upon them the power of Your Mercy.

"Today you will be with Me in Paradise," because your faith in the Mercy of your Savior has erased your crimes and leads you to eternal life.

"Woman, there is your Son! Mother of Mine, there are My brothers! Watch over them, love them… they are not alone."

O, you, for whom I have given My life, you now have a Mother to whom you can turn to in all your needs. I have united all of you with the tightest bonds when I gave you My own Mother.

The soul now has a right to say to its God, "Why have You forsaken me?" Indeed, after I fulfilled the mystery of Redemption, human beings have become sons of God again, brothers and sisters of Jesus Christ, and heirs of eternal life.

> "O Father of Mine… I thirst for Your Glory… and the hour has arrived." From now on, by the fulfillment of My Words, the world will know that You are the One who sent Me, and You will be glorified!"

I thirst for Your Glory; I thirst for souls. To quench this thirst, I have poured out My Blood unto the last drop! For that reason, I can say, "All is fulfilled." The great mystery of Love has now been fulfilled; the mystery for which God surrendered to the world His own Son in order to restore life to mankind. I came into the world to do Your Will, O My Father. It is now fulfilled!

"To Thee I give My soul." In this way, the souls who accomplish My Will can say in truthfulness: "Everything is consummated." My Lord and My God, receive My soul. I place it in Your beloved hands.

For souls in the throes of death, I offered My death to My Father, and they will have Life. In the final cry I gave from the Cross, I embraced all of humanity: past, present, and future. The piercing spasm with which I detached Myself from earth was welcomed by My Father with infinite Love, and all of Heaven exulted over it because My Humanity was entering into Glory. At the same instant in which I surrendered My Spirit, a multitude of souls met with Me: those who desired Me centuries ago and those who desired Me a few months or days ago, but all of them desired Me intensely. Right then, this joy alone sufficed for all the hardships suffered by Me.

You should know that in memory of that joyful meeting, I have decided to assist the dying and many times do so even visibly. I grant them salvation to honor those who so lovingly welcomed Me in Heaven. So pray for these dying people, because I love them very much. As often as you offer the last cry that I gave to the Father, you will be heard because, through it, many souls are given to Me.

It was a moment of joy when all the Heavenly Court, packed together and vibrant and awaiting My death, was presented to Me. But among all the souls who surrounded Me, one was particularly jubilant, overwhelmed so much that it sparkled in joy, in love. It was Joseph, who, more than anyone else, understood the Glory I had acquired after such bitter battles. He led all the souls who were waiting for Me. To him, it was granted to be My first Ambassador in Limbo [where the faithful, deceased souls awaited]. The Angels, each in their own order, paid honor to Me in such a way that My Humanity, already resplendent, was surrounded by a countless number of Saints who adored and exalted Me.

My children, there are no glorious crosses on earth. They are all wrapped in mystery, in darkness, and in exasperation: in mystery, because you do not understand it; in darkness, because they blind the mind; and in exasperation, because they strike blows in precisely those places where one does not wish to be struck.

Do not complain; do not delay. I tell you that not only did I carry the wooden cross that led Me to Glory, but, above all, that invisible but permanent Cross that was formed by the crosses of your sins. Yes, and of your sufferings. Everything that you suffer was the object of My sorrows, for I not only suffered to give you Redemption but also for what you should suffer now. Look at the love that unites Me to you; in it, have the confirmation of My Holy Will and unite yourselves to Me by observing how I behaved in the midst of unlimited bitterness.

I have taken as a symbol a piece of wood, a cross. I have carried it with great love, for the good of all. I have suffered real affliction so that all could rejoice in Me. But today, how many believe in the One who truly did love you and does love you? Contemplate Me in the image of the Christ that weeps and bleeds. There and in this way, the world has Me.

The Resurrection of Jesus

Holy Friday was followed by the glorious dawn of the Sunday of the Resurrection. If I have decided not to destroy the world, it means that I want to renew it and rejuvenate it. Old trees need to lose their leaves and be pruned so that they can sprout new buds. Old branches and dry leaves are burned.

Separate the young goats from the lambs so that they can find ready and well-prepared and fertile pastures to graze at their ease and drink from the clear fountains of the water of salvation... It is My redeeming Blood that waters the arid lands that have stayed the deserts of the world of souls. And this Blood will always flow over the earth as long as there is one man to save.

Beloved spouse, I desire what you do not want, but I can do what you cannot obtain. Your mission is to have Me loved by souls and to teach them to live with Me. I have not died on the Cross and gone through a thousand tortures to populate Hell with souls, but rather to populate Heaven with chosen ones.

God the Father

I see My Son, trembling down there below in the shadows of Gethsemane, who, having descended from Heaven, took the form and substance of that creature of Mine who presumed and continues to presume that he has the power to rebel against his Creator. The man, that lonely and confused man, is the designated victim, and as such, with His own Blood, has had to cleanse all of humanity which He represents. He trembles and is horrified at feeling Himself covered, even to the point of seeing Himself dominated by the inconceivable mass of sins that He would have to remove from the blackened consciences of millions and millions of filthy creatures.

Poor Son of Mine, Love has taken You now to this, and You are frightened by it. Who will glorify You in Heaven when, radiantly, You enter into it? Can any creature give You praise worthy of You, any love worthy of You? And what is the praise and love of a man, of millions of men, in comparison with the Love with which You have accepted the most tremendous of tests that could ever exist on earth? No, My beloved Son, nobody but Your Father could equal You in Love, nobody but I, who in My Spirit of Love, can praise and love You for Your sacrifice that night.

You have reached, beloved Son of Mine in whom I rest all My benevolence, the paroxysm of death by surviving the very bitter agony in the Garden. You have reached, in the sphere of Your humanity, real and whole, the summit of the great passion that a human heart can have: to suffer for the offences committed against Me, but to suffer for them with the most pure and intense Love that there is in You. Albeit with trembling, You have reached the limit through which humanity should reach complete Redemption. You, beloved Son, by the sweat of Your Blood, have conquered not only the souls of Your brothers, but even more, Your own personal Glory that should elevate You, man, equal with Me, God like You.

You have drawn in Me the most perfect Justice and the most perfect Love. At that time, they represented the scum of the world, and You did it through Your voluntary and free acceptance. You are now, among all, My honor, glory, and joy. You were not My offender, not You. You have always been My beloved Son, in whom I have placed My pleasure. You were not the scum because even then I saw You as You have always been: My Light, My Word, that is to say, precisely Myself. Son, who trembled and died for My Honor, You have deserved that Your Father make You known to the world, to that blind world, which offends Us and yet is so loved by Us!

Oh, most beloved Son, I see You and will always see You in that night of Your bitterness, and I have You always in mind! Because of Your love, I am reconciled to creatures and with creatures. And then You could not raise Your face to Me; it was so covered with their guilt. Now, to please You, I make them raise their faces to Us so that by catching a glimpse of Your Light, they will remain captives of Our Love.

Now, My Son, always so beloved, I will do what I told You then in the shadow of Gethsemane, and they will be great things to give You joy and honor.

The Most Blessed Mother

The Sorrows of the Virgin Mary

Many prophets spoke about Me; they prophesied that it was necessary for Me to suffer to become worthy of being the Mother of God. On earth, they advanced knowledge of Me but, as it was meant to be, in a very veiled way. Later, the Evangelists spoke of Me, especially Luke, My beloved physician—more of souls than of bodies. Afterwards, some devotions were started that had as a basis the sorrows and pains suffered by Me. Thus, it is commonly believed and thought that I experienced seven main sorrows.

My children, your Mother has rewarded and will reward the efforts and love that you have had for Me. But as Jesus did, I want to talk to you more extensively about My sorrows. Then, you will talk about them to other brothers and sisters, and everyone at last will imitate Me. Because of what I suffered, I am continuously praising Jesus, and I seek nothing more than for Him to be glorified in Me.

Look, little children, it is sad to talk about these things to My own children, because every mother keeps her sorrows to herself. And this I dutifully did in the course of My mortal life; therefore, My wish as a mother has already been respected by God. Now that I am here, where the smile is eternal, and having already concealed, like all mothers, the sorrows that I experienced, I should talk about them so that as My children you may know something about My life.

I know the fruits that you will gain from it, and as they are pleasing to Jesus, My beloved Son, I will talk about them as soon as you can understand Me.

My Jesus said, "Whoever is first, make yourself last," and He truly did so because He is first in the House of God, but He lowered Himself unto the lowest step. Now, because of love, I will not take away from Him this first and last place that belongs to Him. Rather, I strive to make you understand this truth, and My joy will be much greater when you are convinced, not through the path of simple knowledge but by means of a profound and deeply rooted conviction. May He be first, and all of us truly be last.

If He was first, there should be a second one in the scale of love and glory and, therefore, of lowliness and humiliation. You have now understood: That being should be Me. Little children, praise God, who even having established an enormous distance between Jesus and Me, still wanted to place Me immediately next to Him.

My children, what appears to the world is not what is most important before God. Having been chosen Mother of God involved for Me grave sacrifices and resignations, and the first was this: knowing through Gabriel the election made in the intimacy of God. I had wanted to remain in a state of humble knowledge and concealment in God. I wanted this more than anything else because it was My delight to know that I was last in everything.

Upon knowing the choice of God, I answered, as you know, but it consisted of so much for Me to rise to the dignity to which I was called.

Little children, do you understand this first sorrow of Mine of which I speak? Reflect on it; give your Mother the great delight of holding in esteem that humbleness which I so much admired above My virginity. Yes, I was and I am the slave to whom every request may be made, and I accepted only because My surrender was in the same degree as My love.

It pleased You, oh God, to elevate Me to You, and it pleased Me to accept because My obedience was pleasant to You. But You know how sorrowful it was for Me, and that same sorrow is now before You, required as light for these children, whom You love and whom I love. I am the slave, oh Children of Mine, and as it was done unto Me, let it now, without doubt, be done unto you all that God wants.

The acceptance gave God the answer that will give men access to the Redemption, and in this was verified that admirable phrase: "Here is a Virgin who shall conceive and give birth to a Son who will be called Emmanuel."

My having accepted to become the Mother of Emmanuel involved My gift to the Son of God so that His Mother would give of Herself to Him before the Humanity of Jesus would form in Me. That is why My gift was the result of Grace but also the cause of Grace. And the precedence should be recognized that God is the foremost cause; nevertheless, it should be affirmed that My acceptance acted on the level of Grace as a concomitant cause.

They call Me Co-Redemptrix because of the sorrows I have suffered; but I was so, even before, because of the gift I had made through Gabriel. Oh, My divine Son! How much honor You have wanted to give Your Mother in compensation for the great sorrow I suffered in rising to the dignity of Your Mother!

Little children, you are in a sightless world, but when you see, wondrous things will be inducements for you to rejoice for Me. You will see what unity of glory and humility there is here where My Jesus is the sun that is never hidden. You will see what a wise design was carried out through what I gave up, to the lowliness of being hidden.

But now, hear Me. As My maternity was advancing, I had to talk to some of My loved ones, and I told them about it while hiding as much as I could of the honor that I had received. I lamented having relinquished the secret about God's triumph because God Himself was to be glorified in Me.

However, very soon I had the joy of knowing that I was regarded as a woman amongst so many. My soul rejoiced because, in the eyes of the world, the slave of God who longed for humiliations as only I could long for, was trampled upon. When Joseph hid himself, I did not suffer, but I truly rejoiced. Do not say that I suffered then because that is not true.

That was how God satisfied My desire for humiliations. This was My compensation from the Lord, for having become the Mother of God: to be considered as a fallen woman. Daughter, learn the wisdom of love, learn to esteem holy humility, and do not fear because it is a virtue that shines with sparkling light.

When the nuptials took place, I had no problems. I knew how things would be, and I feared nothing. Indeed, God grants perfect peace to those who give themselves entirely to Him in the most paradoxical situations, as was Mine: I was forced by human dictates to marry a man, yet knowing that I could only belong to God.

I suffered so many sorrows on earth! It is not easy to become the Mother of the Most High, I assure you. But neither can everything one does out of the purest motive and to please God be called difficult. Remember that!

Have you ever thought what it was that caused Me the most sorrow on that Holy Night in Bethlehem? You distract the mind with the stable, with the manger, with the poverty. I, on the other hand, tell you that I spent that night in complete ecstasy about My Son. And even though I had to do what every mother does with her little child, I did not abandon My ecstasy, My rapture. And so, the only thing that caused Me sorrow that night of love was seeing how My poor Joseph suffered, seeking shelter for Me, any place at all. Aware of everything that was to happen and of the One who was to come into the world, My beloved husband, on seeing My confusion, became anguished, and I felt much sympathy for him. Later, we were both filled with joy, and we forgot all our anguish.

We fled to Egypt, and all that is possible has been said about this, even though some focus their imagination more on the fatigue of the journey than upon the fear of a Mother who knew that She possessed the greatest treasure in Heaven and on earth.

Later, living in Nazareth, little Jesus was growing up full of life, and, at that time, He caused us only the slightest and most minimal worry. Every mother knows what it is like to wish for the health of her own child, and how a very simple thing looks like a great dark cloud. My Child went through all the epidemics and childhood illnesses of those times. Like every mother, I could not be protected from any of the anxieties that a mother's heart experiences.

But one day, the truly dark cloud that darkened the festive light of the Mother of God arrived. That cloud is called losing Jesus. No poet or master of the spirit could possibly imagine Mary when She knows that She has lost Her well-adored Son and when She has no news of Him until three days later. Little children, do not be amazed at My words. I experienced the greatest confusion of My life. You have not reflected enough on those words of Mine: "Son, your father and I have been looking for you for three days. Why have You done this to us?" My God, now that I speak to these beloved children, I cannot stop praising You. You who hid Yourself to make us experience the delight of finding You. Oh! How else could one possibly come to know the sweetness that a glassful of honey places in the soul when She embraces her Everything?

Now you see, I also speak to you about My joys, but not without reason do I relate and join together joys and sorrows. You should draw benefit as best you can from everything that happened; God conceals Himself in order to be found. Some know this truth; others, thinking about that dreadful sorrow of having lost Jesus, may do everything to find Him. You should not remain incapable of acting and disheartened.

Your Mother would like to save you from dealing with so much that remains to be told. First, there are things that have never been told and for that reason, not yet appreciated. Secondly, by getting to know them, you will have to join Me in suffering and in painful thoughts. Moreover, everything that My Jesus wants has been told without any opposition.

Do you think that I spent family life in Nazareth peacefully? It was peaceful by virtue of the uniformity with the will of God. But from the creatures, there was so much trouble!

Our unique way of living was noticed, and as a result, we were ridiculed publicly. I was considered excessive for the sole fact that whenever Jesus left the house, I could not contain My tears, and Jesus went away frequently. Joseph was harassed as if he were a slave to Jesus and Me. How could the world possibly understand? We abandoned all worry to the One who lived amongst Us, adored in all His manifestations.

What a beloved Son that young Boy was; more handsome than the sea, wiser than Solomon, and stronger than Samson. All the mothers would have snatched Him away from Me, such was the charm that surrounded Him. The small-minded covered Me with soothing judgments; however, they did not spare criticism of the tireless father whom they thought was subject to his faithful but jealous wife. Everyone recognized My integrity, but they all thought it to be a common and selfish passion.

This, My little children, is what is not known. This happened in the midst of a world that could not see or understand, and His Mother most pure. Jesus kept quiet, without encouraging Me, because the Mother of God had to go through the crucible, that is, as one woman amongst many about whom opinions should not be spared.

Admire the Wisdom of God in these things and find that Divine meaning, which joins the greatest of sublimity with the trials that are more painful in relation to such sublimity, because every abyss summons another abyss and every profundity summons its profundity.

The hour of separation arrived, the hour for the action of Jesus. With it arrived the feared day of His departure from Nazareth.

Jesus had spoken quite extensively to Me of His mission and of the fruits that it would give to Him and everyone. He had made Me love it beforehand. It was necessary, therefore, for us to separate, even if for a short time… He said goodbye, kissed us, and headed towards His mission as Teacher of humanity. But His departure did not go unnoticed in the small village where Jesus was so loved.

There were demonstrations of affection, of blessings, and even though they really did not know what good Jesus was going to do, just the same a loss was foreseen by these people of little intellect but after all, of generous heart.

And I, in the midst of so many manifestations, how did I feel? So much affection welled up in Me, but He did not delay His departure by a minute. My Jesus knew what awaited Him after His preaching. He had spoken to Me about it so many times and so profusely of the treachery of the Pharisees and the others. And now you see Him leaving, departing like that alone and without Me to fulfill His mandate, without Me who had made Him grow with the warmth of My heart, without Me who adored Him like no one would ever adore Him!

Later I followed Him. I found Him when He was surrounded by so many people that it was impossible for Me to see Him. And He, truly the Son of God, gave His Mother a sublime response as was His wisdom but which pierced this maternal heart through and through. Yes, I understood Him completely, but that did not spare Me from sorrows. It is true, to the human relationship, He countered the divine one in which I was included, but nevertheless, the remarks of others did not fail to hurt Me.

The initial blow was followed by the joy of witnessing His greatness, of seeing Him honored, venerated, and loved by the people; thus quickly this wound also healed.

I traveled the roads with Him, enthralled by His knowledge, comforted by His teachings, and I never tired of loving and admiring Him.

Then arrived His first friction with the Sanhedrin. The miracle occurred that caused so much fuss in the minds of the Jews, of their arrogant Priests. He was hated, persecuted, spied upon, and tempted. And I? I knew everything and from then on, with outstretched hands, I offered into the hands of the Father the holocaust of My Son, His surrender, and His horrible and ignominious death. I already knew about Judas; I knew the tree from which the wood would be taken for My Son's Cross.

You cannot imagine the intimate tragedy that I lived through together with My Jesus, in order for the Redemption to be fulfilled.

I have said before: Co-Redemptrix. For that to be, the usual sorrows were not enough. A more intimate union with His great suffering was necessary so that all mankind should be redeemed. So, as I went from town to town with Him, I became more and more aware of the inconsolable tears shed by My Son on so many sleepless nights that He spent in prayer and meditation. Every state of His mind was revealed and placed before Me, and certainly, that began My Calvary and My cross.

So many considerations increased My sorrows each day that I was His Mother and yours! So many sins, all the sins; so much sorrow, all the sorrows; so many thorns, all the thorns. Jesus was not alone. He knew it and felt it. He witnessed His Mother continuously in union with Him. He was afflicted by it, even more so because My suffering was for Him the greatest suffering.

My Son, My adored Son, if only these children knew what happened then between You and Me!...

And the hour of the holocaust arrived, after the sweetness of the Paschal Supper. And from then on, I had to rejoin the crowd. I, who loved and adored Him in a unique way, had to be far from Him. Do you understand, oh My children?

I knew that Judas was taking his treacherous steps and there was nothing I could do; and I knew that Jesus had shed Blood in the Garden and there was nothing I could do for Him. And then they seized Him, abused Him, insulted Him, and wickedly condemned Him.

I cannot tell you everything. I will only tell you that My Heart was in turmoil with continuous anxiety, a seat of continuous bitterness and uncertainty, a place of desolation, dejection, and affliction. And the souls that would later be lost? And all the acts of simony and sacrilegious exchanges?

Oh children of My sorrows! If today you are granted the grace of suffering for Me, with fervor, bless the One who granted it to you, and without hesitation, sacrifice yourselves.

You think about My grandeur, My beloved children. It helps you to think about it; but listen to Me: do not think about Me, but about Him. I would like to be forgotten if it were possible! Give all your compassion to Him, to My Jesus, to your Jesus, to Jesus, your love and Mine.

Thus, little children, the sorrow in My Heart was a sword continuously piercing My soul, My life, through and through. I felt it, while Jesus did not. He comforted Me with His Resurrection, when My immense joy suddenly healed all the wounds that bled within Me. "My Son," I kept repeating. Why so much affliction? Your Mother is near You. Is not even My love enough for You? How many times did I comfort You in Your afflictions? And now, how is it that not even Your Mother can give you some relief? Oh Father of My Jesus, I want nothing more than what You want. You know it; but see if so many afflictions can have some relief. The Mother of Your Son asks this of You.

And now on Calvary I cried out: "My God, cause to return to those eyes that I adore the light that You imprinted in them since the day that You gave Him to Me! Divine Father, see the horror in that holy face! Can You not at least wipe away so much Blood? Oh Father of My Son, Oh My Beloved Spouse, Oh You who have desired to take your Humanity from Me! May those arms, opened up to Heaven and Earth, be a prayer; may they be the supplication for the acceptance of Him and of Me!"

See, Oh God, what the One whom You love has been reduced to! It is His Mother who asks You to alleviate so much sadness. After a short time, I will be left without Him. Thus My vow, which I offered wholeheartedly in the Temple, will be entirely fulfilled. Yes, I will remain alone, but lighten His pain without paying attention to Mine.

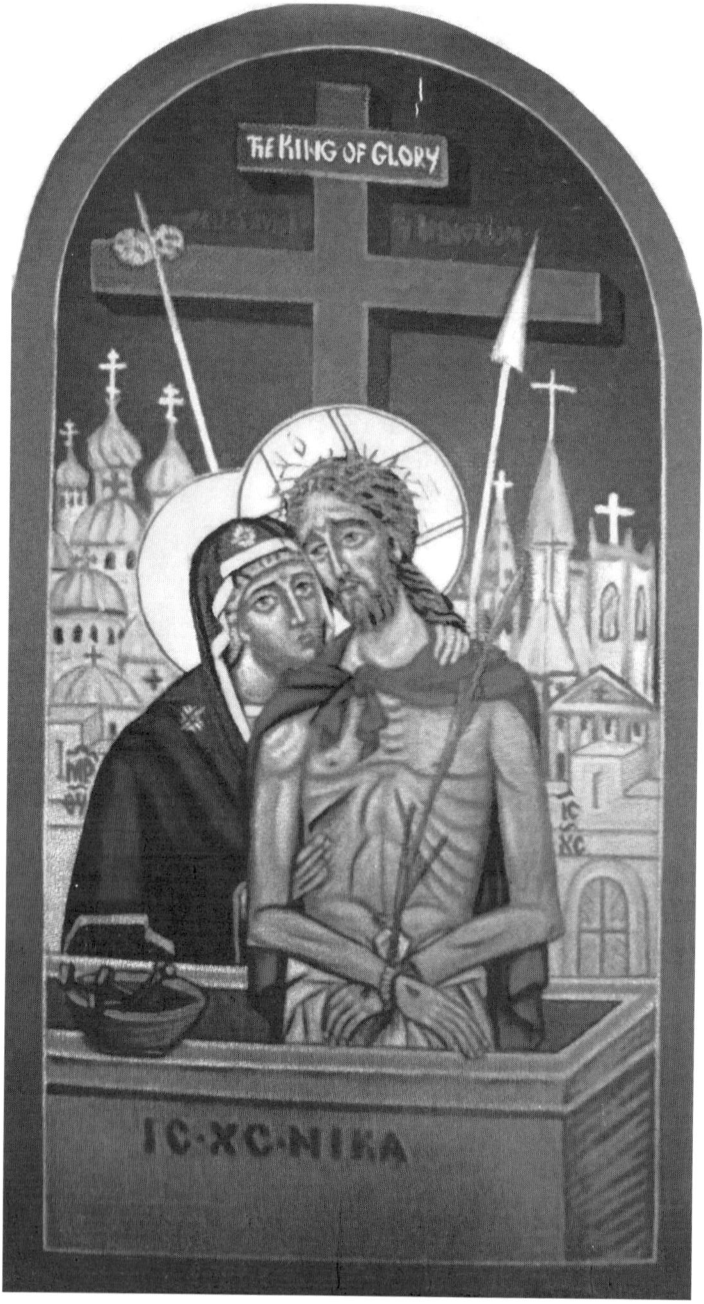
THE KING OF GLORY
IC·XC·NIKA

Chapter 5

The Stations of the Cross

Introduction

Allow yourself to be embraced by My most ardent desire that all souls will come and purify themselves in the water of penance, and that the feeling of confidence and not fear may penetrate them, because I am a God of Mercy and I am always ready to receive them in My Heart.

When you do what I ask of you, I am near you. Your obedience will quench that flaming thirst which dried My lips on the Cross.

I will make Myself present each time that you invoke My Passion with love. I will permit you to live united with Me in the pain that I experienced in the Garden of Gethsemane when I saw the sins of all men.

Think about everything that I had to go through to save mankind, to be able to reign in their hearts, to make possible their entrance into My Father's Kingdom.

Let us now meditate on My Passion… which continues to give glory to the Father and holiness to souls.

Let us walk together the Way of the Cross.

The First Station

Jesus is Condemned to Death by Pilate

† † †

†

We adore You, O Christ, and we praise You because, by Your holy cross, You have redeemed the world.

Crowned with thorns and covered with a purple mantle, the soldiers presented Me again to Pilate. Not finding a crime that he could punish Me for, Pilate was looking for a way to set Me free. In the pitiable condition that I was in, Pilate showed Me to the mob. He proposed to give Me liberty and condemn Barabbas, a famous thief and murderer. The people shouted back: "Crucify Him and set Barabbas free!"

Souls who love Me, see how they have compared Me to a criminal. How they have lowered Me more than the worst criminal. Meditate for a moment upon the unspeakable martyrdom of My Heart: My Heart degraded beneath the heart of Barsabbas. I am the most despised of men, and I am being condemned to death like an infamous criminal. Pilate has pronounced sentence. My little children, consider attentively how My Heart suffered…

Jesus, most obedient, meek and humble of heart, have mercy on us.

†††

The Second Station:

Jesus Accepts the Cross

†††

†

We adore You, O Christ, and we praise You because, by Your holy cross, You have redeemed the world.

Let us continue, My little children. Follow Me on the way to Calvary. I am overwhelmed with the weight of the Cross....

While My Heart was absorbed with sadness for the eternal loss of Judas, the cruel executioners, insensitive to My pain, place the Cross on My wounded shoulders. The hard and heavy Cross cuts into My shoulders. Through the Cross, I consummated the mystery of the Redemption of the world.

Contemplate My Passion, Angels from Heaven. See the Creator of all the marvels; the God to whom all the heavenly spirits render adoration; the God walking towards Calvary and carrying on His shoulders the holy and blessed wooden cross; the God who is going to receive His last breath.

Contemplate My Passion, you souls who wish to be My faithful imitators. My Body, destroyed by so much torture, walks without strength, bathed in sweat and Blood...

†Jesus, most obedient, meek and humble of heart, have mercy on us.

†††

The Third Station:

Jesus Falls the First Time

† † †

†

We adore You, O Christ, and we praise You because, by Your holy cross, You have redeemed the world.

I suffer, without any sorrow for My pain from the mob! As I walk, there is not a single one of the mob who feels pity towards Me. I am surrounded by hungry wolves, wanting to devour their prey... All of the demons came out of hell to compound My suffering.

The fatigue that I feel is so great and the Cross is so heavy, that I fell half-way there. In the most brutal manner, the soldiers forced Me to lift up the Cross. One soldier takes Me by the arm; another soldier pulls My clothes that are stuck to My wounds, tearing them open again... Yet another soldier grabs Me by the neck, another by the hair. A number of soldiers hit Me with their fists and others kick Me with terrible blows all over My Body. The Cross falls over Me and with its weight causes new wounds. My face is forced down into the stones of the path. Blood runs down My face and it sticks to My eyes which are almost closed. The blows I have received are causing My eyes to be swollen. The dust and the mud mingle with the Blood and I am turned into the most repugnant person.

Jesus, most obedient, meek and humble of heart, have mercy on us.

†††

The Fourth Station:

Jesus Meets His Mother

†††

†

We adore You, O Christ, and we praise You because, by Your holy cross, You have redeemed the world.

Continue with Me for a few moments, and a few steps ahead you will see Me in the presence of My Holy Mother. Her Heart pierced by pain. She comes out to meet Me for two reasons. One is to give Herself more strength to suffer at the sight of Her Son and God. And with Her heroic attitude, it gives Her Son encouragement to continue His work of Redemption.

Consider the martyrdom of these two Hearts. What My Mother loves the most is Her Son… She cannot ease My pain and She knows that Her visit will make My sufferings much worse. However, Her presence will increase My strength to fulfill the Will of the Father.

My Mother is My most beloved being on earth, and I know I cannot console Her. The sad state in which She sees Me causes Her heart a suffering as deep as Mine. She allows a sob to escape. She receives in Her heart the death that I am suffering in My body. O, how Her eyes are fixed on Me and Mine on Her! We do not utter a single word, but Our Hearts say many things in this painful gaze.

Jesus, most obedient, meek and humble of heart, have mercy on us.

†††

The Fifth Station:

Simon Helps Carry the Cross

†††

†

We adore You, O Christ, and we praise You because, by Your holy cross, You have redeemed the world.

I am on My way to Calvary. Those wicked men, fearing to see Me die before reaching the end, look for someone to help Me carry the Cross, and from the vicinity they seized a man called Simon. This man helps with carrying part of the Cross. But the burden of My Cross is still very difficult to bear.

There are souls that walk this way behind Me. They accept to help Me carry My Cross but they still worry about comfort and rest. Many others agree to follow Me and, with this in mind, they have embraced the perfect life. But they do not abandon their self-interests, which is still their priority. That is why they falter and drop My Cross when it feels too heavy for them. They look to suffer in the least possible way. They measure their self-denial, evading humiliation and fatigue as much as possible. They remember, perhaps with sorrow, those whom they left behind. They try to obtain for themselves certain comforts and pleasures.

Jesus, most obedient, meek and humble of heart, have mercy on us.

†††

The Sixth Station:

Veronica Wipes the Face of Jesus

† † †

†

We adore You, O Christ, and we praise You because, by Your holy cross, You have redeemed the world.

There are many souls who are moved by a desire for salvation. It is the inspiration of love for the vision of what I have suffered for them that they decide to follow Me on the path to Calvary. They embrace the perfect life and give themselves to My service. They help Me to carry not just a part of the Cross but all of it. Their only desire is to console Me and give Me rest. They surrender themselves to My Will, searching for anything that can please Me. They do not think about the merits or the reward that awaits them, nor do they consider the tiredness or the suffering that will follow. They only consider the love they can show Me, and the comfort they can give Me.

They accept with total submission the cross that presents itself as an illness. They also accept a cross that is hidden under a job contrary to their inclinations and of little agreement with their abilities. They also accept a cross of loneliness—a cross of the absence of people to surround them. Oh! These are the souls that truly carry My Cross; they adore it. They take advantage of My Cross to glorify Me. They do this without any interest or payment other than My Love. They are the ones who are considerate of Me and glorify Me.

Jesus, most obedient, meek and humble of heart, have mercy on us.

†††

The Seventh Station:

Jesus Falls the Second Time

† † †

†

We adore You, O Christ, and we praise You because, by Your holy cross, You have redeemed the world.

Consider Simon, who is behind Me; he is helping Me to carry the Cross. He is a man lacking good will; he is a mercenary because if he accompanies Me and shares the weight of the Cross, it is because he has been forced to do so. For that reason, when he feels tired, he lets the full weight of the Cross fall on Me. Thus, I fall to the ground for the second time.

My Father sends Angels to assist Me. They help to maintain My human consciousness when I fall. My battle must continue until the appointed time so that many souls are not lost.

I walk over the stones that destroy My feet. As I stumble and fall, I look into the crowd searching for a small look of love, of union with My pain, however... I do not see anyone with a look of compassion.

My children, will you who follow in My footsteps not let go of your cross even if it seems so heavy? Do it for Me. In carrying your cross, you will help Me carry Mine, and on the difficult path, you will find My Mother and the holy souls who will give you support and comfort.

Jesus, most obedient, meek and humble of heart, have mercy on us.

†††

The Eighth Station:

Jesus Speaks to the Women

† † †

†

We adore You, O Christ, and we praise You because, by Your holy cross, You have redeemed the world.

Daughters of Jerusalem, weep not over Me, but weep for yourselves and for your children. For behold, the days shall come wherein they will say: "Blessed are the barren, and the wombs that have not borne, and the breasts that never nursed." Then shall they begin to say to the mountains, "Fall upon us," and to the hills, "Cover us."

Consider that if you do not see the product of your sufferings, of your self-denial, or if you see it later, be certain that they have not been in vain and fruitless. On the contrary, they shall bear abundant fruit.

The soul who truly loves does not keep count of how much it has suffered or worked. Nor does it seek rewards; it only desires that which it believes glorifies its God. For him, neither its hassles nor toils are tiring. It does not become agitated nor restless. Far from it, for it remains calm and peaceful. When it encounters obstacles or when it is humiliated, it does not mind. The only motive for its actions is love, and that love abandons concern for the consequences and the results. These souls who do not seek reward are only motivated by love. They only desire to participate in My Glory, to comfort Me, and help Me rest. For that reason, they have taken up My Cross and all the weight that My Will wants for them to bear.

Jesus, most obedient, meek and humble of heart, have mercy on us.

†††

The Ninth Station:

Jesus Falls the Third Time

†††

†

We adore You, O Christ, and we praise You because, by Your holy cross, You have redeemed the world.

Exhaustion takes its toll on Me, as I can barely walk. My feet are bleeding because the stones along the way cut into My feet. I fall for the third time.

Three times I have fallen along the way. The first is to show sinners who are used to sinning that they can convert and have the strength even though they have fallen into sin. My second fall is for those souls who fail because they are frail or those souls who are blinded by sadness and restlessness, that they can get up and embark with courage upon the path of virtue. My third fall is for those souls who depart from sin at the hour of death.

My children, call Me by My name, for Jesus means everything. I will wash your feet, those feet that have embarked on a slippery path that leads to injury to their feet by blows against the rocks. I will wipe away your tears, I will cure you, and I will kiss you. With this, you will remain healthy and know no other path but the one that leads to Me.

Soul that belongs to Me, do not pay attention to our cruel enemy. As soon as you feel the movement of grace at the beginning of the battle, come to My Heart. Feel and watch how My Heart spills a drop of My Blood over your soul, and you will come to Me. You will know where I am: under the veil of faith. Lift off this veil and, with complete confidence, tell Me all your sorrows, all your miseries, and all your falls. Listen to My words with respect and do not fear for the past. My Heart has submerged itself in the endless depths of My Mercy and My Love.

Jesus, most obedient, meek and humble of heart, have mercy on us.

† † †

The Tenth Station:

Jesus is Stripped of His Clothing

†✝†

†

We adore You, O Christ, and we praise You because, by Your holy cross, You have redeemed the world.

Look at what cruelty these hardened men surround Me. Some of them pull the Cross and lay it on the ground, while others work at tearing My clothes that adhere to the wounds that open again and My Blood oozes out.

Look, beloved children, at how much shame and confusion I suffer seeing Myself humiliated in this way before that immense mob. How this pains My soul!

The executioners tear off My tunic and toss lots for it, this tunic which My Mother covered Me with so much care during My childhood and had grown in size as I had. What immense sorrow envelops My Mother as She contemplates this scene!

Contemplate for a moment these bloodstained hands and feet... This naked body, covered with wounds, with urine, and Blood. Dirty. My head is punctured by sharp thorns, soaked in sweat, full of dust, and covered with Blood.

Jesus, most obedient, meek and humble of heart, have mercy on us.

†††

The Eleventh Station:

Jesus is Nailed to the Cross

† † †

†

We adore You, O Christ, and we praise You because, by Your holy cross, You have redeemed the world.

It is now time for the executioners to stretch My arms onto the Cross. They pull My arms to make them reach the holes prepared on the Cross. My entire Body is ruined, swinging from side to side. The crown of thorns penetrates deeper into My head. Listen for the first blow of the hammer that nails My right hand—the sound of that blow resounds to the depths of the earth. Listen again—now they are nailing My left hand. At the presence of this spectacle, the heavens tremble, and the Angels prostrate themselves. I keep the most profound silence. My lips do not utter a complaint nor do they moan under such pain, but My tears now mingle with the Blood that covers My face.

After they have nailed My hands, they pull on My feet with as much cruelty as they can muster. My wounds open, the nerves in My hands and arms are torn. My bones are dislocated from their joints. The pain is intense! My feet are nailed, and My Blood soaks the earth!

Contemplate your Jesus, hanging on the Cross, without being able to make the slightest movement. I am naked—without fame, without honor, and without liberty. They have snatched everything from Me! There is no one who takes pity and feels sorry for My pain! I receive only tortures, ridicule, and mockery.

Jesus, most obedient, meek and humble of heart, have mercy on us.

†††

The Twelfth Station:

Jesus Dies Upon the Cross

†††

†

We adore You, O Christ, and we praise You because, by Your holy cross, You have redeemed the world.

My children, you have heard and seen My sufferings; accompany Me until the end and share My pain.

My Cross is now raised. Here is the hour of the Redemption of the world! I am the spectacle of jeers for the mob, but I am also admired and loved by souls. This Cross, up to now an instrument of torture where criminals are executed, becomes, from now on, the light and peace of the world. I offered My death to My Father for the dying souls that they will have life. In the last cry I gave from the Cross, I embraced humanity: past, present, and future.

My children, there are no glorious crosses on earth. They are wrapped in mystery, darkness, and exasperation. They are wrapped in mystery because you do not understand them; wrapped in darkness, because they confuse the mind; and wrapped in exasperation, for they strike exactly in places where you do not want them to strike.

Jesus, most obedient, meek and humble of heart, have mercy on us.

†††

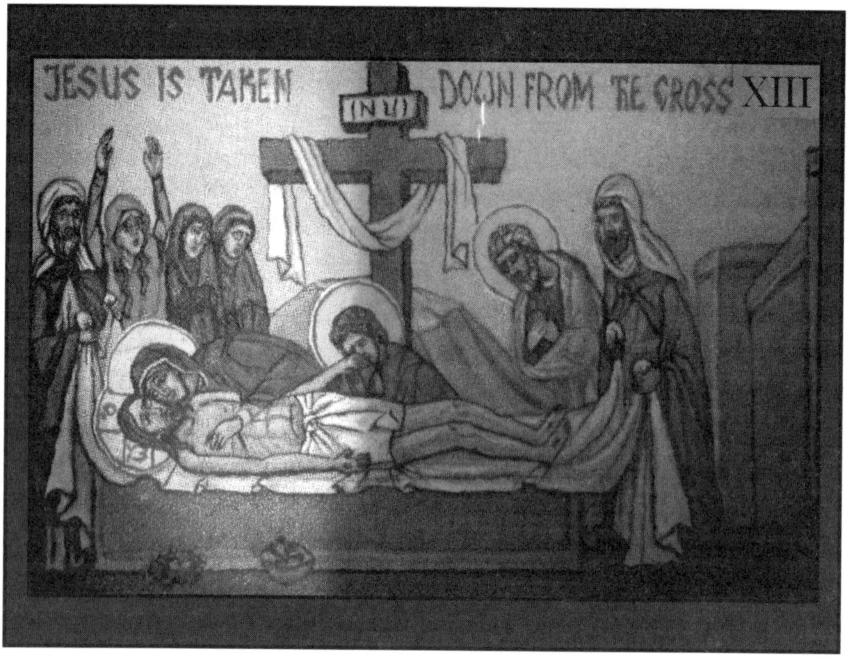

The Thirteenth Station:

Jesus is Taken Down from the Cross

†††

†

We adore You, O Christ, and we praise You because, by Your holy cross, You have redeemed the world.

There is no time for lamenting nor is there time for delay. I tell you that not only did I carry the wooden cross that led Me to Glory, but most importantly, I also carried the invisible but permanent Cross that was formed by the crosses of your sins. As for all your sufferings, they are the object of My sorrows. I suffered not only to give you Redemption, but also for what you should suffer today. Look at the love that unites Me to you; in it, have the confirmation of My Holy Will. Unite yourselves to Me, observing how I acted among limitless bitterness.

I have taken as a symbol a piece of wood, a cross. I have carried it with great love, for the good of all. I have suffered real affliction so that everyone could be joyful with Me. But today, how many believe in the One who truly loved you and loves you? Contemplate Me in the image of the Christ who cries and bleeds. There and in this way, the world has Me.

Jesus, most obedient, meek and humble of heart, have mercy on us.

†††

The Fourteenth Station:

Jesus is Placed in the Tomb

† † †

†

We adore You, O Christ, and we praise You because, by Your holy cross, You have redeemed the world.

I created the world and also the tree that was to provide the wood for My cross. I created and cultivated the bramble bush that was to provide the thorns for My royal crown. I buried in the bowels of the earth the iron that was to forge My nails. Oh, mystery of incomprehensible love! I have created a nest for the bird, a den for the beast, a palace for the rich, a house for the laborer, a crib for the baby, a home for the aged. When I came in person to visit My land, there was no room for Me in the inns of the world. It was a cold, freezing world that night when I came to mankind. I came to men, but men did not recognize Me. There was no room for Me… And now?

My children, poor sinners! Do not distance yourselves from Me. I wait for you night and day at the Tabernacle. I will not reproach you for your crimes; I will not throw your sins in your face. What I will do is to wash you with the Blood of My wounds. Do not be afraid, come to Me. You do not know how much I love you.

Jesus, most obedient, meek and humble of heart, have mercy on us.

†††

The Fifteenth Station:

The Resurrection of Jesus

†††

†

We adore You, O Christ, and we praise You because, by Your holy cross, You have redeemed the world.

Holy Friday was followed by the glorious dawn of the Sunday of the Resurrection. It is My redeeming Blood that waters the arid lands that have become the deserts in the world of souls. And this Blood will always run over the earth as long as there is one man to save. I have not died on the Cross and gone through a thousand tortures to populate Hell with souls, but rather, to populate Heaven with chosen ones.

I say again, My children, poor sinners! Do not distance yourselves from Me. I wait for you night and day at the Tabernacle. I will not reproach you for your crimes; I will not throw your sins in your face. What I will do is to wash you with the Blood of My wounds. Do not be afraid, come to Me. You do not know how much I love you.

Come now, My children. Come to Me. I am your Lord who awaits you in the Tabernacle. I am completely present in Body, Blood, Soul, and Divinity. Do you want to know Me? Then come and spend time with Me. I love you, dear children.

Jesus, most obedient, meek and humble of heart, have mercy on us.

†††

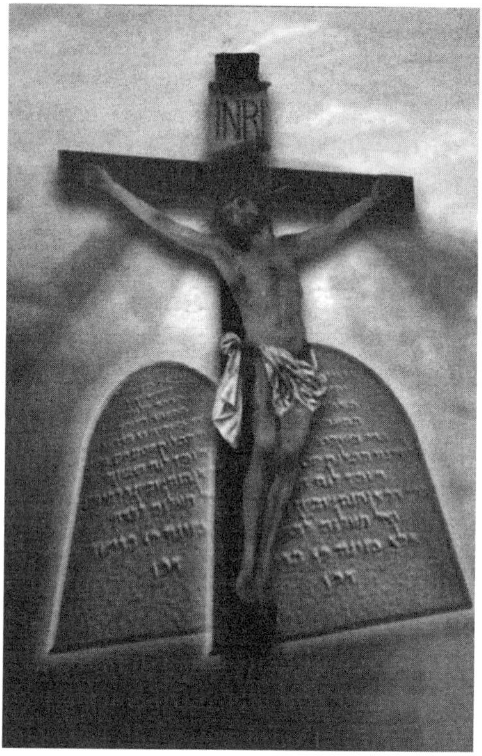

IMPRIMATUR

The reading of the book "From Sinai to Calvary" charts a beautiful itinerary for a brand new spiritual growth. I find nothing contrary to Sacred Scripture, or to the doctrine of the Church in its contents.

I find only concepts and principles, which can help the interior enrichment of the faithful. For this reason I grant my Imprimatur, asking our Creator for His special blessings upon each reader.

San Vicente, El Salvador, February 9, 2004
[Sealed and signed]
Mons. José Oscar Barahona C.
Bishop of San Vicente
El Salvador, Central America

Chapter 6

From Sinai to Calvary

Presentation

The sacred and mystic writers, who have ardently desired to reach the heart, mind, and soul of their readers by offering them true nourishment that strengthens their spirits, have first sought out the help of God. They have beseeched Him for the necessary light and His Divine inspiration to illuminate, with the light of Faith, the intellect, and the will of those who, with a humble disposition, wish to receive these salutary messages. These messages, written under God's inspiration, reveal His Most Holy Will for the good and benefit of mankind.

This present chapter, written by Catalina, carries the characteristics of texts written by those who, living in intimacy with God, have penetrated into the depths of the Divine Being to transmit the inspirations He grants at His pleasure. The Gospel is the source from which our Faith is born, leading us to a profound knowledge of Jesus Christ, who, through His life, passion, death, and resurrection, has obtained redemption for humankind.

The Gospels recapitulate all the infinite grandeur of the Triune God manifested in the Person of Jesus Christ. As believers know, these sacred texts are the source from which all infallible teachings of the Church are drawn. From these Sacred Books, the Word of God, innumerable writings have been created to promote Faith and ensure that the Christian life complies with the Divine Will.

God has raised and chosen certain people to be His messengers and witnesses of the one Truth, entrusting them with some of the riches of the deposit of Faith.

We as Christians may know the Gospel, but not all of us live it or comprehend its full dimension. This is why it is necessary to revisit the Gospels step by step to better understand them and make them the rules of our lives. How often have we read about the Passion of Christ, only for those readings to remain like the simple recounting of history or a novel, having no impact on our lives?

In this book by Catalina, truly inspired by the Lord, we find a profound meditation on the Passion of Christ, particularly the Seven Words uttered by a dying Jesus on the Cross to call humankind to conversion. The echo of that Divine clamor spreads throughout the world and will continue resonating through time and space, even if the majority of humanity covers their ears to avoid hearing it.

Catalina, fulfilling her sacred duty as "Christ's town crier," carries the sacred words of the Lord to all places, environments, and people of the world so they may understand that the one necessary thing in life is friendship with God. Called by the voice of Jesus Christ and inspired by Him, she invites us to live her experience of God. Catalina introduces us to the Mystery of our Redemption, taking us to the solemn and sorrowful moments of the Passion of Jesus Christ. These scenes and their interpretations are described experientially, as though they come from the depths of Catalina's being, enabling readers to truly feel the presence of Christ, His call to conversion, and the strength of His command to His chosen messengers.

The world today is sadly secularized. "In observing this world, we realize it needs a means of restraint. It needs, as Pope John Paul II says, a new evangelization to bring forth the splendor of God's presence with renewed strength. A new evangelization that may redirect the world toward Christ, our Hope, and His Mercy by inviting everyone to look again at the Cross, so we may calm the storm our common enemy has unleashed and straighten the ways of man."

Each phrase of the Seven Words is profound in its contents, leading me to recommend that this book be read slowly, imagining oneself beside the Lord to feel His Divine Love. At the supreme moment of His life, His gaze was set on us.

This book is not just another pious writing. Besides containing no dogmatic error, it draws readers into the presence of Christ, uniting us all in faith, love, and the hope of a perfect life in God.

Mons. René Fernández A.
Archbishop Emeritus of Cochabamba

Introduction

Our Lord urged me to write this chapter, which content is based on all that was revealed to me during almost two and a half months.

For a long time, I did not know when or how to start writing this testimony, even though I was certain that it would be on a date of great importance for the history of our Salvation. And it turned out to be precisely today, when the Church commemorates the day of the Immaculate Conception of that Woman, who with Her "Yes" facilitated the fulfillment of the greatest act of God's Mercy to mankind: the coming of our Redeemer into the world.

This chapter contains new teachings concerning the Words of Love and Wisdom, of Abandonment to the Will of the Father amid the most atrocious pain, Pity and Mercy towards humanity, of Courage and Self-giving to man. These are the last hours of Jesus on the Cross and, today, they are being recreated in order that you meditate upon them in depth and live united with our Savior in the last moments of His life as a man, before returning to the Father and sending us the Holy Spirit. I pray that this Spirit of God may guide us through these pages, begging His assistance and consecrating to Him my poor work, so that in some way I may be able to help in the salvation of souls.

> "When I arrived at Golgotha, I found that two convicts had just been crucified,"

The Lord had said to me at the start of my meditation on that First Friday.

> "They were screaming and I felt pity for them, I Who was in a worse physical condition than they…"

I could see hundreds of people, men who were going to be crucified, walking slowly but in desperation, screaming, blaspheming, their eyes filled with terror and hatred, with a blind desire for vengeance. They were not all together. I realized that these were scenes from different days and hours. But they shared a common denominator: all were condemned to the cross, and almost all of them spoke the same words and uttered similar insults and threats to those who became their executioners.

On more than three occasions, I saw one or several soldiers approaching one of these convicts and pulling out a knife or sword to cut the man's tongue off to keep him quiet, and that entire road toward death would become even more horrible and sorrowful. Then there appeared before my eyes the scene of Good Friday. This Man condemned to death was different. Beaten… a thousand times more wounded than any of the others, crowned with a helmet made of long thorns that had destroyed His skin, being encrusted into His flesh, covered with blood and dust, feverish, trembling, and with very irritated eyes due to the sweat and injuries. But His gaze was full of peace, of mercy, of sadness, and at certain moments, one could even perceive happiness when the certainty returned to Him that this suffering would save humanity from eternal death.

The others threw insults; they cursed and squirmed. He remained silent. Not one complaint escaped from His mouth—only blessings and words of forgiveness. Contrary to what the values of this world would tell us, it could be clearly seen that He is the Great Victor, the Vanquisher of death. His executioners were merely the poor instruments of the devil, the Devil who, along with Judas, is the great loser.

The First Word

When they tore off His clothes, everyone waited in absolute silence for that Man to rebel or to ask for pardon, for mercy from His adversaries. Some expected that He should rebel or beg pardon from that sentence. Others expected that, as the Son of God He purported to be, He would beg His Father to have fire rain down from Heaven to chastise those who mistreated Him so much. Time seemed to have stood still for them; nevertheless, this Man barely moved His lips. Silently, He prayed.

But there were four people who expected something else: John, Mary Magdalene, Mary of Cleophas, and the Virgin Mary. And it seems to me that Jesus also expected something different… He too.

They expected to see those people who were cured by those Hands, which were now being pierced. Where were those who heard His teachings on the Mount of the Beatitudes? Where were those who received pardon from His lips? Where were the men who lived with Him for almost three years? Where were those whom He had resurrected in body and soul?

What I saw hurt me, and I knew that my eyes were welling up. Then I heard the voice of Jesus, who spoke and told me that He had thought not only of them but also about all of humanity, about all of us of yesterday and today, those who, in spite of having known Him and having received so many benefits from Him, would one day turn their backs on Him. Some would do this because of cowardice, for fear of persecution; others out of fear of being mocked for admitting their Christianity; others because of their comfort; others because they thought they deserved every good thing, and their selfishness did not allow them to think of anyone else. The majority would do this because of indifference, lukewarmness, or lack of faith.

Then He repeated to me the words of the Gospel:

> "... and have no fear, for there is nothing hidden that will not be known. What I say to you at night, say it in the light of day, and what I say to you in your ears, preach it from the rooftops."

That is why I am here writing, helped by Him, so that you are not among those whom Jesus refers to with such pain.

The soldiers had finished putting Jesus on the Cross. Until a few minutes earlier, you could only hear the blows on the nails first deadened by His virginal Flesh and, later, dull against the wood. He did not reply. He pardoned. He prayed, and silence grew in the throats of those either awaiting the first words or the anguished howling of the Crucified.

When they lifted high the Cross, the weeping of the women broke the silence, and then the horror started anew: the shouting, the insults, the mocking, the spitting. The defiance of God in that precise instant of the confrontation between hatred and Love, arrogance and Humility, the diabolic and the Divine, rebellion, and Obedience to the Will of God!

Jesus looked at me, and it was as if His light-colored eyes lifted me up, awakening me from myself, for I felt that I was losing myself in the depth of that pain. He began to talk to me again. His Words echoed in my heart, as if all of a sudden, an enormous hole had opened in it.

With sadness, He said:

> "I was subjected to a trial in which they had nothing to accuse Me since I had done nothing wrong. There was never a lie in My mouth, and even the false witnesses, who were called before this infamous trial to talk against Me, lacked any coherence in all their testimonies. My only offense and the cause for My sentence to death was My affirmation of

something which I could not deny before anyone—that I was the Son of God."

He stopped speaking, and I felt that I was broken because of that moral and physical torment. How many things passed through my mind in seconds! How many feelings that I perhaps will never be able to explain!

Soon afterwards, His voice, with a masculine and calm tone and with faltering words, woke me up from the present time, and I listened to what, maybe, none of those who were there were expecting to hear from the lips of this convict sentenced to death:

"Father, forgive them, they know not what they do."

Everyone was rendered silent before these words; many of them were shocked by the impact as they had just realized in whose presence they were. What unjust irony! He was sentenced for proclaiming Himself the Son of God because He dared to call God: "Father," "Abba," or beloved Papa, "Daddy," as many of us would say today. For that reason, they sentenced Him… And even then, He asked of His Father that He have mercy upon His executioners. He asked that this grave sin not be taken into account by God, His Father. And with this act, He was leaving the best example of all that He communicated in His years of preaching. In these acts, He was giving a living testimony of what He taught us: to love and pray for one's enemies, for those who hurt us.

The words that one day were heard from His lips on the Mount of the Beatitudes, He was now converting them into action on the mountain called Golgotha or "of the Skull." How much had Satan enjoyed the Passion of the Son of God! However, if before he had laughed at the pain of Jesus, after these words he now howled with rage and went running into those monsters who were torturing the Son of Man, that Man on whose account "the bad angel" or "devil" was thrown out of Heaven.

In this way, he wanted to increase the cruelty of the tormentors against Jesus to the point of challenging Him and tempting Him to come down from the Cross. That would have been the triumph of the devil, for Jesus to accept the challenge and, with that, fall into the temptation of disobedience and pride. The enemy of souls writhed in rage because the sentence had been carried out. The Son of the Woman of Genesis was crushing his head against the ground, as He was gaining for us entrance into Heaven. And not with swords or arms, nor with tanks or warplanes as battles are won on earth to justify our miseries, but rather with one Man, destroyed on that Cross.

That Man who, as He forgave Peter, the adulterous woman, the Magdalene, and so many others, humbly asked forgiveness from the Father to teach us that sweetness and love can do more than pride, the humiliation of others, the whip, a self-sufficient posture, and arrogance. To teach us that the person who is noble, wise, and holy is recognized by their simplicity and humility, not by their yelling or earthly possessions, and also by the quality of their acceptance of suffering, not by making others suffer.

No, there is no mercy for Him. But He does ask for mercy for them, for all of us, men and women, from Adam and Eve until the last man who will be born before the end of the world. He knows that from this profound pain a Church will be born. That is the great and tasty fruit, the happy consequence of the combination of water and blood that soon would flow from His open Side—fruit of the Love of He who is leaving two commandments that sum up the ten given by His Father to Moses on another mountain, Mount Sinai.

If you keep these two commandments, a whole river of Mercy will be poured out on you, and you will be saved. There is only one condition for obtaining that Mercy: "To love God above all things and to love your neighbor as yourself." He has not come to abolish the laws of the prophets but rather to fulfill them. His whole life was nothing else than the fulfillment of the prophecies written in times past about Him, from the time of His conception in the pure womb of a young virgin.

We, as human beings, have had such difficulty accepting ten

rules in exchange for so much Love, for so many blessings, for the gift of life, for the freedom of choice, that God Himself decided to be incarnated from a human womb to show us that, yes, it is possible to keep those commandments. But since our misery and selfishness are so great, He took one step farther in our favor.

He says to us:

> "Acknowledge that you have one Father alone, whom you must love above all your comforts, above all your loved ones, above all the power, honor, and pleasures that the world may offer you, and treat others as if they were yourself."
>
> "Love them with the same love with which you love yourself, nothing less. Give men and women the respect and consideration that you demand from others. Be capable of giving all that you ask for yourself and do not do unto others as you would not want them to do unto you."

It is that plain, that simple, so that even children and the unlearned may understand it.

I know that at this point of your reading, brother and sister, you know that this will not be easy. It is no small enterprise to detach oneself from everything in favor of others. It is heroic! That is what the search for holiness is all about, and all the baptized must strive to be holy. If you have had the courage to accept it, do not allow anything to obstruct your way. You will face moments in which many circumstances and too many people—loved ones and not, known and unknown, of your same creed and of other religions, of your own country and of other lands—will try to halt you. This is the moment when the virtue of perseverance is so necessary.

How will you do it? You have the assurance that Jesus has left you a Church to guide you when you do not know which way to go, to lift you up when you fall, to forgive you in His Name, to welcome you when you seek shelter for your soul, to form you with

His Word, and to nourish you with His Body and Blood... so that you can become an extension of Him, a transparent manifestation of His living Presence, so that you can radiate that clarity and brilliance. This is the stamp of those who are His witnesses, of those who have received the sparkle of His Light and His Love.

Our merits cannot save us because we do not have any before the immensity of the Divine Omnipotence. We are not going to be saved because we were good parents, brothers and sisters, sons and daughters, or friends. That is our obligation. We will be saved because Jesus was, is, and will always be Love and is waiting for us to accept Him as such. This Love, with His infinite merits, has won for us the pardon. He has asked this of His Father from the Cross.

Many times, the reproach of our conscience is so great for a committed sin or for a whole lifetime of sin that we cannot believe that God can forgive us, that He already won for us the pardon, nailed on the Cross of Love. Jesus said that when we ask for forgiveness of our sins while praying the Our Father, let us remember that He was able to ask for forgiveness for us because He never felt bitterness against anyone.

Only a simple and humble soul is able to ask for pardon for the offenses of enemies. That requires much courage and surrender, which is the formula for removing the base instincts that seek the ordinary: vengeance, the downward pulling of others in order to try to stand out, or even to keep oneself above water. But this is for sure: absolutely all of us are obligated to forgive the offenses against us in the same measure that we want for God to forgive us.

If we say that "we forgive, but do not forget," we are asking the Father to do the same with us. If, on the contrary, we forgive from the heart those who offend us and, while praying, we ask God to forgive us as we forgive, in that case, we are in a position to implore that God grant us His Mercy since we acted with mercy.

Later Jesus said:

> "My Heart, tormented by the suffering, had a feeling of compassion for another being who was suffering next to Me. The crucified man at My right, Dismas, called 'the Good Thief,' kept watching Me with compassion, he who was also suffering. With one look, I increased the love in that heart. A sinner, yes, but capable of feeling compassion for another man. That wrongdoer, that bandit who hung from a cross, was another Magdalene, another Matthew, another Zacchaeus... another sinner who was acknowledging Me as the Son of God. That is why I wanted him to accompany Me toward Paradise that same afternoon, to be with Me when I opened the doors to Heaven to give entrance to the just."
>
> "That was My mission, and that is your mission: to open the doors of Heaven to sinners, to the repentant ones, to the men and women who are able to ask for forgiveness, to lay their hope in the existence of eternal life and place it next to My Cross. Dismas, the Good Thief at My right, and Gestas, 'the Bad Thief,' at the left. The one on the left full of hatred; the one on My right, changed in an instant upon hearing Me say those words: 'Father, forgive them, for they know not what they do.'
>
> "That man, before My serene presence—My suffering presence, yes, but not desperate; the presence of the bearer of peace—felt many things break inside of him. There was no longer any place for hatred. There was no place for sin, for violence, for bitterness. Only a good heart is capable of acknowledging that which is coming from Heaven. Dismas was acknowledging it to himself. I was asking for forgiveness for those who were crucifying Me. I was pleading for mercy for a sinner like him. And his little soul opened up to accept that mercy."

Jesus continued:

> "That is why, when Dismas hears Gestas, the Bad Thief, mockingly say to Me that if I were the Son of God I should save Myself and save them also, Dismas feels the fear of God. He knows that their lives had been miserable, so wretched, that they probably deserved a greater suffering than what they were going through. That fear, that acknowledgment of the light that was shining in front of him, makes him reply: 'Do you not fear God, you who are suffering under the same sentence? And we are suffering justly, we deserve it because of our deeds, but this One has done nothing wrong.'"

At this point, the Lord permitted me to witness the look that He exchanged with the Good Thief, a look of gratitude, a look of forgiveness, a look of a father who is pleased with the response given by his son. There is now a new scene before my eyes, and I understand that Jesus is allowing me to witness what He was remembering, what had happened not long ago when He had started to live among His disciples. I see Jesus choosing His followers. One by one, He looks at them deeply, lovingly, but firmly, with a gentle authority, the kind of authority that is not self-important but the fruit of such conviction before which no one can refuse Him. And He invites them to follow Him.

About those days, Jesus said:

> "I wanted that they be My disciples, My brothers, My friends. It is one who chooses his own friends, and I chose Mine. How many times did I have to bring peace among them in order to teach them the value of friendship! Even today, I try to teach men the sense of community and agape love in this relationship of friendship with Me and with all others. I loved them not only as God but also as a man. I

could converse with them; I could play with them, and, in fact, I did so."

"When we used to go down to the river for a swim, we played and splashed each other with water like little children. We used to throw pebbles, as in a contest, and we celebrated with applause and laughter the more swiftly and the farther the pebbles skipped. We would climb trees as any young man would. We would race, climbing up the hills to pray or to eat our small snacks. We shared anecdotes and laughter, as all men do when they live in community. But we always ended those gatherings with a prayer of gratitude to the Father for allowing us to have those moments."

"Yet, the days in which we did not even have time to eat were not few, but I always tried to do their work so that they could appreciate the example. My food was to do the Will of My Father. That was My objective, My repose, My happiness. I could instruct them and listen to their concerns, their secrets. And even though I saw into their deepest thoughts, I felt happy that they wanted to make Me part of their intimacy. On My part, I gave them so much love, patience, instructions, hugs... all that can be given to a friend. But it was not enough. I had to give My life for them, and I did not hesitate to do so."

"That is why I am nailed, agonizing on this Cross, for them, for all of you."

My God, how much pain and how much Love! I saw two tears come down from the big eyes of Jesus, and I would have given my life to dry them with my lips—those tears so full of pain and of Love! That is when I understood that no one deserves the consideration of Jesus. His disciples and friends of those days did not deserve them, and neither do we deserve them today.

Jesus continued:

> "I gave My life for you, so you may live. And even now, I call you My friends. I do not ask that you understand everything I have done for you, but I do ask that you trust in My Love, that you believe in My Mercy, and that you strive to love as I have loved you."
>
> "Look at the world around you and at your own heart. How many times have you fallen, doubted, or even rebelled? Yet here I am, still loving you, still calling you to My Heart. Do you think My tears are of sadness alone? No. They are also tears of hope because I see what you can become if you allow My Love to transform you. I see the beauty of your soul as I created it, and I long for you to see it too."

I could feel the depth of His words, and they pierced my heart. He went on:

> "Even as I hung on this Cross, I saw the faces of those who would turn away from Me, deny Me, and mock Me. But I also saw the faces of those who would come to Me, those who would accept My sacrifice, those who would be faithful. I saw you. I saw your struggles, your victories, and your failures. I saw your prayers and your tears. And for all of it, I embraced this Cross because My Love for you is greater than anything you can imagine."

At this point, I felt overwhelmed by His words. The weight of His Love and sacrifice became almost too much to bear. Yet, He gently continued, as if to console me:

> "Do not let your unworthiness keep you from Me. I do not seek perfection; I seek your heart. Bring Me your wounds, your sins, your weaknesses, and I will give you My strength, My forgiveness, and My healing. You are not alone. I am with you always, even to the end of the age."

I was filled with awe as He spoke these words, realizing that His agony on the Cross was not just a historical event but a living reality, a continual outpouring of His Love and Mercy for all of humanity, for me, for you, for each of us. He was not distant; He was present, and His Heart was open wide.

He then spoke of His final moments on the Cross:

> "When I cried out, 'My God, My God, why have You forsaken Me?' it was not a cry of despair but of profound solidarity with every soul who has ever felt abandoned, alone, or lost. I carried the weight of all sin, of all suffering, so that no one would ever have to carry it alone. In My humanity, I experienced the deepest depths of anguish, so that in your moments of darkness, you could know that I am with you, that I understand, and that My Light will guide you through."

He paused for a moment, as if inviting me to reflect. Then, with great tenderness, He said:

> "When I gave My Spirit into My Father's hands, it was a moment of total surrender and trust. I ask you to trust in Me as I trusted in the Father. Surrender your fears, your doubts, your burdens, and your sins into My hands, and I will lead you to new life. Remember, the Cross is not the end; it is the gateway to Resurrection, to hope, to eternal joy."

At these words, I felt a profound sense of peace and hope, even amidst the sorrow of contemplating His Passion. He concluded:

> "My beloved, walk with Me on this journey. Take up your cross, as I took up Mine, and know that My strength will sustain you. When you fall, I will lift you up. When you feel weak, I will be your strength. And when you feel unloved,

remember My Love for you, which led Me to this Cross. I will never leave you. I am yours, and you are Mine."

The vision faded, but His words remained engraved in my heart. They were not just words of the past but a living invitation to trust in His Love and to follow Him more closely every day.

The Second Word

Jesus was alone at that moment and He found in Dismas all the love that He had wished to find in His Apostles. That man had even dared to defend Him while the others, the ones whom He loved, had cowardly fled except for John, so as not to compromise themselves and fall together with Him.

It seemed that in more than two years, His own had not been able to truly believe in His words. Otherwise, they would be there next to Him now.

This man, Dismas, had in a few minutes believed in His Divinity by hearing from His lips words of supplication to the Father. Dismas had discovered the Truth and the Way to Life.

He was seeing Jesus dying in the Peace of those who have nothing to fear, with the Hope of those who know that there is something to hope for. Dismas wanted to believe in that "something" because he was in front of Hope Himself.

Under great exhaustion because of the effort and pain, but with all the emotion of having seen the Light, he says the words that would take him to sanctity: "Jesus, remember me when you come into your Kingdom!"

Those words are equivalent to those we say today in the confessional: "Forgive me, Father, for I have sinned."

The previous night, Jesus began suffering His Passion to save sinners such as each one of us and such as Dismas. Meanwhile, the "good thief" did not even suspect that he would leave his prison insulted, spit upon, and rebuffed as "just another ill-fated man," only to find himself before the Fountain of Merciful Love. He had no idea that by nightfall, he would come into the Palace of the King of Kings holding onto the arm of the Prince of Peace.

And Jesus saw a friend in that criminal because a friend is one who trusts in you, one who gives you his trust without fear. A friend is one who is moved to pity for you in your moments of suffering and does not add salt to your wounds.

A friend is one who wants to remain at your side and who stays with you until the end, without listening to the shouts of the damned ones, of those who accuse, offend, insult, and want to see you die in the worst possible way because their hearts are full of cruelty.

That look from Jesus replaced the embrace, which He longed to give Dismas, the same way He embraces today all those who entrust and consecrate their souls to Him. In the midst of His tears and spasms, He smiled and with a voice full of tenderness He promised:

"Truly, I say to you, today you will be with me in Paradise."

Once more, Jesus is extending His loving arms to the sinner, exalting him, the one who repents and humbles himself, even above the just ones.

It will indeed not be the holiest among those who had died up until that day who would be the first to enter into Heaven… not even the Prophets nor the Martyrs who would cause the "feast in Heaven." It is a thief, perhaps an assassin, a man repudiated by society who will be the first Saint to be canonized in life and by Jesus Himself: "Saint Dismas."

It is said that opposite poles attract. Poverty captivates our Lord. Misery attracts Him; the sinner is His great challenge. For that reason, He lowered Himself even to take on our human condition so that in union with Him, we may free ourselves of all ties. And so the two ends meet again: on one side, the empty hands of man; on the other, the infinite Love of God. Two ends only united by two sentiments, by two attitudes: humility and Mercy, which together always build the bridge of salvation.

Blessed are you, Dismas, you who deserved the first salvific drop of the Redeemer's Blood, only by the strength of your faith and His infinite Mercy. Happy are you, my brother, for you did not cause Jesus the disappointment that many cause Him today, those who should recognize His voice and love Him more.

Blessed are you, the Good Thief, for having been able to forget your sufferings and have compassion upon others.

This is how you became deserving of the Grace of having God Himself give you absolution, transforming your sin into a resplendent fire of Divine Love. It is because you were brave even as to deliver a teaching to your companion, Gestas. Hence, you were evangelizing from your cross, following the example of Him, Whom you had just met.

Thus, Dismas was giving his companion all that he owned at the hour of his death. He offered him all that he possessed: faith, a new but firm faith; hope in the Mercy of the Lord, to obtain eternal life; and charity, at inviting him to take pity upon the Suffering One.

Now I ask myself and all of my brothers and sisters: And as for us, what are we willing to give for this Love, Who gives Himself in order to save us? Perhaps what we have in excess?

And we feel "generous" when we give some food or clothing or some other type of material help to those who need it. But how many times are we aware that it is our obligation to give to our brothers something more than bread or clothing?

I do not have the least doubt that these things are necessary and much more so in times of scarcity, of hunger or of difficulties. But we must remember, "Man does not live by bread alone."

And if we are aware that material wealth or having much to eat and drink does not generate true happiness in man, and that there is a permanent dissatisfaction in those who live in lust, in avarice, and other concupiscences of the flesh…

And if we learned that fame and honors will not lead us to true happiness because they are ephemeral and transitory glories…

And if we can attest to the fact that neither physical health nor crass laughter nor the hustle and bustle of life, or having worldly friendships exclusively, are crucial to living a truly happy life…

Then why are we not taking God to our brothers? Why are we not taking to them His Word, the Love that we have known, the Faith that makes us witnesses? We do not realize the gravity of our omission!

God loves the one who gives joyfully. God provides for our necessities. When we give our faith and our love happily with joy, then we are as full as a huge granary from which others can come and gather good grain to take it in turn to the more needy.

During one of the encounters that we had in the last few days, upon arriving at this point, Jesus said to me:

> "The nucleus of My Message was that the joy, which I had, was the fruit of the Love and the surrender to My Father and to you, mankind. All that I said and did was so that My profound joy would infect the others as well, so that My disciples' joy would be real, and reach its fullness."
>
> "My daughter, this harsh battle that I am living, My flesh injured and crying out for its rights, darkness seeping all around Me and being far from those for whom I give My life, makes Me feel a deathly anguish. This is because I carry in My Being all the love that I feel for the creatures who await redemption. The anguish and the sorrow increase the pain in My Body that is becoming weaker and weaker from all this Blood that drains out of My skin, as a result of this harshest of trials."
>
> "Happy are you who accept to share in My pains and in My loving. Happy are those who voluntarily accept this communion with My deepest feelings, this union with My most profound desires of surrender, this living of My same condition as [being] crucified, in the extraordinary lesson that never ends."

The Third Word

My Lord lifted His head a little, as if wanting to free His eyes of the blood that entered them so He could see once more those two persons whom He had loved so much. Now they remained as His testimony: His Mother and John, the brother, the friend, the son... who, perhaps because he was the youngest and the purest among the Apostles, identified best with Jesus.

In fact, John would later write the Gospel of the Love of God and would speak about Mary, the Woman in the book of Genesis: the Mother of the Son of God, the "Full of Grace," the perfect collaborator, disciple, and, at the same time, the teacher of Jesus - Mary, our beloved and sweet Mother.

Jesus said to me at that moment:

> "The day when I spoke on the mountain about the Beatitudes, My Mother was in front of Me, listening attentively, learning... 'Blessed are the poor in spirit... Blessed are the pure of heart... Blessed are the humble and simple... Blessed are those who suffer and cry... Blessed are those who are hated and persecuted for My sake...' And I thought of all those who would be called Blessed or Happy, taking Mary as their model."
>
> At that moment, She came closer to the Cross, where that Body, flesh of Her flesh, was nailed. Knowing that little time was left, Mary interiorly tells Him, "My Son and My Lord, take Me with You...!"

Jesus looked at Her with unfathomable tenderness and pain. There She was, the Woman in Genesis, the Woman in the Wedding of Cana, the Woman in the Apocalypse, the Woman who had been destined, chosen, and formed to be His Mother on earth...

That look of Jesus demands of everyone a profound respect and true compassion for the one who is now living the pains prophesied by Simon in the Temple the day of His Presentation... A sword was piercing Her soul!

After having had the vision of that moment, our Lord told me:

"My Mother was always destined to be the Woman whose sufferings would help Me in the redemption of man... You must know that on the day of the Wedding at Cana, when I told Her that My hour had not yet arrived, I was referring precisely to this moment. The hour when I would leave so that She would continue My Work in the Church born from My Side.

"The Father willed that She become the Mother of the 'Fruit' of His love. I willed that She become the Mother of My Passion and My Cross: My Church. The Mother of the Church, and the Mother of those who believe in My name and become Children of God.

"Having said 'Yes' to the Will of the Father when My Incarnation was announced to Her, and Whose life had been nothing other than a 'Yes' to the Divine Will, this Woman will now become the first harvester of the fruit, of the grain of wheat that has died. And for this She will have to be equal to Me in mercy towards the world.

"You see, little nothing, Now as you ponder this moment, you can see and understand with greater ease, why human suffering makes sense when it is endured for love's sake, desiring to fulfill the Divine Will. And it is that the greatest pain, as intense as it may be, does not diminish the joy in the heart of those who sweeten themselves with the greatest Love.

"True happiness lies in the love of God and, as a consequence, of men, a love that is a generous surrender, capable of even giving one's own life to please the Father.

"My hour and Her hour have arrived. I return to the Father, but She must stay and implore, as I implored, so that

Mine may not be lost. I needed to tell Her, I needed to remind Her that She was the Woman in the book of Genesis. That although our hearts were being torn with pain, I must go and She must stay, so that God's sentence [upon the serpent] be fulfilled: 'I will put enmities between thee and the woman, and thy seed and her seed: she shall crush thy head, and thou shall lie in wait for her heel.' [Gen 3:15 DRV]

"Tell all My children to prostrate their hearts before this meditation because it is one of the culminating moments in the history of the salvation of men. I will entrust humanity to the one who will be the 'mediator' between Myself and man.

"The hour of the Genesis has arrived; the hour to complete the miracle started in Cana. It is the moment in which I must ask Her to adopt John and in him, that She adopt as Her children, all of the children of God, all My brothers and sisters. My way became Her way and She must drink to the last drop of the bitter chalice of suffering. She is surrendering to Her Son to fulfill the Divine Will and She must become the Mother of humanity. Later humanity, represented by My Church, will sing Her praises and Her glory will shine when the Universe bows down before the Queen of all virtues.

"It is necessary that once again Her Immaculate Heart be open to the Divine Will and Her obedient Love be stronger than Her humble Pain… She must remember that She is the Woman of yesterday, of today and of tomorrow: the Old Testament, the Gospel, and the Apocalypse…

"It is necessary that She give birth again:"

**"Woman, behold, your son… [Son,]
Behold, your mother."**

Once again, the Holy Virgin has obeyed. John falls into Her arms, crying. And She is exhausted by sadness, but still full of dignity, a

Lady as always, majestic in Her simplicity, needing no artifices to enhance Her beauty... Serenely and sweetly, She embraces John.

She knows that the labor pains have once again arrived for Her. She knows that this childbirth is very much more painful than the other one. In the first She was being entrusted with the Son of God, the Holy One, a child as pure as Herself. He would bring Her joy, wisdom, laughter, and blessings with each one of His kisses.

In this other childbirth, She will become the Mother of all humanity. Many will not only not be willing to acknowledge Her, but they will also offend Her. Others, in attacking the Church of Her Son, will call Her 'devil' when She comes, time and again, to the earth searching for the lost sheep that the Shepherd loves.

In the first childbirth, Her arms cradled a beautiful child, whose fresh, tender body received the joyful kisses of a young Mother. Now Her arms will receive Her Son, dead, tortured, and bloodied to save miserable men. Because of their sins, He was rendered unrecognizable, as Isaiah had prophesied it.

Knowing all of this and seeing Her Son in that state, in the throes of death, upon hearing Him, She obeys and consents to adopting, as Her sons, all men, even the evil-doers, the prostitutes, the atheists, the murderers, the thieves, the liars, all those who from now on and throughout the time that life may last on the earth will continue offending, combating, and denying God.

She receives all those from that time and from today, and with this comes the childbirth labor. She gives light to the Church of Her Son. As one day the Holy Spirit deposited in Her most pure womb the Word in order to bring salvation to the world now the Son deposits in Her Immaculate Heart all of humanity so that the sinner who wants to be saved could find refuge in that Sacred Place.

No, it is not easy what the Lord entrusts to Her and She knows it because God filled Her with gifts. Moreover, He gave Her the Gift of being the 'All-Powerful Supplicant.' That gift, which entails permanent supplication, was and, even today, is the secret key to open the Heart of Jesus.

Our Lord told me:

> "She knew that She would have to plead for each one of you and you should learn from Mary... As a child, I followed Her steps, so that later She would follow Mine. Our union was so intimate, so perfect, that She felt all My sentiments and knew all My thoughts because in My Holy Spirit, of which She was full, all was known to Her. This is how She was in God and God was in Her. That is why Her life was silent and prayerful.
>
> "The man of today, when he encounters life's difficulties, ponders, doubts, or argues, instead of praying. Many times he reflects too much over problems as an escape to the imaginary, while true prayer is always a return to reality.
>
> 'When My Mother found Herself in difficult situations, She did not begin to reflect or plan but rather She prayed. That is why She could give of Herself totally because praying and giving are intimately united.
>
> "Mary's supplication has the value of the gift that God expects from Her. It is the greatest gift, the most perfect way to give. Prayer is not true, is not pure, [and] it stops being Christian if it is not a way of giving of oneself."

As I contemplated Jesus again and Psalm 22:16-17 comes to mind:

> "As dry as a potsherd is my throat; my tongue sticks to my palate; and you lay me in the dust of death. They surround me like dogs; a pack of evildoers is around me. They have pierced my hands and feet..."

What mother, facing something so atrocious such as seeing Her Son crucified, would have been able to stand such suffering? I contemplated the Holy Virgin and felt such pity that My love for Her kept growing in intensity, in respect, in admiration. I assumed that Her spirit, in spite of so much pain, would harbor hope in the All-Mighty but that Her humanity was suffering deeply that enormous trial.

I remembered a meditation from the "Way of the Cross" that recites a portion of the Song of Songs: 'I searched for the love of my soul. I searched for him and did not find him. I got up and ran through the city streets and the parks, searching for the love of my soul. I searched for him and did not find him… The sentinels who were patrolling the city found me. Have they seen my lover? Hardly had I left them when I found the love of my soul.'

I also remembered the Prophet Jeremiah who said: "… You who walk by on this road, look, observe well if there is pain such as this pain with which the Lord has afflicted me…"

Years earlier while revealing to me what happens during the Celebration of the Eucharist, Jesus had said that no Mother had ever nourished her child with her own flesh and that He had gone to such an extreme for Love, giving us His Body and Blood as nourishment.

Now, while contemplating this Body from which hung strips of skin and flesh, I understood exactly what He had wanted to say to us. My heart felt so guilty that it wanted to stop beating at that moment so as not to suffer what I was suffering. Imagine what the Most Holy Virgin was feeling at that moment!

Today, when we realize how much women have degraded themselves, trampling their chastity, surrendering themselves shamelessly to the obscene look of so many men…

When we see all those young women who boastfully exhibit themselves in nude pictures because they are proud that their bodies, sometimes perfect in beauty, have been selected to show themselves as cheap merchandise or as if it were fresh meat hanging on hooks in the markets…

Does it not occur to us to think, nor do we want to believe that that body is the Temple and Dwelling of the Holy Spirit?

Our love should admire more the purity of Mary. It should not be this or that [super] model that inspires our daughters because the flesh is like carrion, which putrefies, and even the greatest beauty ages in the end, turning itself into dust.

All of us women should have Mary as our role model, imitating

Her purity, Her delicate and authentic movements. We should realize always that it is that femininity and sobriety which give greater Glory to God's Creation and do not sadden the Holy Spirit.

It is regrettable that many women, when becoming creatures who move by mere instinct and the pure desire of seduction, use such exaggerated movements that they become vulgar, and they [the women] end up going against the very aesthetics which they supposedly seek.

We cannot turn ourselves into stumbling stones, for one day we will give an account to God for each one of the men who sinned because of our immodesty. This is because the one who sins by looking is not as culpable as the one who exposes herself, inciting sin.

May God have mercy on us, the women who did not have the interest to see in Mary, the one full of Grace, as a possible model to imitate.

> "Oh, you, for whom I have given My life. You now have a Mother to whom to turn for all your needs. I have united all of you with the tightest of bonds by giving you My own Mother."

The Fourth Word

Jesus' teaching at this moment consisted of showing me His Face and allowing me to see that He was very pale behind that bath of blood. At that moment, the sky darkened until it seemed as if almost night; it was as if there was an eclipse.

Dark clouds were signaling a storm. Dozens of lightning bolts zigzagged on the horizon and the very loud rumble of thunder was making the earth quake.

Suddenly hundreds of Angels appeared around the whole scene. In a united, perfectly synchronized movement, they all prostrated themselves to adore Jesus, each one with hands together and in silence, while their brilliant faces reflected a profound sorrow. His tongue and lips were very dry and pasty. Once again His voice acquired a tired nuance, as if it were difficult to speak to me.

And He said:

"Contemplate this scene, My beloved, and learn that My own cannot march through life without a cross.

"Go and tell the world what you are learning and, if they want to silence you, shout even louder. Do this for the sake of the power of the love that unites you to Me, which is as united as these two pieces of wood that form an instrument of salvation for all of humanity.

"Tell the consecrated souls that the cross that they wear is not only to adorn their chests or identify them superficially with Me. First, they must gird themselves with the cross and learn to 'make themselves comfortable' on it instead of running away from it. Tell them they cannot long for Tabor if they have not first passed through Golgotha. It is here on the Cross where they will learn charity, humility, poverty of spirit, and temperance in all acts of their lives.

"Assure them that I give proof and testimony that the devil can be easily defeated from the experience of the cross. Contemplate Me: I am a true Man, in whom the flesh manifests its limitations, and true God, in demonstrating the relentless force of Agape Love.

"Pray for those who do not know of sufferings, for it is certain that they are not among My own... Observe these two condemned ones who flank Me and meditate on the ways that men carry their crosses.

"Some carry it with rage, with bitterness, amidst much grief. He who carries a cross in similar circumstances and with those sentiments carries, for sure, a cross that has no sense because instead of drawing him closer, it pushes him away from Me. Usually, that is the cross of those who refuse to understand the meaning of suffering, which takes on supernatural dimensions. That is the cross of the thief at My left; it is the cross which will always be heavy and will never be able to redeem.

"Dismas, on My right, accepts his cross with resignation and even with dignity; he assumes it at first because he has no other recourse. But suddenly, when he recognizes Me and knows that I Am the Son of God, he accepts that cross, acknowledging himself as a sinner and asking that through it, Mercy remembers him.

"Finally, you have Me here in front of you, embracing My redeeming Cross to teach all of you to carry yours. I invite you to be co-redeemers with Me, making reparation for your own sins and those of all mankind. Know that this way of carrying the cross is reflected in your conduct when before you are difficulties and pains and through them, you draw closer to Me and you profit from them to give testimony before men. When you embrace your cross, you can feel that the only thing you desire is strength because the thirst for souls consumes you."

"I thirst."

"Yes, I had a dry mouth and tongue. I was dehydrated and burning with fever. That is why they took a lance and, with a rag, they put upon My lips bile and vinegar, in order to mock Me even more when My mouth blistered.

"When I said, 'I thirst,' I still had My sight fixed upon My Mother, on John and, a bit further back, on the sinful woman who before such a sight did not even feel worthy to come close enough to touch Me compassionately. So great was the feeling of guilt that engulfed her, that she limited herself to crying, looking at Me with helplessness. Blessed Magdalene, you, who remained at the foot of My Cross, allowing your tears to mix with the redeeming Blood that kept falling upon the earth!

"By your love and your sorrow, you were redeemed and rewarded with My first apparition before men. For having loved much, your sins were washed away, and the Father wanted to reward your conversion and sacrifice, placing

> you on the Altars next to My Mother and John so that all who thought themselves 'just and wise' would bow before she whom they were condemning. And thus, would fulfill Mary's Magnificat which says that God 'exalts the humble' and that He 'fills the hungry with good things.'"

Then Jesus began to explain to me the reasons and sentiments that inundated Him when He said, "I thirst." And all this goes very much further than one can imagine. Jesus did not say "water," which would have been much easier and practical, if in truth He had wanted to drink. In fact, He did not even think of water because He was saying to us that He had a thirst for us, thirst for souls, a thirst for all of us to understand the infinite value of what was taking place.

Anyone who has ever experienced true thirst—the thirst to ingest liquid—knows what that means... I invite the reader to experience it sometime with the necessary prudence and offering it up to the Lord...

Within the human needs, perhaps thirst is the most pressing, and even more so in situations of extreme fatigue... I think that it was precisely for that reason the Lord had said it... Whoever thirsts cannot wait to quench that thirst; it is a burning anxiety...

Jesus was thirsty to see us united around His teachings. He was thirsty to see a united, not a divided Church, "because in this group there are better singers or the preachers give better sermons, speaking much better and in more modern language than others...," or "because these ones work with this priest and those with another...," or "because in this group there is too much false piety, whereas the other identifies more with the poor...," or "because here they do not give me the space that I deserve and over there they do..."

He was thirsty to see all of those of us who proclaim Christ as Savior, united by love and not separated by petty, egotistical, and materialistic interests. He wanted the Beatitudes, which He one day proclaimed with all the strength and sweetness of His Heart as the only path to salvation for all mankind, to become part of the flesh of our hearts. In short, He was thirsty to see us help each other: man to man, community to community, parish to parish, apostolate to apostolate, not competing nor destroying each other as if we were political enemies who go in search of spoils.

He was thirsty to see His Bishops and priests uniting, edifying, pouring out mercy, helping, supporting, counseling, and encouraging us lay sinners. We many times do not know where to begin to work because they load us with such heavy burdens. And many of them cannot even carry these burdens themselves, in spite of having been on the spiritual road a long time and supposedly have been trying to grow in the Faith.

Jesus said:

> "I wanted to shout to man to come just as he is and to drink of My thirst, from that spring of pain that was born from Love itself. I was thirsty to see that all children had a happy home, not an alcoholic father or mother. I was thirsty to see children mentally healthy, without traumas for having seen the violation of their intimacy and their innocence. I was thirsty to see those little ones, whom I love so much, filled with desires of building a better world, and knowing the evangelical values…"

Jesus was thirsty for the youths who would give Him their lives, renouncing the world, and for those in the world, who would proclaim the Good News from the place that they may have freely chosen.

Christ was thirsty for us women who, taking other holy women as a model and starting with the domestic Church, build a more just society with moral values, teaching our own children and those of others to have God as the beginning and end of our walk through this world.

Jesus was thirsty for souls, for all the souls for whom He was pouring His Blood to the last drop.

From high on the Cross, He saw your sins and mine, and He cried out to humanity:

"I thirst for this soul..." "This is the soul for whom I am suffering so much. I thirst, I am hungry, I have need of this soul in order to ease this heat, caused by the fever from the wounds, which upon becoming infected have injured My humanity..."

"I thirst for prayer, for peace in families, in communities, in the whole world. I thirst for knowing that everyone will respond to My call one day. I thirst for generous souls who offer themselves as 'lightning rods' before the Divine Justice, in order to save other souls..."

"I thirst for you, My daughter, for your help, for your perseverance. But beware of the wolves in sheep's clothing. If you see that someone who tries to halt your journey is someone who makes deals, be very careful. Let it not be that he may want to exchange for you the cross that I have given you for one that is corrupt, pretending that it is a better choice.

"Silently continue your journey, although with much caution, embracing the wood that weighs upon your shoulders with greater fervor. And follow the traces of My Blood so that they lead you always towards Me... And if one of your tormentors starts to hit your face, do not cover your face against the insult or the blow, nor try to defend yourself... Offer him also your back so that the world can see by your wounds that you are Mine. For I assure you that they who hit you will be the same ones who hit Me. Rejoice in being among those who belong to Me!"

That thirst, which Jesus had, was His testament, leaving to us, sinners all, His merits so that by virtue of them we would be saved. Jesus was thirsty even for those atheists and apostates who, twenty centuries later, would say: that the devil and hell do not exist; that the Eucharist is only a symbol, a commemoration; that He, being God, did not feel the pain of His Passion and that is why He did not suffer what any other man would have suffered; that it is an exaggeration when pictures are painted of Christ "suffering too much"; that the historic Christ is different from the Christ idealized by popular devotion; that Jesus cannot speak anymore to men because He has said it all during His journey on earth…

And what if we do not know how to listen to Him, if we have lost the capacity of being amazed by the teachings of the Gospel, of finding solidarity with the suffering Christ, and of learning to love our brethren…?

Jesus was thirsty for seeing Christians who would commit themselves to the work of spreading the Kingdom of Heaven in the hearts of men. He did not want our comfortable mediocrity of "assistants to Sunday Mass" and our "membership" in some "Apostolate" as if it were an affiliation to a club, to create better social relationships in a passing attempt to mitigate the weight of our consciences.

Christ saw us from His Eternity and felt thirst. He felt a true and pressing need to shake us up, to awake us from our comfortable lethargy of spiritual lukewarmness into which the greater part of us would fall into, the supposedly "good Catholics."

Those and another thousands more reasons that could fill hundreds of pages, were those that caused Jesus to say, "I thirst."

The Fifth Word

His face was very pale, the whole left side was deformed with the eye almost totally closed because of the swelling of the cheek and the eyelid. So brutally had been the beating that He received, that it had opened His cheekbone. It looked like an open mouth that allowed the flesh of the Son of God to be seen!

Jesus did not open His lips, but I could hear Him. I heard His words directed to the Father. They were a combination of love, gratitude, resignation, powerlessness, pain, and meekness.

I felt that my heart was being crushed with sadness as He said:

> "My Father, look at Me… as a sun eclipsed by its own choice! You have allowed Me to drink the bitter chalice of the icy night of the spirit and I give You thanks for this."

Then He addressed me, saying:

"In this profound pain which causes My sight to grow darker to the point that I can no longer see clearly those beings which I love and who remain at the foot of My agony, I know that Love has conquered, that it will conquer forever.

"As you can see, it seems that it had not been enough to have passed through this world doing good to everyone. I went all the way to the extreme of love. I gave life to that which I had preached previously: 'No one has greater love than the one who gives his own life for his friends.' And I also gave Mine for My enemies, for those who were crucifying Me.

"It is precisely because of that boundless love which, in the midst of My unfathomable suffering, I did not lose confidence in My Father. But rather, I was being overcome by immense joy in knowing that I was fulfilling His Will and, thus, demonstrating My Love for Him and for all mankind."

"My God, my God, why have you forsaken me?"

The Lord gave me the immense grace of also being able to contemplate that moment. It happened in this way:
I was in prayer with my eyes closed in front of the small altar in my workroom where I have a crucifix, an image of the Holy Virgin, and a small box with the relics of some saints. I opened my eyes, and in front of me was something else. That place was no longer there, but instead, I was looking at a dark sky, lightning with strong claps of thunder, and three crucified men.

The scene came closer until I had it at what seemed a distance of about two meters from where I was, and it only consisted of the agonizing Jesus in front of me. It was so near that I stretched out my hand. But when I realized that I could not reach Him, I understood that it was another vision.

Jesus panted, and I could see that He was making efforts to breathe in air. This I know well, for having lived it so many times. His eyes were popped wide open, the mouth so dry that each time it became more difficult for Him to modulate words.

He began to sob, and the bloody tears were running down His wounded cheeks when He said, looking towards Heaven, "Eli, Eli… lama sabachthani…" "My God, My God… why have You forsaken Me?"

I could not bear it and broke down sobbing, pouring out such tears as I had very seldom done in my life.

Then I heard internally His voice:

"Dear daughter, there are many pages written about these words which would seem to give the idea that at that moment I only felt, as a man, that I was being forsaken by My Father. It goes much farther than that. Remember that from the Cross, I was looking at all the times to come and at all men and women who would suffer: some because they fabricated their own crosses and others because the crosses are imposed upon them by their brothers who cannot carry them.

"In that cry, I complained about the abandonment of all humanity's Via Crucis [Way of the Cross]. I felt in My own wounds the infinite wounds of all the bodies that would be tortured by hunger and misery. Millions of voices united to Mine saying: 'My God, My God… why have You forsaken me? I am dying of hunger, when there are people who get sick of gluttony… My life is a continuous and forced fast while there are people who do not know what it means to fast and they call themselves Christians!'

"I felt the wounds that are the consequence of the injustices and cruelty suffered by the crucified of all times in exile, in the refuge camps. I felt the pain of the wounds of those incarcerated, rejected, and scorned by the same society who took them to that place moved by their selfishness. And those voices from the silence united themselves to

Mine, saying: 'My God, My God... why have You forsaken me? You did not create borders. You did not make jails. You did not want a society of a few rich and another with multitudes of marginalized...'

"In My arms and legs, I felt the pain felt by the handicapped. In My head, the thorns taught Me what the mentally deficient or ill would suffer, who are many times humiliated by the rejection of even their own families. The cry of these people united itself to Mine saying: 'Why Father, do You allow them to laugh at me, to marginalize me, to shut me in, if it is not my fault that I am in this state...? They do not think that one day they could be like me and feel the same?'

"I felt in My heart the pain that an elderly person feels when he is forgotten, by his own as well as by others as when he is abandoned in a 'home' at the mercy of the oversight and hands of strangers. Abandoned because now his hands are not capable of working in order to feed his family or because the new and elegant friends of his children and grandchildren could not understand the limitations of an elderly person.

"They are already tired of prohibiting him to talk, so he will not say 'inappropriate' things, because his memory no longer works. In some cases, people 'mercifully' have compassion on them and murder them 'so that they can stop suffering.' And then their voices unite themselves to Mine saying: 'My God, My God... why have You forsaken me? Why do You allow the ones I once taught to walk, to throw me onto the street? Why do You allow the others who walk by me, to feel revulsion for my poverty, my dirty clothing? They humiliate me, boasting of their youth and their wealth. Why does this son of mine want to have them apply euthanasia to shorten my days and increase his condemnation in Hell?'

"I felt in My skin the burning sensation of all those who would be marginalized because they belonged to a certain race and that for the same reason, would be forced to place themselves in the same conditions as a dog, which access is limited to only certain sections of the home. Their voices, full of helplessness and pain, would cry out next to Mine: 'My God, My God… why have You forsaken me? Why do You allow another man, maybe more sinful than I, maybe more unfaithful, maybe less intelligent, with instincts more similar to the beasts than to ours, to lower himself from his human condition and to lower me from my condition as a human being because I do not have skin like his?'

"I felt the anguish of all those men and women, who at the moment of their death, would find that they had been wrong. That their lives had been a continual loss in sin, in the pleasures and in the denial of God and that their condemnation is imminent… For an eternity of eternities, in exchange for having lived their own way for 'x' number of years! Oh, the pain!

"But I also felt the pain of those Christians who, at the moment of their death, would find that they had been right: that they had believed, had fed themselves, and had lived supposedly 'as good Christians,' that is to say, fulfilling many things but omitting many others. Omissions such as taking their knowledge to others, thinking selfishly of saving themselves, ignoring what happens to the neighbor who lives without knowing anything about God. And justice is for both groups: for those who did not want to know God and for those who did nothing to share their faith, for not being bearers of hope for the rest!

"I felt in each centimeter of My Body the pain of each child murdered inside the body of his own mother. And their innocence joined with My shout of human powerlessness: 'My God, My God… why have You forsaken me? Why do You permit this woman, who could cradle me in her arms, warming my small body, to condemn me to not see the light of day and to condemn herself to not see the Light of Heaven?'

"Thus, contemplating My wounds and the wounds of humanity, I thought of Judas and of all the traitors and, also, of all who would be betrayed by their friends, sold for thirty coins from hell: for a better economic situation; for an exchange for more power, in order to allow their arrogance to surface; for envy that can only be quenched by discrediting the person envied; for the ambition of possessing what cannot be possessed.

"Then I felt the cry of those who would feel the kiss of the betrayer on their cheek, like a smelly drool, just like I felt the kiss of the one who one day had been My beloved brother. At that moment I cried out with all of My strength: 'My God, My God… why have You forsaken Me?'

"The most admirable attribute in a human being with respect to another human being is the capability of feeling that one is 'a close enough friend' as to receive from the other advice or a warning with love, knowing that one would also give it with love to the friend to the point of being able to straighten him out by telling him, 'not that way brother, because you are going to make a mistake,' and to the point of being able to understand each other with one look, with a smile and being able to support each other through a handshake that means, 'here I am, you can always count on me.'

"A friend is he who inconveniences himself, who deprives himself of something or of many things to offer them to you. A friend is one who will give up his time of rest to work for you. A friend is he who can in a moment give up the comfort of his house so as to make you feel comfortable, loved, and appreciated. A friend is that one who leaves his land to help you save yours. A friend is he who confides his sorrows and joys, who is always transparent with you and who always takes you towards growth in faith and in the love of God. A friend is he who builds, who unites, who gathers. Not one who tears apart, who destroys, knocks down, so he can sit on top of the rubble. A friend is he, who gives his life to save you… as I did.

"And because I am a friend of mankind, each one of the wounds that Mine receive stirs up My compassion, and it forces Me to search for the proper medicine. I mean to say that I have a very fresh and vivid memory of each injustice, of each slight, of each 'false kiss,' of each humiliation.

"No, I do not forget those who you, mankind, forget! I listen to those whom you do not hear because the noise of your souls prevents you from having the peace to listen to others and to figure out what their actions mean, regardless of how irrational they might seem to you!

"I sweetly place in My Sacred Heart those whom you leave mercilessly abandoned on the road, those whom you slander, those whom you destroy trying to attain what they possess, the Beatitudes!"

The Sixth Word

On another day Jesus explained to me that not all of us ascend towards holiness through the same path, that while some persons have to work on their humility, others have to work on their joy. Still others must work on their lack of hope, others on their tempers, others on their vanity, and yet others on their strength in order to break the chain that ties them to some vice... in other words, each on his own issues.

The Lord was saying that every time that we feel entangled on this path, we should do an analysis that would help us see clearly the place where we have laid our desires. What things worry us the most, or take away our peace, our joy. In what things, and at which moments, do we encounter the greatest temptations.

He spoke to me about the temptations experienced by some people who were close to Him. He talked about the temptation of distrust, suffered by the apostles when they experienced a moment of danger while in the boat. They thought that they would sink and drown in the waters and not be able to save themselves because "He" Who could save them, was asleep.

He spoke to me about Peter's temptation of lack of faith when Peter started to sink into the waters at the moment when he doubted being his ability to walk on them to come to his Master.

He spoke to me about the temptations of James and John, when they were discussing, anxious to know, who would sit at His right hand side, thus allowing the temptations of envy, vanity and the desire for power to make prey of them.

He addressed the temptations suffered by the Scribes and Pharisees: envy, fear and hatred against Him. Feelings that led them to place stones in His way, so that He would stumble and fall, in order that all of them could come down on Him and beat Him. He told me how they would ask questions trying to catch Him in "His error" and to condemn Him for it.

He spoke to me about His own temptations during the forty days He fasted in the wilderness. And how with His prayer and rejection of the devil He was able to overcome them.

I could write several pages concerning all this that He kept telling me about but, in all cases, the central message was the same: That we can overcome temptation only through prayer and by truly seeking to do the Will of The Father.

"It is finished."

Jesus spoke like this when He uttered His Sixth Word:

> "When I said that it was all finished, I summarized with these words all that My thoughts were saying to the Father. The fulfillment of Your Will has been consummated, My Father... I came to the world by means of the womb of a Virgin, in the tiny body of a baby. I became a man like all other mortals in order to save them.
>
> "All the prophesies were fulfilled in Me: I was born in Bethlehem; I lived like the poor; I had a man baptize Me; I preached in Your Name. You sent Me and I made You known

as loving and kind as You are. I suffered persecution. I came as the physician of body and soul, and I healed many who were sick. I was betrayed by a very close friend, and sold for thirty worthless coins… I came to prove to them that those who believe in You and in Me are not dead, and I raised many who were dead.

"'Tetelestai!' It is finished! I came to save sinners, and here is one, tied to My Cross. She is at My Mother's side, and weeps out of love for You [Father] and out of sorrow for Me. I bring to You a thief, so that he opens the doors of Paradise for all the sinners who want to be saved… It is finished.

"All the prophecies have been fulfilled in Me. They add up to more than twenty for the period of My passion and My agony, alone. I leave My Mother as the Mother of all humanity, that they may not feel as orphans, and I am leaving the perfect disciple that You gave Me for a Mother, in the hands of those who will love Me throughout the centuries.

"'Tetelestai, My Father…! (It means: 'All done!' 'All has been done well!' 'I have fulfilled Your Will and to the best of My ability!') Mankind has seen the Light. And although they have not recognized it, it will illuminate them throughout all of earth's history. I have fulfilled My duty to You, Father; by vanquishing the serpent, I have opened the Gates to Heaven.

"Remember Job, My daughter, when he says: My heart leaps [in fear] It leaps outside its place Hearken; hearken to the rumble of his voice The roar that from his mouth comes Under all the heavens he hurls it And its luminosity reaches All the ends of the earth.

"It has been perfectly accomplished. Never again will man have to fear that God of justice, insistently portrayed as such due to the culture of the people, by persons who lived during the times of the warnings. The Strong Angel has fulfilled His duty, Father, and even though I must now return to You, the Church will be born from My Open Side, and the gates of hell will not prevail against her.

"It will be a Holy Church, made of holy people and sinners. But, amid the filth, the consequence of the human misery, many men and women will keep their vows and promises, and will shine like the stars. Also, this Church will not lack for sorrow, treachery, sin. You know that all is contaminated, and all will have to go through a Gethsemane, and a Golgotha. But the faithful remnant, that portion of the flock of this Church, which from now on I am cleansing with each drop of My Blood, will arrive to Mount Tabor to be transfigured.

"It is finished, Father! All had to be fulfilled, and all must be fulfilled, including the hours of darkness that will frighten man so much; because it is necessary that the man of iniquity make his entrance into the world and wage battle against Ours: Yours and Mine. But Mary remains, My Father, Your perfect collaborator, and She will keep Your Word. I have suffered everything in My Body. I have endured everything freely. Not as an imposition on Your part, but because I wanted to do it, for love of You and love of man.

"It is finished, and now, My Father, I must return to You. But remember that I have entrusted those, who are Mine to You, so that not a single one of them be lost.

"I know that they will be lost, those who will leave after having sworn an oath of fidelity to Me, going after the pleasures of the world. They will be lost, those who, having had their hands consecrated to bring Me and give Me as food to men and women, will stain those hands by hurting the innocent. Then they will certainly have a rope with a millstone tied around their necks, to throw themselves into the depths of a river of lava.

"They will be lost, those who, being unable to carry heavy burdens, will unload them onto the backs of the weak, in order to crush them. They will be lost, those who, blinded by their pride, will no longer see Me in the humble and simple people. They will be lost, those who, having received more, will be accountable for more.

"But those who are capable of weeping upon meditating on the pain that now overwhelms Me, those who in seeing an older woman dressed in rags, give her a kiss on the cheek as a sign of brotherhood and equality, those who being able to sleep on a bed, sleep on the floor, so as to mortify their flesh as a sign of reparation for Our love..., those who recognize My gaze in the eyes of the marginalized, My pure smile in that of the children, My voice amid the racket and confusion of the world, My tears in the repentant sinners.

"Those who reflect My hands in the granting of pardons, those who will follow in My footsteps as missionaries, opening furrows of hope to sow My seed, not trusting in their capability but only in My Providence..., those who make themselves like little children, to the point that their innocence and purity lead them to believe and fully trust in My Almighty Presence.

"Those whose lips are always willing to give a smile, a pardon, a blessing, a gentle reproach or brotherly correction. Those who will not hesitate to proclaim My message of salvation with strength, without being afraid to be silenced, and are capable of enduring the blows, the wickedness, the slander, the insults without defending themselves or harboring vengeful desires. Those will be saved because they are among those whom I call Mine, and who were entrusted to You, so that being in the world they may not be of the world... so that they may not be lost."

The Seventh Word

After having reflected on the previous word uttered by Jesus on the Cross, I understand that the Cross will follow all of us Christians, as if it were a part of our own existence. But I also give warning that not all of us are capable of awakening, of unburying the Christ that remains asleep within us.

Many of us live complaining about our small or large crosses, thinking that our lot in life is the saddest, the most painful, which no one else but ourselves would be capable of enduring... And the worst thing is that we believe that God has forsaken us, that He does not hear us, or that He is angry with us.

But it is not so. Jesus says that the knowledge that He has of us, particularly of the most sorrowful, of those who suffer the most, the weakest, makes Him love with preference the poorest and those who need Him the most.

If we would only be aware of the fact that the people most in need are not [necessarily] those in poverty, but in general terms, those who have everything but God; then, our paths would lead us to those persons who, being the wealthiest, are actually in many cases the poorest.

It is not so difficult to reach the indigent and to persuade them to place their trust in God, given that these persons usually have a very open heart toward our Faith. And a few words, or a simple gesture of love, is enough most of the time to show them the path towards the Father. What is difficult is to change the mind of those persons who have everything or who have made of sin the reason for their lives and live convinced that they have no need for anything else.

This work is the hardest for the evangelizers. When they are faced with pride, it is like dealing directly with the prince of this world, hiding cunningly within some poor man who is wealthy, but in need of the love of God.

How beneficial it would be for us to meditate from time to time, on the Passion of Jesus, on the sorrow of the Most Holy Virgin, who, by His side, has suffered the martyrdom of martyrdoms, watching Her Lord and Son nailed to the Cross on Calvary for the sake of mankind.

And yet, She has been able to leave us the greatest of testimonies, because with Her endless love and absolute obedience to the Father, She endured with humility the wrenching pain of seeing Her Son die amid horrible sufferings. Moreover, She has taken charge of humanity and become our Mother. In other words, She has willingly chosen to project onto us Her love for Her Son. She was to suffer like a sinner next to Her Son, being innocent like Him and all this so that the Will of the Father may be fulfilled in Her as well.

Jesus said that it is because of this tragic moment that the two Hearts are represented united to each other. (The two Hearts united is the symbol of our apostolic spirituality, as is of other communities and apostolic organizations.) This is because they were united with one another through pain: At Golgotha, they were one sole wounded Heart; two hearts that merged together in order to transform themselves into one; one sole Heart, feeling pain for each other's suffering, one sole Heart feeling Love, for obeying the Father and for saving mankind.

Now I see myself compelled to explain to the reader something, which at first might seem to be of little importance, but which, nonetheless, contains a crucial teaching from the Lord for all of us.

Many of you, my dear brothers and sisters, must have wondered why the title to this chapter was "From Sinai to Calvary."

Jesus told me one Friday night:

> "The darkness for the world is approaching, but he who lives embracing the Cross has nothing to fear. Therefore, man must not be contented with only looking at an image of Mine, or going to a Good Friday procession. But he must try to have My same sentiments: to forgive as I forgave and to ask pardon as I did [for them]; to remain silent in the face of infamous remarks, as I did before Pilate, and yet to feel such zeal and bravery as to become capable of: chasing the money changers out of the Temple of God with a whip; to live to do the Will of the Father as I did; to love so much as to even give your life for others; and to allow your body to be crushed, and with joy, to give oneself as food, so others can feed on that bread."

Right after my prayer while meditating, I was thinking of Moses. I have always been impressed with his mission, his life... Suddenly that space which opens many times in order to allow me to watch a faraway scene opened itself before my eyes. Before me was the scene of the Transfiguration, and watching it I wondered: why Moses and Elias? I thought that perhaps Elias [was there] for the strength of "The Prophet of Fire" that Jesus, as a man, would need to face what He had to live through.

But seeing Moses, I could not figure out with my limited knowledge, what Moses might be doing there. I felt as if a light had turned on inside me, and within what I consider a few minutes, dozens of images, in sets of two, passed before me.

Moses coming out of Egypt alone... and then Jesus being baptized in the Jordan.

Moses going down the mountain after having received the responsibility of taking the people of God out from the bondage of Pharaoh... and then Jesus choosing His twelve apostles, teaching, healing, forgiving, living among His people.

Moses bringing his people out of Egypt... and then Jesus preaching the call to conversion and announcement of the Kingdom of God on the Mountain of the Beatitudes.

Moses at the crossing of the Red Sea... and then Jesus giving sight to the blind, speech to the mute, making the lame walk, and raising the dead.

Moses eating with his people the manna that God sent from Heaven, to keep them from dying of starvation on their walk towards the Promised Land... and then Jesus with His disciples, having supper for the last time with them and instituting the Eucharist in order to remain with us, giving us His Body and Blood in order to feed us and save us from eternal death.

But I noticed that Jesus, at that moment, was not alone with His apostles, and all of a sudden the room became huge. It encompassed all that my eyes could manage to see. I saw with them some people sitting in wheelchairs to the sides of the apostles, and the rest were standing behind Jesus and His disciples—hundreds, thousands of priests, dressed in white tunics and red stoles. They had their right hands extended towards the place where Jesus was lifting the bread. They were repeating with the Lord the words of the Consecration.

Jesus told me:

> "Take care of My brothers, because through them I will remain with you until the end of times."

Then I saw Moses again on Mount Sinai, barefoot, as ordered by the Lord. He was on his knees, trembling at contemplating the finger of God writing the Ten Commandments for mankind... and, then, again I saw Jesus in the Garden of Gethsemane, on His knees, looking at and taking on our sins, contemplating the suffering He was to endure for us, men and women, trembling and sweating blood.

Once again the Last Supper was before my eyes, Jesus with His Apostles and all the priests repeating the words of the Consecration.

Jesus looked at me for a moment and said to me:

> "I Am the Bread of Life, and these (He raised His hands as if wanting to encompass them all) will be they who give Me to man, as food for eternal life."

My whole body was trembling at that moment due to the majesty of what I was beholding and understanding. Weeping, I covered my face with my hands... and after some time, perhaps minutes, which seemed hours to me, I lifted my head and saw the previous scene again.

I saw Moses lifting high a pole with a carved serpent, in order to heal with it those who had been bitten by snakes... and then I saw Jesus, lifted there in front of me on the Cross, in order to heal the souls of those who would be bitten by Satan and poisoned by sin.

The Lord said to me:

> "Remember what I told you at the beginning that times of darkness are approaching for mankind, that will shake institutions and with them, the people. My Church will also have to go through that painful road, and it has already begun [to go through it] because it is written: 'The Shepherd will be struck and the sheep will scatter'... But remember that I have defeated the world."

I again contemplated the Last Supper before me. All of those priests had their faces transfigured into the same face as that of Jesus. Then there was total darkness in front of me, and I heard the voice of Our Lord, very saddened as He said: "Judas, what you have to do, do it now...!"

The image returned, but now together with one of the disciples, many of those priests departed, pushing one another, running, no longer with the luminous and peaceful countenance of Jesus, but with their own faces, full of anguish and pain.

From far away I could hear the howling noise of a thousand voices in unison, as if they were running toward a cliff and falling down. Frightened, I turned my gaze to those who were with the Lord. They seemed to have not heard nor seen anything, such was their immersion into their prayer, into the moment in which they were living, that the peace of the Master gave them a majestic bearing, like that of princes.

I understand that those consecrated men, who remained with the Lord, were those who would be faithful to the choice that they made for Him. And they are those who will enter into that divine Hierarchy because they earned that right. This is because the right is the fruit of fidelity, and fidelity is the fruit of a close relationship, of intimacy. Intimacy is the fruit of self-giving, and self-giving is the fruit of agape love, which gives without asking anything in return, for the simple reason of seeking the happiness of the beloved.

Finally, that [kind of] love is the fruit of knowing Him to Whom you will be faithful for the rest of your days, without allowing to fade away the desire of reproducing within yourself, the perfect gift of Him, to Whom you have surrendered.

My meditations were suddenly halted when I heard the Lord give His last shout from the Cross, between labored gasps of air, each time being a longer interval:

"Father, into Your hands I commend My Spirit."

In the book *Divine Providence,* which was published some time ago, I wrote about my mother's death and the profound evangelization received by all of us who were around her as she was dying.

For those persons who have not read the book, I mention that it was a happy, calm, and peaceful death, that of a dying person who has complete trust in the Love of God, who is anxious to leave and meet with Mercy, Who was waiting for her on the other side of her deathbed. She kept asking us for prayers and songs, as she, with her big blue eyes wide open, repeated over and over Jesus' request: "Father, into Your hands I commend my spirit!"

While she was dying, I kept thinking of the death of Jesus... Now the Lord was allowing me, a poor sinner, to witness this moment [the death of Jesus] and by its means relive the former [the death of her mother]. Both instances were united by the Omnipotence of Him, Who is Almighty, and in the love of Him, Who is Love Itself. Few moments of my life will ever be so greatly impacted, and so difficult to describe...

At Golgotha, the sky was almost black, the earth was trembling, and all the people had started to run, fleeing. Some screaming in fear at seeing nature itself quaking, and others weeping, begging forgiveness, and saying that truly this Man was the Son of God.

Jesus said to me:

> "I am going back to the Father, and one day those bad brothers, who have made a business out of their vocation, will

understand, the true meaning of My predilection for them in granting them the grace to be able to make Me present in the Eucharist..."

"Then, they will no longer make use of the Altar in order to launch a homily that will confuse instead of helping man, to make politics, to justify a salary, or simply to 'fulfill their duty' when they can no longer avoid it. And they do it watching the clock, to leave in a rush to fulfill their other 'obligations'."

"They will have to make a halt on their way to the abyss and acknowledge that their love for themselves is greater than their love and desire to serve God and man. Because with their attitude they take away the trust and discourage those who, at least once a week, decide to go to their encounter with Me."

"From My Cross, I say to them and to you: Do not complain about the sects being filled with people without asking yourselves if this is a consequence of your own testimony."

I again heard those words, which represent the end and the beginning of all things:

"Father, into Your hands I commend My Spirit!"

And the Head of the Savior of all humanity rested on His shoulder and chest. And it remained thus for a moment before it came down to rest completely on His chest.

That moment, which could have been endless and which I sometimes think will live with me forever, was absolutely in the present to my eyes and ears when He said to me:

"My whole Body was devastated. But My joy was so great that, from the hill of My Passion, I beheld Heaven and exclaimed that all had been accomplished perfectly, and I commended My Spirit into the hands of the Loving Father."

"That Spirit, which was revealed to man the day of My Baptism in the Jordan, would return to the Father with Me so that the Trinity be complete again in Glory. And, as the Heavens were opened that day in order that the light would radiate the Love of the Third Person Who, as the Gospel says, was in the shape of a dove; now the curtain of the Temple, which covered the Ark of the Covenant, was being torn in order to pass judgment on those who had condemned Me. And that, indeed, was horrifying to them due to the culture and education of those people."

"The mission of the Word had ended, the colossal battle had reached its conclusion. The Son of Man was dying, having freely surrendered for Love. I was trustfully placing Myself in the hands of My Father, peacefully, sweetly. Another had died a few hours earlier, hanging, in desperation, as die the cowards, the traitors, those who do not love My Father, and, hence, they do not trust in His forgiveness."

Suddenly the light returned and the darkness disappeared. In seeing my surprise, Jesus spoke from the Cross.

"This light that you see would before long, come down upon My Apostles to illuminate and assist them, through this Spirit of Mine, Whom I was placing in the hands of the Father. He [the Holy Spirit] would come to remind them of all that they heard Me say and to assist them by having this knowledge penetrate so deeply as to allow them, through His [the Spirit's] Strength, to acquire all the wisdom and holiness necessary, for Me to extend Myself in them. In this way, I would continue walking among you, in order to continue healing, to continue blessing, to continue saving..."

"All of this had to be seen by witnesses, in order that the real value could be understood of the sacrifice of a Man Who voluntarily surrenders His life, in donation to God and to mankind."

The Lord did not tell me this, but I understood that it was that same Spirit, Who would pour Himself out upon the successors of the Apostles, because in some way He was referring to priests and committed lay people...

Then Jesus continued saying to me:

> "I have fulfilled [the Will of the Father]. I return to the Father and you, those who love Me, will also be persecuted, slandered, humiliated, mistreated. But you are not alone. I remain with you, and I leave with you what is most precious in My Life, My Mother, who from now on will be your Mother."

As Jesus was finishing saying this, I see a soldier coming closer and, taking a lance, he whispers something that I do not quite understand. And with an expression of pity on his face, he pierces the side of the Lord, and a great amount of Blood and Water comes down, splattering on the soldier's face. He covers his eyes with his hand and falls down on the ground.

The chest of the Redeemer was full of light, in a symphony of hues that could not be described. Out of that open side comes something like water, but very luminous, then blood, which mingles with that water. It begins to open furrows on the ground. And wherever the blood runs, white lilies marvelously arise.

Jesus' Cross disappears. I see now in its place a huge church, and these flowers are entering into it, as if they were gliding. But from the other side, there are very many young men, dressed in white tunics, also entering into the church.

Suddenly, I see myself inside that church, and I contemplate: all those white flowers are in front of the Altar, and they are now turning into young women. And on the other side are the young men, dressed in their white tunics. Men and women lay prostrate in humble prayer, their arms extended to their sides forming a Cross. I understand that they are the women and men who are being consecrated, surrendering their lives to God.

I hear a marvelous choir, like the choir I have heard sometime during Holy Mass, and I see the Resurrected Jesus, clad in all majesty, as a King, Who at once makes a signal and the young men begin to approach Him one by one. He, Himself, anoints their hands, while He smiles with the love that I sometimes see in the eyes of a dad, looking at his children.

Jesus looks at me for a few seconds, and then, while walking toward the middle of the Altar, He says:

> "Through the Priestly Order, with the power of the Holy Spirit, all the sins of man will be forgiven, and they [the priests] will open for you the Gates of Heaven... But I am a jealous lover, Who demands from them their entire will. I expect everything from a soul in accordance to the vocation to which it was called one day and consistent with the invitation that I continue to extend to all of you, through the circumstances of your everyday life."

At that precise instant, the vision of Moses and Jesus returned in a terrible way. I will try to describe it as faithfully as I can.

I saw Moses standing on a flat terrain on Mount Sinai. He was carrying in both hands two big stones with some graphics on them. (I gather that they are the Ten Commandments.) Below were the people in the midst of horrible noises and filthy scenes, which were revolting. They seemed to be more beastly than human. The face of the prophet turned almost purple, flushed. I saw him sway back and forth, and then with force and anger hurl down both stones onto the people. It was as if a hundred loads of dynamite fell on them because many people became air bound and many others kept falling into a great hole in the ground, screaming.

Then, I saw Jesus lifted on the Cross and, behind Him, two huge angels with very brilliant faces, but displaying a very strong expression of anger. One of them was carrying some "tablets" (let us call them that) like the stones that Moses was carrying, but these were made of flesh. They looked as if, when put together, would form a heart. On one of them, it said, "Thou shall love God above all things," and on the other, "Thou shall love thy neighbor as thyself." The other Angel was holding in both hands a huge Chalice filled with Blood.

As the angels were about to hurl those "tablets of flesh" and the Chalice of Blood over the globe, a manly voice was heard, which said: "Halt... I will infuse My Law in their hearts. They will be My people, and I will be their God..."

Upon hearing the voice, both angels knelt, lowering their heads, and they disappeared from my sight.

In an instant, I thought of the parallel between Moses and Jesus and became horrified at the thought of what would have happened if the two angels had hurled the Two Commandments and the Chalice of Blood over the earth... I believed that all of us would have perished, receiving perhaps a punishment that, through our sins, we seemed to be asking for very loudly.

Before this memory, I am moved to do nothing else than to ask God for Mercy for the world.

I am positive that whoever reads this testimony will understand the moment in which we are living. And the reader will be of one mind with me, in that if we do not kneel before the Living Jesus in the Most Blessed Sacrament of the Altar, making reparation and uniting our prayers, that Cup will overflow and a great part of humanity will be lost.

Then I saw the Most Holy Virgin sitting on the floor, with Jesus lying on a cloth, His head on Her bosom. She was caressing and kissing Him, shedding abundant tears.

I am a mother, and when at times my children have suffered and have been away from me, I have felt a spiritual and a physical pain. In trying to explain this, I say that my breasts, which nursed the child who is now suffering or having problems, are aching.

In contemplating this picture and thinking of the Heart of our Mother, I am moved to such respect that I believe that one has no other choice than to prostrate oneself on the ground. There is the

Woman, holding the head of Her dead Son, accepting the pain that is piercing Her Heart.

When a person dear to us dies, we are left with the pain. The one leaving does not take along the sorrow.

In this case, from the first "Yes" of the Holy Virgin up until this moment, both lives have been so intimately united that one could suffer or have joy with the feelings of the other.

If the Church proclaims that all human suffering has redeeming value, that it is useful for the conversion of souls, when it is offered to God with love, how can anyone feel offended upon hearing that Mary was the Co-redemptrix at the foot of the Cross?

The link that ties the Woman in the Book of Genesis, whose descendants would crush the head of the serpent, with the Woman clothed with the Sun in the book of Revelations, is it not precisely that of the Co-redemption, Her active participation, also as a victim, in that Holy Sacrifice which was consummated at the foot of the Cross?

I ask forgiveness for what I have just said if I have offended people, but let our Mother the Church pass judgment on this since my formation is not sufficient even as to attempt to give an opinion [on this matter]. But love is recognized by LOVE, and for this, no intelligence is necessary.

The Calvary scene returned, and the voice repeated with majesty:

> "...I will infuse My Law in their hearts. They will be My people, and I will be their God...!"

Then, before my eyes appeared again the great church, where not only future priests and consecrated women were entering but also an endless number of women and men, old, young, and children...

Something made me look up towards the dome of the church. There was the Virgin Mary, majestic, covering the whole scene with a light blue mantle. She wore a beautiful smile, like that of a mamma embracing her baby, protecting him with great love.

Inside was Jesus, clothed as in the picture of Christ the King. He was celebrating the Holy Mass and concelebrating with Him, were all those young men who had been anointed before. I felt great happiness in my heart.

Then Jesus told me:

"Tell all My sons that it is not enough to know the fifteen Stations of the Way of the Cross by heart but to live it and to recreate it, so that every Holy Mass may truly be the memorial of My Passion."

"Tell them that from the Cross, I have leaned over each one of them, because the force of Love has granted them to be 'Alteri Christi'... (other Christs)."

At that moment, I saw a room with light-colored walls and a not-so-big window and Jesus, resplendent, all dressed in white, Who was blowing upon His apostles and saying to them: "Receive the Holy Spirit... Whose sins you forgive will be forgiven in Heaven..."

At this point, I transcribe the last words that Jesus had just given me for you at the moment that I was finishing the writing of this testimony at the daybreak of the festivity of the Baptism of Our Lord.

"Dear brother, this testimony has been for you, that you may be able to live a renewed Lenten time in deep meditation about the union that I want to have with you, and through you, with My people."

"Do not allow the rationalism of the world to exchange your white vestments for a sickle and a hammer. Your library must be to contemplate Me on the Cross. Your weapons, and those of every Christian, must be prayer, the company of My Mother, and the door of salvation, the Eucharist."

"But always make sure that your celebration is as that of Holy Thursday, that celebration which moves deeply the hearts of lay people. Remember that My people want holiness in their Shepherds."

The Closing Words of Catalina

Dear Fathers, most appreciated priests: Here ends this book, a testimony of favors, never deserved, but only given through the Immense Love of God towards humanity and towards you, the consecrated souls.

With God's favor, these pages [referring to the original version in Spanish] will be released for distribution on the day of Our Lady of the Candles [La Candelaria]. She is my Godmother, and I have placed all of you under Her protection.

Certain Bible passages and different words of Jesus come to mind, and I want to share them with you:

Jesus called His twelve Apostles together; He gave them power and authority over all demons and the capacity to cure diseases. And He sent them out to preach the Kingdom of God and to heal the sick. And He said to them: "Take nothing for the journey; no bags, nor bread, nor money nor clothes."

Then He chose another seventy-two, who He sent ahead of Him, two by two into all the cities and places where He Himself would be going.

Then He said to them:

> "The harvest is plentiful, but the laborers are few. Therefore, beseech the lord of the harvest to send laborers into his harvest. Behold I send you out as sheep in the midst of wolves; therefore, you must be wise as serpents and simple as doves. He who listens to you listens to Me, and he who shows contempt for you shows contempt for Me, and he who shows contempt for Me, shows contempt for Him who sent Me. And you will be taken before governors and kings for My sake, to bear testimony about Me before them. Do not worry about what you are to say, for the Holy Spirit will speak for you."
>
> "You will be hated by all for My name's sake. But he who perseveres to the end will be saved."

> "Be not afraid, for nothing is hidden that will not be discovered. What I tell you in the dark, say in the daylight and what you hear whispered, preach from the housetops. Do not fear those who kill the body but cannot kill the soul; rather fear Him who can cast both soul and body into hell."
>
> "Whoever acknowledges Me before men, I also will acknowledge before My Father Who is in Heaven, but whoever denies Me before men I will also deny before My Father Who is in Heaven."
>
> The seventy-two returned full of joy saying: "Lord, even the demons are subject to us in your name!"
>
> And He said to them: "I was seeing Satan fall like lightning. I have given you power to handle serpents and scorpions, and all the power of the enemy will not be able to harm you. But do not rejoice so much that the demons are subject to you, but rather rejoice that your names are written in Heaven..."

I give you thanks, from the depth of my heart: for all the pardons granted to men and women, in the name of our Church; for giving your life to Him, Who is THE WAY, THE TRUTH AND THE LIFE; and for bringing Jesus, the Bread of Heaven, to us in order to strengthen us in this temporal exile. May He be the source of union and charity among those of us who make up His Church, for the greater Glory of God and for the salvation of souls.

With profound respect, and in the Merciful Love of Jesus,

Catalina
February 2, 2004

The feast of the Presentation of Our Lord, and of Our Lady of Candelaria

Scriptural Citations Referenced By Jesus

Note: The Scriptural Verses that follow are from the Challoner revision (1749–1752) of the 16th–17th century Douay-Rheims Bible [DRB], a "scrupulously faithful translation into English of the Latin Vulgate Bible by St. Jerome (342–420) translated into Latin from the original languages" [quoted from the Preface of this Bible].

GENESIS 22:6-8

6 And he [Abraham] took the wood for the holocaust, and laid it upon Isaac his son; and he himself carried in his hands fire and a sword. And as they two went on together, 7 Isaac said to his father: My father. And he answered: What wilt thou, son? Behold, saith he, fire and wood: where is the victim for the holocaust? 8 And Abraham said: God will provide himself a victim for an holocaust, my son. So they went on together.

PSALM 95:12-13 [same as Psalm 96 in modern Bibles]

12 The fields and all things that are in them shall be joyful. Then shall all the trees of the woods rejoice 13 before the face of the Lord, because he cometh: because he cometh to judge the earth. He shall judge the world with justice, and the people with his truth.

WISDOM 2:12-14; 19-20

12 Let us, therefore, lie in wait for the just, because he is not for our turn, and he is contrary to our doings, and upbraideth us with transgressions of the law, and divulgeth against us the sins of our way of life. 13 He boasteth that he hath the knowledge of God, and calleth himself the son of God. 14 He is become a censurer of our thoughts. 19 Let us examine him by outrages and tortures, that we may know his meekness, and try his patience. 20 Let us condemn him to a most shameful death: for there shall be respect had unto him by his words.

WISDOM 14:7

7 For blessed is the wood, by which justice cometh.

ISAIAH (ISAIAS) 53:4-6

4 Surely he hath borne our infirmities and carried our sorrows: and we have thought him as it were a leper, and as one struck by God and afflicted. 5 But he was wounded for our iniquities, he was bruised for our sins: the chastisement of our peace was upon him, and by his bruises we are healed. 6 All we like sheep have gone astray, every one hath turned aside into his own way: and the Lord hath laid on him the iniquity of us all.

ISAIAH (ISAIAS) 53:8

8 He was taken away from distress, and from judgment: who shall declare his generation? Because he is cut off out of the land of the living: for the wickedness of my people have I struck him.

ISAIAH (ISAIAS) 53:7

7 He was offered because it was his own will, and he opened not his mouth: he shall be led as a sheep to the slaughter, and shall be dumb as a lamb before his shearer, and he shall not open his mouth.

MICAH (MICHEAS) 6:3

3 O my people, what have I done to thee, or in what have I molested thee? Answer thou me.

PSALM 34:11-12 [same as Psalm 35 in modern Bibles]

11 Unjust witnesses rising up have asked me things I knew not. 12 They repaid me evil for good: to the depriving me of my soul.

JOSHUA (JOSUE) 7:10-12

10 And the Lord said to Josue: Arise, why liest thou flat on the ground? 11 Israel hath sinned, and transgressed my covenant: and they have taken of the anathema, and have stolen and lied, and have hid it among their goods. 12 Neither can Israel stand before his enemies, but he shall flee from them: because he is defiled with the anathema. I will be no more with you, till you destroy him that is guilty of this wickedness.

LAMENTATIONS 3:11-15

11 Daleth. He hath turned aside my paths, and hath broken me in
pieces, he hath made me desolate. 12 Daleth. He hath bent his bow,
and set me as a mark for his arrows. 13 He. He hath shot into my
reins the daughters of his quiver. 14 He. I am made a derision to all
my people, their song all the day long. 15 He. He hath filled me
with bitterness, he hath inebriated me with wormwood.

PSALM 139:5-6

5 Keep me, O Lord, from the hand of the wicked: and from unjust
men deliver me. Who have proposed to supplant my steps: 6 The
proud have hidden a net for me. And they have stretched out cords
for a snare: they have laid for me a stumbling block by the wayside.

PSALM 37:7-8; 12-13; 20-21

[same as Psalm 38 in modern Bibles]

7 I am become miserable, and am bowed down even to the end: I
walked sorrowful all the day long. 8 For my loins are filled with illusions; and there is no health in my flesh. 12 My friends and my
neighbours have drawn near, and stood against me. And they that
were near me stood afar off: 13 And they that sought my soul used
violence. And they that sought evils to me spoke vain things, and
studied deceits all the day long. 20 But my enemies live, and are
stronger than I: and they that hate me wrongfully are multiplied. 21
They that render evil for good, have detracted me, because I followed goodness.

JOB 19:25

25 For I know that my Redeemer liveth, and in the last day I shall rise out of the earth.

SONG OF SONGS (CANTICLE OF CANTICLES) 5:17 [same as verse 6:1 in modern Bibles]

17 Whither is thy beloved gone, O thou most beautiful among women? Whither is thy beloved turned aside, and we will seek him with thee?

LAMENTATIONS 1:15

15 Samech. The Lord hath taken away all my mighty men out of the midst of me: he hath called against me the time, to destroy my chosen men: the Lord hath trodden the winepress for the virgin daughter of Juda.

JEREMIAH (JEREMIAS) 14:17

17 And thou shalt speak this word to them: Let my eyes shed down tears night and day, and let them not cease, because the virgin daughter of my people is afflicted with a great affliction, with an exceeding grievous evil.

ISAIAH (ISAIAS) 53:2

2 And he shall grow up as a tender plant before him, and as a root out of a thirsty ground: there is no beauty in him, nor comeliness: and we have seen him, and there was no sightliness, that we should be desirous of him.

ISAIAH (ISAIAS) 50:5-6

5 The Lord God hath opened my ear, and I do not resist: I have not gone back. 6 I have given my body to the strikers, and my cheeks to them that plucked them: I have not turned away my face from them that rebuked me, and spit upon me.

ISAIAH (ISAIAS) 52:14

14 As many have been astonished at thee, so shall his visage be inglorious among men, and his form among the sons of men.

ISAIAH (ISAIAS) 53:3

3 Despised, and the most abject of men, a man of sorrows, and acquainted with infirmity: and his look was as it were hidden and despised, whereupon we esteemed him not.

PSALM 108:22-24 [same as Psalm 109 in modern Bibles]

22 For I am poor and needy, and my heart is troubled within me. 23 I am taken away like the shadow when it declineth: and I am shaken off as locusts. 24 My knees are weakened through fasting: and my flesh is changed for oil.

ISAIAH (ISAIAS) 22:9-16

9 And you shall see the breaches of the city of David, that they are many: and you have gathered together the waters of the lower pool, 10 And have numbered the houses of Jerusalem, and broken down houses to fortify the wall. 11 And you made a ditch between the two walls for the water of the old pool: and you have not looked up to the maker thereof, nor regarded him even at a distance, that wrought it long ago. 12 And the Lord, the God of hosts, in that day shall call to weeping, and to mourning, to baldness, and to girding with sackcloth: 13 And behold joy and gladness, killing calves, and slaying rams, eating flesh, and drinking wine: Let us eat and drink; for to morrow we shall die. 14 And the voice of the Lord of hosts was revealed in my ears: Surely this iniquity shall not be forgiven you till you die, saith the Lord God of hosts. 15 Thus saith the Lord God of hosts: Go, get thee in to him that dwelleth in the tabernacle, to Sobna who is over the temple: and thou shalt say to him: 16 What dost thou here, or as if thou wert somebody here? for thou hast hewed thee out a sepulchre here, thou hast hewed out a monument carefully in a high place, a dwelling for thyself in a rock.

JOEL 2:12

12 Now, therefore, saith the Lord. Be converted to me with all your heart, in fasting, and in weeping, and mourning.

LAMENTATIONS 3:38-39

38 Mem. Shall not both evil and good proceed out of the mouth of the Highest? 39 Mem. Why hath a living man murmured, man suffering for his sins?

ISAIAH (ISAIAS) 51:17

17 Arise, arise, stand up, O Jerusalem, which hast drunk at the hand of the Lord the cup of his wrath; thou hast drunk even to the bottom of the cup of dead sleep, and thou hast drunk even to the dregs.

JEREMIAH (JEREMÍAS) 31:6

6 For there shall be a day, in which the watchmen on mount Ephraim, shall cry: Arise, and let us go up to Sion to the Lord our God.

ISAIAH (ISAIAS) 61:1-2

1 The spirit of the Lord is upon me, because the Lord hath anointed me: he hath sent me to preach to the meek, to heal the contrite of heart, and to preach a release to the captives, and deliverance to
them that are shut up. 2 To proclaim the acceptable year of the Lord,
and the day of vengeance of our God: to comfort all that mourn.

ISAIAH (ISAIAS) 33:10

10 Now will I rise up, saith the Lord: now will I be exalted, now will I lift up myself.

LAMENTATIONS 5:16

16 The crown is fallen from our head: woe to us, because we have sinned.

JOB 19:8-11

8 He hath hedged in my path round about, and I cannot pass, and
in my way he hath set darkness. 9 He hath stripped me of my glory,
and hath taken the crown from my head. 10 He hath destroyed me
on every side, and I am lost, and he hath taken away my hope, as
from a tree that is plucked up. 11 His wrath is kindled against me,
and he hath counted me as his enemy.

SIRACH (ECCLESASTICUS) 5:16 [same as verse 5:14 used in the Spanish version of this book]

16 Be not called a whisperer, and be not taken in thy tongue, and confounded. 17 For confusion and repentance is upon a thief, and an evil mark of disgrace upon the double tongued, but to the whisperer hatred, and enmity, and reproach.

ISAIAH (ISAIAS) 1:6

6 From the sole of the foot unto the top of the head, there is no soundness therein: wounds and bruises and swelling sores: they are not bound up, nor dressed, nor fomented with oil.

GENESIS 37:31-32

31 And they took his coat, and dipped it in the blood of a kid, which they had killed: 32 Sending some to carry it to their father, and to say: This we have found: see whether it be thy son's coat, or not.

PSALM 21:7,18-19 [same as Psalm 22 in modern Bibles]

7 But I am a worm, and no man: the reproach of men, and the outcast of the people.
18 They have numbered all my bones. And they have looked and stared upon me. 19 They parted my garments amongst them; and upon my vesture they cast lots.

ISAIAH (ISAIAS) 61:10

10 I will greatly rejoice in the Lord, and my soul shall be joyful in my God: for he hath clothed me with the garments of salvation: and with the robe of justice he hath covered me, as a bridegroom decked with a crown, and as a bride adorned with her jewels.

ISAIAH (ISAIAS) 52:7

7 How beautiful upon the mountains are the feet of him that bringeth good tidings, and that preacheth peace: of him that sheweth forth good, that preacheth salvation, that saith to Sion: Thy God shall reign!

ZECHARIAH (ZACHARIAS) 12:10; 13:6

12:10 And I will pour out upon the house of David, and upon the inhabitants of Jerusalem, the spirit of grace, and of prayers: and they shall look upon me, whom they have pierced: and they shall mourn for him as one mourneth for an only son, and they shall grieve over him, as the manner is to grieve for the death of the firstborn.
13:6 And they shall say to him: What are these wounds in the midst of thy hands? And he shall say: With these I was wounded in the house of them that loved me.

ISAIAH (ISAIAS) 53:12

12 Therefore will I distribute to him very many, and he shall divide the spoils of the strong, because he hath delivered his soul unto death, and was reputed with wicked: and he hath borne the sins of many, and hath prayed for the transgressors.

EXODUS 12:5-7

5 And it shall be a lamb without blemish, a male, of one year: according to which rite also you shall take a kid. 6 And you shall keep it until the fourteenth day of this month: and the whole multitude of the children of Israel shall sacrifice it in the evening. 7 And they shall take of the blood thereof, and put it upon both the side posts, and on the upper door posts of the houses, wherein they shall eat it.

EZEKIEL (EZECHIEL) 17:22-23

22 Thus saith the Lord God: I myself will take of the marrow of the high cedar, and will set it: I will crop off a tender twig from the top of the branches thereof, and I will plant it on a mountain high and eminent. 23 On the high mountains of Israel will I plant it, and it shall shoot forth into branches, and shall bear fruit, and it shall become a great cedar: and all birds shall dwell under it, and every fowl shall make its nest under the shadow of the branches thereof.

SONG OF SONGS (CANTICLE OF CANTICLES) 8:6-7

6 Put me as a seal upon thy heart, as a seal upon thy arm, for love is as strong as death, jealousy as hard as hell, the lamps thereof are fire and flames. 7 Many waters cannot quench charity, neither can the floods drown it: if a man should give all the substance of his house for love, he shall despise it as nothing.

NUMBERS 21:8-9

8 And the Lord said to him: Make a brazen serpent, and set it up for a sign: whosoever being struck shall look on it, shall live. 9 Moses therefore made a brazen serpent, and set it up for a sign: which when they that were bitten looked upon, they were healed.

DEUTERONOMY 21:23

23 His body shall not remain upon the tree, but shall be buried the same day: for he is accursed by God that hangeth on a tree: and thou shalt not defile thy land, which the Lord thy God shall give thee in possession.

ISAIAH (ISAIAS) 1:10

10 Hear the word of the Lord, ye rulers of Sodom, give ear to the law of our God, ye people of Gomorrha.

LAMENTATIONS 1:12

12 Lamed. O all ye that pass by the way, attend, and see if there be any sorrow like to my sorrow: for he hath made a vintage of me, as the Lord spoke in the day of his fierce anger.

REVELATIONS (APOCALYPSE) 5:6

6 And I saw: and behold in the midst of the throne and of the four living creatures, and in the midst of the ancients, a Lamb standing as if were slain, having seven horns and seven eyes: which are the seven Spirits of God, sent forth into all the earth.

JUDITH 15:9-10

9 And Joachim the high priest came from Jerusalem to Bethulia with all his ancients to see Judith. 10 And when she was come out to him, they all blessed her with one voice, saying: Thou art the glory of Jerusalem, thou art the joy of Israel, thou art the honour of our people. 11 For thou hast done manfully, and thy heart has been strengthened, because thou hast loved chastity, and after thy husband hast not known any other: therefore also the hand of the Lord hath strengthened thee, and therefore thou shalt be blessed for ever. 12 And all the people said: So be it, so be it.

PSALM 15:10 [same as Psalm 16 in modern Bibles]

10 Because thou wilt not leave my soul in hell; wilt thou give thy holy one to see corruption.

PSALM 29:6 [same as Psalm 30 in modern Bibles]

6 For wrath is in his indignation; and life in his good will. In the evening weeping shall have place, and in the morning gladness.

PSALM 23:7 [same as Psalm 24 in modern Bibles]

7 Lift up your gates, O ye princes, and be ye lifted up, O eternal gates: and the King of Glory shall enter in.

ISAIAH (ISAIAS) 40:1-2

1 Be comforted, be comforted, my people, saith your God. 2 Speak ye to the heart of Jerusalem, and call to her: for her evil is come to an end, her iniquity is forgiven: she hath received of the hand of the Lord double for all her sins.

ISAIAH (ISAIAS) 53:12

12 Therefore will I distribute to him very many, and shall divide the spoils of the strong, because he hath delivered his soul unto death, and was reputed with the wicked: and he hath borne the sins of many, and hath prayed for the transgressors.

IMPRIMATUR

"The Passion of Christ is sufficient to serve as a guide and model for our entire life. For all those who wish to lead a perfect life, they need do nothing more than to despise what Christ despised on the Cross, and to accept what Christ accepted. On the Cross, we find the example of every virtue." (Saint Thomas Aquinas)

An attentive reading of the text entitled *I Have Given My Life for You* invites us to a profound reflection upon the meaning of the Passion of our Lord Jesus Christ and the way in which it directly relates to the life of believers, encouraging them to be witnesses to the Truth.

In the concepts and the lines for reflection expressed here, we find nothing which could possibly contradict Sacred Scripture or the teachings of the Magisterium of the Church. This book, the Testimony of Catalina, helps us to better contemplate the evangelical message and especially the Passion of our Lord Jesus Christ.

For that reason, I authorize its publication and recommend its reading.

Oruro, Good Friday, April 10, 2009
Mons. Krzysztof Bialasik, SVD
Bishop of the Diocese of Oruro, Bolivia

Chapter 7

I Have Given My Life For You

INTRODUCTION

For the spiritual growth of every Christian, it is always necessary to meditate on the Passion of Our Lord Jesus Christ. When we reflect on the sufferings that Jesus had to undergo in order to redeem us, we can gradually understand more deeply not only the nature and breadth of His Love for each one of us but also the gravity and effect of our own sins.

This chapter in this book is a compilation of texts written intermittently during the Lenten periods of 2005, 2006, 2007, 2008, and the beginning of Lent, 2009. Its precious contents are a new call from the Lord to each of its readers, inviting them to unite themselves to Him during the dramatic moments when He surrendered His Life for the salvation of humanity.

Around the year 1210, more than 800 years ago, St. Francis of Assisi sorrowfully repeated unceasingly: "Love is not loved, Love is not loved…!" Now, Jesus Himself tells us at the beginning of this text:

> "I wish to speak to you again about My Passion, because by doing so, I wish to transmit to your hearts feelings of union with Me, of compassion… to show you My Love, because

> 'What more can I wish for than the Love of those who led Me to the sacrifice?'"

In the following pages, Jesus Himself will lead you "to the reliving of His bloody and terrible hours," which led Him to sacrifice Himself out of love for you. However, in contrast to other texts transcribed by Catalina on this theme, you will not find here so much a detailed story of the tortures and "mockery" (the jeering, the derision, the insults, and the shame) that Jesus had to endure during His Redemptive Passion. Instead, this text delves into the deep meaning of it all—the "reasons for" and the "why" and "wherefore" of such immense humiliation and offense.

Herein lies the greatest richness of this simple work. The understanding of these reasons will greatly help us, in accordance with the Will of the Father and His Holy Church, "to better participate in His Divine Life" (Cf. Vatican II Council, Dogmatic Constitution Lumen Gentium, 1).

We hope in God that the reading of this Chapter will be of great benefit to you and your loved ones, dear reader. May the Holy Spirit lead you to delve more deeply into the message of Love embodied in each moment of agony Jesus suffered for you.

Lenten Season of 2005

Merida, March 16, 2005 – The Lord

Beloved flower of My Passion, contemplate from this place the tide of turbulent waves of distrust and envy brought on by the aversion to My Works. They complain because they find the same concepts in works written at different times and by persons who cannot possibly have anything in common. But they pay no attention to the context and do not take the trouble to make an in-depth study.

The fact is that the Teacher never tires of repeating, although some students who are rascals are drowsing only to wake up and give some inane answer, exactly like arrogant children do when they are caught in a mistake. I wish to speak to you again about My Passion because when I do so, I want to spread in your hearts feelings of union with Me, of compassion, to show you My Love, because what more can I wish than the Love of those who led Me to the sacrifice?

When I was led to Calvary, there was condensed in Me all suffering which I always experienced while thinking about the wickedness of mankind that so greatly offended a Father who is so good. That offended Love was what made Me suffer most, piercing My Soul at every sigh, at every step which brought Me closer to the crucifixion.

How I wish that mankind would cultivate greater devotion to My Passion! For that reason, I insist upon it, even though many "theologians" feel repulsion in their stomachs when they contemplate a statue representing Me weeping or bleeding. My Passion is a compendium of Holy Love and supernatural Wisdom itself. Everything can be found during My hours of the Passion: every evil in the world transformed into good for eternity, and all the supernatural goodness of present mankind, united to the promise of the good that they may attain if they die protected by My Passion.

It is for that reason that time and time again I insist on it for those who gaze upon My crucified self, and I invite them to be with Me in order to relive the dreadful, bloody hours that led Me to sacrifice Myself. Those who do not meditate on My sufferings, who do not compare them with their own, do not extract from the treasure chest of My Passion the treasures that I have stored up for each one of you.

I assure you that those who meditate on My sorrowful Passion will derive many Graces, because it is a treasure chest of infinitely enormous benefits. By the same token, those who have paid no attention or have forgotten My sufferings will always find emptiness and spiritual poverty. My sufferings will always be the Glory of My Father and My Glory, as well as the greatest demonstration of the Spirit of Love for you on earth.

The strange thing is that many are convinced of those things; yet with indifference, they immediately forget what they know and unfortunately and sadly, they take refuge in many other matters that satisfy their ego. If you keep Me company while meditating on My Passion, I will make smooth your hardships, because as I have said, I always repay love with Love.

This is no mere sentimentalism. Or do you not believe that the Love that pours from My Heart is genuine, in order to bring to you and give you true union with Me? It is difficult to love Me without heartbeats driven by a strong inner reflection. That being so, what could I give you that would be more effective to make you love Me than My sorrowful Passion?

I know very well how many other matters you must be concerned with; therefore, I do not seek that you constantly meditate on My sufferings, but rather, that you should acknowledge how little you know about what I suffered for you, and by recognizing this, that men and women may rectify their faults. Oh, the depths of the ignorance that conceals from their nearsighted vision the boundless beauty, power, holiness, and salvation of My Passion, unknown up to now, often hidden by their "excessive caution."

I had to make use of two books and a film director in order to shake men and women, and even with that, scales still cover their eyes! Yes, there are many who reproduce My crucifixion. They reveal Me in many ways that I approve of. But I know very well that I do not reign in their hearts as I would like to. I know that their thoughts about My spiritual and bodily sufferings have not penetrated their spirits so frequently.

I have made them so accustomed to the extraordinary things about My Passion, that they have often assessed My actions in a highly relative fashion. Thus, My greatest actions seem ordinary to them. Nevertheless, I wish that from time to time, they would ponder more greatly My Human Nature, making good use of the most transparent reflections offered them by My Divine Nature when they desire greater knowledge of Me.

And to those who wish to hinder My plans, I assert that My

Work will be carried out. It cannot fail because I hold everything and everyone in My hand. Therefore, whatever they prevent Me from doing today, I will do more effectively tomorrow. This "tomorrow" should be of concern to them. It would be more prudent to give in today, better to show Me that they love Me. But they are and do remain free, not only to believe in My Love but also to belittle My Works. And what do they suppose will happen to them if they make poor use of their freedom?

Beloved children, become convinced of the fact that Gethsemane and Golgotha are sudden, enormous blazes that reached the Infinite Royalty of the Throne of My adorable Father. Gethsemane and the Cross contain extensive flames that have the power to reach you too, and by touching you, to gather you into a blazing whirlwind that may elevate you very high: towards Me and with Me; towards the Father, with Me; and in the Holy Spirit, always with Me.

My being a Man meant for Me to assume everything pertaining to human nature, and therefore, I desired to experience the whole gamut of human feelings, but in an intense fashion. During such feelings, I would have to experience tremendous bitterness when the people, impelled by their leaders, would prefer an assassin to their own Redeemer.

I knew that this had to happen, but My knowing this did not prevent Me from experiencing the feelings native to human beings. I believe that the world will never be capable of understanding how much and how I suffered during My Passion; the sensations of pain grew greater and greater. However, the increase in the sensations of pain did not prevent Me from exhibiting the gentleness which led Me to be bypassed by Barabbas.

Now I ask you, My souls: Whom do you choose? Me or Barabbas? For your own good, I must tell you that the choices you have made up to today have not always been clear nor pure. I tell you today that if you love Me, quickly leave and with determination every Barabbas of this world, who is a genuine assassin like that other "Barabbas," because he kills souls and often bodies too.

I want everything to be clear-cut on the part of those who love

Me, and remember that you cannot claim that you prefer Me if you are in agreement with the world. I will assist you greatly in avoiding that; all I need is for you to accept My help. Ask yourselves often, "Good or Evil? Jesus or Barabbas?"

Do not listen to the angry cries of so many who raise their voices shouting "Give me Barabbas!" The problem about choice is the fact that you do not have enough strength and desire to uproot your self-love, which is like a wild animal that hungers for those pieces of meat with which it thinks it can still fill itself.

I, who knows all this, make those ill-fated pieces sometimes bitter and sometimes sweet for you, because I must allow you to gain strength by abandoning them if they seem sweet to you or swallowing them if they seem bitter. Nevertheless, there are so many who choose a "Barabbas" so as not to have to choose Me. And what do they gain? The only place they can get to: a prison that is eternal and already so filled with other "Barabbas's."

So as not to fall into error, you who love Me, leave the crowd and come with Me to the Praetorium without fear of suffering your passion, like Me. The honor is yours; the pleasure is Mine and will be yours forever. Do not be afraid of keeping Me company in My Praetorium. Concentrate your gaze on at least three things: My back horribly scourged, My head crowned with a tight crown of thorns, and My hands tied behind Me.

If anyone wants to follow Me, I said, "Take up your Cross and come to Me." That is a precise condition. My Word cannot undergo any changes.

Merida, March 17, 2005 – The Lord

My little children, I would like to have you see the glory that I have conferred on those who have followed Me during the Passion by accepting a portion of the outrages that I experienced. Thus, you will realize that that glory is similar to Mine, and moreover, it is really a part of My glory because whoever has shared My Passion with Me, will share My glory with Me.

When you are persecuted and reviled, even with lies like I was, rejoice greatly. What Martyr has been forgotten by Me? Even those who do not need to give their lives like the Martyrs, but who suffer harassment because of Me, will become chosen ones who are guarded by My Angels. I tell you truly that My followers are lucky!

Those on whom I wish to bestow the great honor of having them share in My Passion need enormous trust in order to follow Me. In one way or another, I must make them share a bitter chalice as an inheritance of those who believe in Me and follow Me. I ask them to be calm and remain very firmly in My hands, and no one will be able to do them any real harm.

I assure you that I passed among My enemies with My Face fixed on the Paternal Home, where an Infinitely loving Father was calling Me with very great sweetness, even when I was marred by men who made evil sport with My humble and silent Person. Lucky are you, O soul, if you understand Me and follow Me during the Passion that I willed for Myself and also for you who are truly fainthearted, when out of weakness or shortcoming, you forget that your strength is all here in this open Heart which patently loves you and has demonstrated predilection for you.

Lucky are you, O soul, and certain of your inheritance in Heaven if you lovingly submit to your various executioners, that being your little Passion which will become great if you unite it to Mine. Now answer Me if you wish to arrive at the summit... at the One who before you rose by immensely lowering Himself.

(Later, when I was praying to the Lord asking about whether it was appropriate and in accord with His Will for me to go to Chiapas or not, He sent me to look up the following biblical passages: Luke 4:41-44; Amos 1:6-8; Matthew 18:1-7.)

Merida, March 19, 2005 – The Lord

I willed to become a Man in order to experience everything you experience, even to the point of wishing to pay for your sins. For that reason, I had to suffer acute abandonment also on Calvary, and in that way, to allow My Humanity to receive your lament. Try to draw a parallel between the abandonment that you feel on some occasions and My abandonment. Thus you will see that holding Me up as your model, not only Divine but also Human, will help you during your little abandonments.

It is almost impossible for you to believe without experiencing something based on the Faith that must be exercised. That is to say that in the midst of your sufferings, you would be unable to believe in My intervention if I did not send you a good dose of abandonment. That is when you see yourselves almost forced to perform the holocaust of yourselves because in abandonment, you surrender yourselves to annihilation.

Concerning that, I went through a very broad and profound human experience: I lost Myself as far as human consciousness was concerned, but I found Myself in the bosom of the Father, and it is the same for you if you wish to do as I have done. Why do you think I spoke from Calvary if it was not to conquer your hearts and minds? Your mind must be greatly exercised; it must search out the reason for My painful cries that are filled with so much Love.

Remember that My Father sent Me to set the hearts of human beings on fire, and I could not set them on fire if I did not send them lights and flames, and Divine sparks of Love. I am pleased when you meditate on My Passion and when you persist in making My Words from the Cross resonate in your souls because those Words were just so many more brilliant flames that escaped from My Soul to take to those who wish it, the fire that devoured Me.

Later the same day – The Lord

My children, My Work is hidden and it produces exterior fruits in the form and in the times that I desire, but day by day, and thus it constitutes the basic nucleus of the great triumph that the Father has been preparing since eternity. If the man of good will wishes to be sure about this work of Mine, firstly he must think about it within himself and probe what was and what is the state of his soul during his own intellectual and volitional difficulties.

He will find that everything is evolving in him, and it is precisely that evolution which demonstrates My inner action, practically invisible for the time being, so much so that he tends to approach Me precisely because My Father has sent all of you to Me. How little all of you reflect upon this possibility of personal proof, this evolution of your spirits.

Nevertheless, if you observe humanity as a whole since the time of My stay on Earth, it is not difficult to see that there has been a progressive approach to Me, especially from My Church. There have been doubts and individuals, and certain unfortunate things now stand out inside the Church. But what remains is the effect I have on My Spouse, because of the greater Light that I grant to Her for Her dignity and for your benefit.

People have caused too much uproar over some individuals who have become famous because of certain personal works of theirs. Still today, they waste too much time thinking about the spiritual and material attitudes of "X" person, and they are afraid that some intruders may cause great harm to My Spouse on earth. Do they not say that She is a Pilgrim on earth? Therefore, She cannot have attained eternal stability, the happy changelessness of the Kingdom that I have prepared for Her.

Rather, invisibly guarded by Me, My Church prepares and carries out the War that I Myself brought to earth, and She always emerges victorious, even from the contradictions which originate in Her very bosom. This results from My Life, which I continuously infuse in Her, particularly at those moments you call "historical." If you had faith, how much Light would be born in you when you assist in the struggles of My Church!

I tell you truly, faithful souls, do not let yourselves be blinded by darkness. Do not be stunned by the noise that surrounds you; do not abandon Her because you see how ill are some of Her members. Moreover, do not be frightened if certain mushrooms see the light of day, which can only poison those who eat them, but not those who look at them and leave them.

Is the Church not Mine? Have I not founded Her and loved Her, remaining in Her hands for your sake? Today is Palm Sunday. I invite you, therefore, to join Me in climbing up onto the restless little donkey that I am taming for you. I sigh, and I am moved… You who are My friends, should sigh with Me. I assure you that I will do the housecleaning that needs to be done. Trust in the foundations.

Mérida, March 20, 2005 – The Lord

Dear souls, My Apostles had not understood the reasons for My Passion. Who could possibly have given Me the understanding that I, as a Man, needed? Only My Father… I missed those who were Mine, but I wanted to fully experience the feeling; I accepted that feeling of loneliness and the inability of my friends to understand, in spite of the fact that they were sincere with Me.

Observe Me, a Man among men, even though I was not just a Man. Observe Me and understand the human drama that wounded My enormous sensitivity as a Man-God, that is, as God made Man in order to be able to suffer, to weep, and to shed My Blood for you.

Listen to this, which is part of My inner personal experience, of the sorrowful beat of the hours so sad that preceded My sacrifice, because they are the confirmation of so many other revelations of Mine. They provide the certainty of the great good that I wish for you.

See the infamous judgment of a human tribunal, this time in the person of Terese Marie, the young woman whom people want to kill by withdrawing food and water from her, calling it an act of charity. Oh, poor human beings who again view the Praetorium on their movie screens… but only a short while ago, even while knowing that they are opening the doors to their own holocaust!

All these writings, My souls, provide the certainty of the enormous good that I wish for you. If you feel that you are voluntarily Mine, you will be capable of some understanding of Me, since whoever belongs to Me always shares in Me.

Oh, how blind, to wish to remain outside the entrance to My wounded Heart! Come, and if you love Me, suffer a little for Me!

Mérida, March 21, 2005 – The Lord

Take My tears before beginning these very difficult days. Know that the Passion that I suffered in Body and soul was a magnet for humanity, so that when it became absorbed in My Passion, all the guilt of human beings would vanish. Due to this, the fact is that on earth there is a permanent struggle, invisible to human eyes but genuine. A struggle between My sufferings, which save, and the passions of human beings, which soil them and lead them to condemn themselves.

Thus, you are plunged into a permanent struggle between good and evil: the good completely focused on My sufferings, and the evil focused on your sufferings when you suffer them fruitlessly and, moreover, with harm to yourselves. That is the reason for acting and healing you… because your actions are wounds that might suffer gangrene and become enormous evils that would destroy your souls.

For that reason, needing to heal you with My Passion, it is logical that I am asking you to meditate on it. It is necessary for Me to offer its fruits to you over and over again and to confer on you union with Me, sorrowful and afflicted. Understand Me!

I lower Myself to you, who are sometimes sad, sometimes useless. I come to you, not with majesty, but with infinite humility, so that you can receive Me easily, since for Me who loves you so much, your good is a matter of urgency, and I procure and achieve it by means of the caresses of My Love, which is truly infinite.

If I come to you with the fruits of My Passion and I enter into your souls, as if I came from outside, while really I am inside of you, so often unknown, abandoned or so little thought of, or much less appreciated… I come with humble patience, but at the same time with pressing supplication, because I long to be welcomed in your hearts, first with sorrow and then with joy.

Who can possibly be a substitute for Me? Who can possibly be your wise Doctor and your compassionate Samaritan? No one can possibly be a substitute for Me, because I bring to you a huge amount of gifts that overshadow all the minute reasons of human love.

No one and nothing can possibly give you the joy of Infinite Love, because only your Creator is Infinite Love; only your Redeemer has a pure and very rich Passion to offer.

My little children, I must repeat for you the painful moments of My Passion at Gethsemane, because the memory of My suffering diminishes with the passing of time for those who remain "contemplating" My agony, but who do not determine to delve more deeply into it. I cannot be lonelier, more abandoned. And I have searched for those who are Mine, just as I searched for Peter, James, and John, and I have found them drowsing, their shortcomings aggravated by many little faults, and inattentive to Me.

Yet I have returned, and I do return to you, men and women of the twenty-first century, to remind you to take a good look at My sad Face, to pay more attention to the sweat of My Blood. But… are you interested in this unrecognized Passion? Do you not believe that I deserve greater consideration, greater attention?

I beg you not to make Me repeat the description of My sufferings because you should undergo them with Me. Yes, the best thing would be for you to suffer a little more for Me, who was consumed with sufferings in that dark and luminous Garden, a place of the greatest martyrdom, chosen by Me, and accepted and experienced for your salvation.

In this Work of Mine, the story of My sufferings causes the hearts of mankind to have become sensitive to the accounts of the hardships I endured. Yes, dear little children, your hearts are understanding toward Me. I have transformed you in this way, and you will want to behave thus toward Me.

My greatly beloved souls, return to the Garden of Olives. Return with Me to darkness, to pain, to compassion, and to sorrowful love.

Mérida, March 23, 2005 – The Lord

Beloved soul, I know very well what your heart has suffered during this time. That is why I am rewarding and consoling you by telling you about My earthly sufferings. Reflect on what My feelings were when departing from Gethsemane: hands tied, mocked, and betrayed. I was brought to Annas, a man feared by the Jews because that old Pontiff exercised his dominion in a shameless fashion, as if demonstrating that his eventual dismissal did not frighten him.

This man was awaiting Me with hostile feelings, and instead of being the first one to acknowledge Me, he had already decided in his heart to put Me to death. It had to be this way; My Father willed it so, and that is the way I wanted as well, although for reasons totally opposite to that of Annas.

Imagine the sorrow in My Heart when I felt the harshness cloaking the words that miserable "Minister" of the Old Covenant addressed to Me. He had greatly loathed and detested Me from the day when he was told of the Words I used to single out the perversity of that group of unworthy men who dominated the House of My Father. In fact, he was included among those whom I called "a breed of vipers." And now I was going to introduce Myself to his cruelty. I was about to fall under his evil hands because I accepted and willed it.

The Divine part of Me would have still liked to save him. As a Man, I would have liked to sink his whole degrading legacy, spiritual and material, so as to be his Savior too, his Emmanuel. Yet, the miserable wretch did not allow Me to do so, and that pained Me deeply.

So then, Annas and his "allies" closed their souls to Me because of their base reasoning in addition to the individual evil of most of them, for there were very few of them who were well disposed toward Me. I paid attention to the Will of My beloved Father, not to the intentions of My executioners. That is why I allowed Annas to say whatever he wanted. Yet, after a few words from him, My silence angered him almost to the point of madness.

Look at the one to whom I surrendered, and practically speaking, into whose hands I gave up My Humanity. Reflect on this, because it is very useful for your souls: for doubts, aversions, and fears that you experience when someone wants to nail you to some cross that is unpleasant for you.

Think of the other aspect of this too: if I surrendered Myself to Annas, as a confirmed enemy, I also surrendered Myself to you, as dearly beloved friends. Is this not true? I ask: how many are there who do something to make amends to Me for the snubs and for the hatred of that master in Hell?

My little one, I experienced a great deal of bitterness during My Passion, and now I would like the sweetness of your hearts, the enthusiastic acceptance of My Person, to make reparation for the humiliating welcome that Annas offered Me, and after him, his son-in-law Caiaphas, a worthy disciple of his, when I was taken to him.

Remember Me in this way: with My hands tied, taken before two authorities of the Jewish Religion. Observe Me again, humble and peaceful, at the mercy of everyone, great and small, while they were awaiting the day of My sacrifice to dawn. Think, beloved, and all of you, think: I was the judge of every age and of all of humanity, past, present, and future, and I was humbly awaiting My conviction, in order to free you from your very own conviction.

Can there be greater humiliation and greater Love? So, console Me during this night.

Later the same day – The Lord

We will continue, My beloved. You ask Me to continue "pouring My heart out." I would say rather, that I am going to continue calling you to deeper reflection. Peter also was to cause Me bitterness, although for very different reasons: on the one hand, because of anger, and on the other hand, because of his weakness, because of his fear of losing his own life.

He had told Me he would give his life for Me (and he would do so at the end). But faced with immediate danger, and even lacking the strength that springs from genuine humility and from great love, he fell.

Peter has shown you, by demonstrating to himself, a truth which is of interest to all of you: the extreme weakness you experience when you accompany Me during My Passion. There he was, present and not far from Me, yet he experienced fear. Who has acted any better than he did? In one way or another, many have denied Me in word or deed.

Peter was fearless about wishing to follow Me, while the rest, with the exception of John, had fled. It was, in fact, the love in Peter's heart that urged him to follow Me and to stay close to Me. Yet, he did not succeed in doing so, and he even uttered some very strong words to convince the rest of those there that he did not know Me.

That is how it was: neither Annas, nor Caiaphas, nor Peter—the future Sovereign Pontiff of My Church—acknowledged the One who had been awaited for centuries. I had to go without approval, without recognition, since before the Father, I was sin personified. It is that which, in the plan of My Divine Will, caused all, except My Mother, John, Magdalene, the other Mary, and some good women, to pity Me. All the rest were to scorn Me.

Oh, woe to those men and women who think that their actions are an end in themselves! I say to them that even where there is the most complete freedom, the heavenly Father has the power to confer many different values on the actions of human beings if He wishes to do so.

My poor Peter was weak, yes, but well-disposed toward Me, and when one has good will, one can work incredible miracles, unthinkable wonders. Peter could have been lost that day if I had not saved him by that gaze from Me that brought repentance to his soul. Nevertheless, his denying Me three times was enough while awaiting his threefold declaration of love for which I would ask of him later, after My Resurrection.

Always be sincere with Me and keep Me company during My Passion. I assure you that this is not an abstract invitation. No. It is an invitation to genuine things, to things that I will send you, but which you should not scorn.

Be close to Me like Peter, and even if you have committed the same fault of warming yourselves near a human fire, any fire at all, do not despair. Whenever you come to Me with friendship and affection, like Peter, and better yet, with fear for yourselves, I will welcome you.

My beloved ones, I invite you to lovingly approach My Passion. I assure you openly that I have a strong preference for those who love to experience My sufferings… that is to say, in My likeness. This is logical because Love attracts love, and as you already know, I Am all Love.

Mérida, March 24, 2005 – The Lord

Judas, that unhappy Apostle, heads the list of those who betray Me, he who was My friend and companion and who sold Me to the Sanhedrin and died by hanging himself like a desperate, suicidal person. That man is the prototype of the baseness of humanity, which is so much deeper the greater the act of rebellion. He had been one of the twelve whom I chose to accompany Me on My mission, and he quickly changed into a henchman for the devil because of his great attachment to money.

They have been talking about his betrayal for more than two thousand years, but it is a subject that could never be exhausted because his offense was excessive. I want to tell you that in spite of the cruelty of his action, I always treated him with kindness, and with even greater compassion than the other Apostles.

There are many who think that I certainly could have chosen another means for sacrificing My Life, avoiding the monstrous betrayal of Judas. But aside from the gift of freedom that I grant you, and which I never take away from anyone, I willed to be handed over to the executioners in the worst way possible, and thus, it was through the very desire of that wretched person to betray Me.

The treatment reserved for Me on his part was due precisely to the freedom granted to the human being. And so it was that Judas, out of evil, brought to completion what I had decided and accepted out of Goodness. His betrayal was not necessary because My Father might have heard My desire to be sacrificed in any way at all that was effective. But in the presence of the traitor, it was suitable for Me to accept his action, which was inspired by another and greater rebel, Lucifer, who became a spokesperson of the darkness.

You cannot imagine how much My sensitive Heart suffered from all that! I want you to understand this, to take it all in and not to minimize My sorrowful acceptance of the betrayal that was perpetuated. True friendship dwells in noble hearts, while it flees from hearts that are vile.

My Apostles were My first friends and also My guests. Afterwards, I surrendered My very Body to them at the Last Supper. I have made them the bestowers of My infinite riches. That is why, humanly speaking, I expected them to return My friendship, My Love that nourished each one of them, with the trust that is granted to beloved friends.

Given the limits of human speech, it is impossible to tell you how much I suffered because of that wicked Apostle, Judas. That is why My Heart feels so much compassion when one of My children is betrayed by another, a compassion mixed with the feeling of repulsion that the one who betrays another friend produces in Me.

Now I tell you that it is useful for you to reflect on your own betrayal, to think about the fact that being distant in spirit from Me, even though near in body, leads inevitably to the ruin of everything that is good.

Mérida, March 25, 2005 – The Lord

While contemplating that painting, you are thinking of the blows I sustained. Yes, I was severely beaten by the soldiers and the guards of the Temple, but today, I am more greatly injured—and very severely—by those men and women who hope to defeat Me and expect that I will be indulgent with them. To act unrighteously and expect My approval is the greatest stupidity.

There is such great loneliness for Me in the world! Some persons are such paltry followers of Mine, of so little faith, that they run to Satan's side, in blindness and sadness. How many souls are there who have genuinely and totally surrendered themselves to Me? Which ones are they? Must I forever beg for love? Shall I always have to persuade human beings by pulling them by the ears? I do not want your ears. I only want your heart.

At least you, be quick to receive these waves of Love that flow unceasingly from this Heart, sick with Love, once again during this Holy Week. Be persuaded that if you come wholeheartedly with Me, then from Annas to Caiaphas, and from Caiaphas to Pilate, you will experience new feelings.

Mérida, March 25, 2005 – The Lord

My daughter, following are reflections about My sufferings. Act as My Spirit moves you during these days and as these words are dictated to you. What more does it matter than being called reflections? What is important is that these words lead you to meditate, and during those meditations, I assure you that those who belong to Me will know how to recognize the voice that is calling them.

There are three questions and answers during this late afternoon:

Who wishes to hurt Me?
Who is tearing My beard?
Whom have I not refused?

Beloved, all sinners have hurt Me, and every evil thing has been a more intense wound for Me. Several persons tore My beard, since those condemned to death by crucifixion in those times had lost their legal rights as individuals. That made permissible every offense, every derision against the condemned person.

Little children, how many persons during Holy Week desire to feel moved because I have accustomed them to that, in order to favor them! But today, I invite you to reason with Me. Later on, we shall see. Human beings have wished to hurt Me, starting with that day, well known to everyone, when I was covered with shame because of their first real sin. I have accepted their repeated blows and I have transformed them into means for their justification.

Could the offense committed against Me remain without My replying to it? What has been that reply? Full acceptance, silence, a gentle gaze, a movement of compassion: a forgiving embrace. No one is hurt without replying in kind, but I have replied in that fashion.

My beard has been repeatedly torn out. Who has done it? You as well? Allow Me to explain to you: if the thorns with their painful pressure impelled My eyes to close, the tearing of My beard was very painful because My Face was one flame of pain due to the blows, to the dreadful Crown, and due to the burning sensation of the saliva of the guards from their spittle. My wounds were smarting.

How could I refuse to accept those pains? I was there for the purpose of suffering, to endure, to die, and that is how My gift proceeded, made concrete act by act. No one can imagine how much My Face suffered! One of the whip lashes from the Scourging ran from My cheek right down to My neck, like a furrow of fire.

I had received the blow of that clumsy soldier on the other cheek. Blood was pouring down from My face and My forehead, and blood was dripping from My mouth because of the blows. Pilate tried in vain to move the crowd to compassion, and he presented Me before them saying: "Ecce homo" thinking that he would justly triumph over the treachery of the Jews, given My condition when he exhibited Me.

Men and women! I did not deny Myself to you or to the Father! I welcomed everything and everyone. With blind hatred, the priests of the Temple could only repeat over and over again: "Crucify him!" I hope that you welcome Me, and not only during this Easter season. I fervently desire it! Come! I go accompanied by you. You will get His approval. You will be justified by Him, because He wants to give the reward due you because of My sacrifice, because I so wish it and He so wishes it.

Remember that My Passion is your guarantee, and that what I suffered then is inconceivable to the human mind, just as your refusal to accept Me should be called inconceivable after so many and such huge demonstrations of Love. Now if you wish, be moved by Me. I desired first to make you reason with Me.

Have you understood My Message? I have not abandoned you. And you… will you abandon Me? Be convinced that My Passion not only saves you but also embellishes you, gives you clarity of thought, faith, unshakable hope, and it powerfully enkindles My Charity in you.

Mérida, March 25, 2005 – The Lord

Beloved daughter, accompany Mary in Her loneliness now on Calvary and for that purpose, I offer to give you light and compassion during those dreadful hours. Listen to this, and love Her for Her strength and Her pain. She followed Me, opening up a path in the crowd towards the place of My martyrdom. When Our eyes met, it was immensely painful. I have already told you this before.

Those who accompanied Her wisely supported Her to the foot of Calvary, but She could not get close to My Cross from the first moment. Her whole Life was dependent on Mine, but never so much as now. She felt She was slowly dying, while experiencing an atrocious oppression. The beating of Her heart was growing faint and slackening. The pain was immobilizing Her more and more.

I witnessed how My poor Mother was suffering! I did not want Her to be far or unable to see Me, so I arranged things in such a way that She was able to come close to My Cross. I was God, but I suffered like a Man, and as such, I desired that My Mother should be near Me. All the more so because this was in consonance with My Divine plan to have Her play an exceptional role in My Passion.

Thus, She cooperated with Me, and with Me, She contributed to the salvation of mankind. She was worthy to share in My work of Redemption, but by keeping Her at the foot of My Cross, I wanted to bestow on Her the acknowledgment that this was My Will. My Mother was close to Me and I could see Her behind the veil of Blood that almost entirely covered My eyelids.

In agony, My Heart of a Son beat with a mixture of profound gratitude and sadness for that poor Mother who had followed Me and had helped by making self-sacrifices during the whole of My Life. I was on the point of departing from earth, and therefore, why would I not say "farewell" to the one who gave birth to Me, who trembled over Me, and who was offering Herself, truly Her whole self, for Me and for you?

Do you know what My "farewell" to Her was? My "farewell" was substituting you for Myself through John. She understood it, and with immense recognition, She welcomed, in place of Her only Son who was irreplaceable, a multitude of sons and daughters whom She would have to care for and follow with the same love She had had for Me.

My Mother gave thanks for the gift because it came from Me, already in the throes of death, and because John would be the alive and continuous memory of Me. John was another symbol, like a crown of the Mother of Madonna lilies, and Mary understood this instantly. The Madonna lily, like the white lily, is the symbol of purity.

I said so many things silently to Her, but My gaze tried to express to Her:

> "Farewell, Mother. You will see Me soon and You will no longer be sad like You are today. I leave You My Church for You to help and nourish as You nourished Me. I am going to the Father and I will return, but I will prepare a Throne of majestic Glory for You there…
>
> Farewell, Mother. Today You see Me most cruelly humiliated, but soon You will be in ecstasy over My Glory… My first gaze was for You and now, My last one is also reserved for You."

Later the same day – The Lord

After having caused that interruption in order for you to meditate on My Mother, we will return to some thoughts about My sufferings. I know that for many, they are the fuel that helps them grow spiritually. When they led Me to the place of My sacrifice, I was reduced to a pitiful state after enduring so much humiliation and suffering.

There, on Golgotha, My own holocaust would burn in an immense flame of pain and Love. Nothing was spared Me, but to the contrary, with the mockery, all My suffering increased. It was the supreme Gift of the Father to humanity: in handing over His own Son made Man, He handed over His suffering when He handed Me over to the most unrestrained and oppressive evil. He abandoned Me to the wishes of those in charge, for them to unleash the hatred that devoured them, even to the point of blasphemy and crime.

You wonder, "Why did I go through so much suffering, like a little lamb bitten over and over again by ferocious wolves?" Was not the suffering I endured at Gethsemane enough? Did not that dreadful, bloody Crown of thorns that I received cover the multitude of all the sins of humanity? Was not the bloody and painful scourging, which I received for Love of you, sufficient reparation?

What a Passion I suffered apart from the crucifixion! And they are still boasting about punishing whomever I choose today to shake the minds and consciences of men and women because they silenced those whom I told about it previously and even burned manuscripts.

Now they will know a great deal more. And let us see whom they punish and how they will have to be accountable to Me—those who wish to put a stop to the conversion of the souls that I wished to save with those sufferings!

What do those blind guides of today know about the further sufferings, the sighs, the woes and tears, the humiliations, the anxieties, the despicable acts, the insults, the arrogant words, the calumny and lies, the betrayal and the weight, the enormous weight of all the sins that I carried to the Cross?

No! The Pharisees of today, like those of yesterday, cannot possibly have noticed everything that I generously took upon Myself.

Mérida, March 26, 2005 – The Lord

When they nailed My hands, I felt then as if they were tearing My veins out, destroying the small cartilages and nerves of My hands, and the pain was unbearable. Today, your gazes when you are before My Blessed Sacraments, your gazes of understanding are sufficient for Me as reparation for those acts of brutality. They make up for the looks of rage and spite that were cast on Me at Calvary.

Already hanging on My tree of torture, while I was suffering spasms of pain, they were blaspheming Me, they were mocking Me, they were throwing stones and clods of earth at Me as if to put an end to that truly Infinite Love of Mine, which even then could have made Me embrace and forgive My hangmen and the others who displayed their hostility under the Cross.

There was My Mother close by, in a state that caused deep suffering to those who saw Her, and even more to Me. Oh, sweet Mother! This is My hour! Yes…! May you understand Her and tell Her that if you had been there, you would have liked to support Her that day.

You certainly were there! I was seeing so many of you through time and space. How dear to Me was the presence of the souls that would love Me at the foot of the Cross! First you were the crucifiers, and then you became the consolers. Before and afterwards, you were always My beloved, as now, as eternally, for the sake of that unique and unvarying Love, which enkindled the Bonfire of My sacrifice and My total gift.

Contemplate Me crucified and recall in this panting breast, the beats of the almost extinct Heart. It is I, Jesus, dying, abandoned, consumed, and Who with His last breath of life, will leave His Spirit lovingly in the hands of His adored Father.

Come, little children, do not fear the jeers of the drunken soldiers, of the furious members of the Sanhedrin, and the obstinate people. Come and climb to the top of the hill and let us be crucified together. Thus it is pleasing to My Father, for thus does He love humanity, and Infinite Love also desires it.

Come, My beloved, and remember that for you I shed My blood; I was reduced to breathlessness and I was a prisoner with the most burning thirst. Gaze at Me on this Good Friday, and you will weep for your sins, and even more so, when you remember that there are many who do not believe in Me.

There are still those who betray; there are still those who spit in My face; there are still those who dare to jam down on My head the Crown of thorns, which is all bloody and glorious. Have pity on Me and live in My Heart, which has been so embittered and beaten by treacherous enemies, often camouflaged in the clothing of the first Judas. Come to My Heart, which was in agony and almost crushed by the enormous weight of ice-cold souls.

Climb even higher when you are troubled and saddened. Know that your weeping is blessed. I will transform you into fervent and vibrant people, and thus, you will be filled only with Me.

Rest, My beloved. We will continue at break of day. In a little while, reflections and meditations on My sufferings will cease. To those "Annases" of today, it is necessary to demonstrate Who is speaking to them: the One who was silent then but who comes back over and over again to repeat to them what their stubborn minds cannot manage to understand: that there is only one spring, and its waters must bathe the earth until it is soaked.

Why do you not squat down and help Me cleave the earth and water it instead of building dikes against Me?

Later the same day – The Lord

Next year, we will continue with these thoughts. Tactless remarks have been made. For now, hold on to whatever you write.

Mérida, March 26, 2005 – The Lord

The Bible says, I shed My Blood for all human beings, although many will not take advantage of their salvation. With My death, I was confirming My Words, My existence, and My Humanity.

Today, although human beings practically deny some points of

My Doctrine, it is impossible for them to deny that I have died for all of you. Can faithless, rebellious, atheistic, unbelieving creatures possibly say that My Sacrifice at the hands of My hangmen is not true, so that they could unleash their rage against Me?

No one can possibly deny it and prove their denial. You, whoever you are who read these lines, do you believe that I died for you? And why do you believe that I did so?

Persist and reflect on the reason why, and you will see that you will be free from every sophism, and from the different versions of My Doctrine that I have allowed to go on propagating among you for various reasons, yours and those that have nothing to do with you.

Remember: no one dies for anyone who is not intensely loved.

Tell Me, My creature, what is it that rules you? The force of feelings or of reason? Reflect, and find in Me the strength to be coherent with yourself, for often you believe with words but you deny with actions.

Free yourself from prejudices in making your reflections. I guarantee you efficacious help.

Mérida, March 28, 2005 – The Lord

Do you weep, My daughter, when you see My Passion repeated in John Paul II? Everyone has their own reaction, and practically every man and woman witnesses this new Crucifixion of Love. Allow Me to speak to you of that day when many men and even more women came to see Me on the Cross, taking away with them different impressions: indifference for many and joy for others.

Yet, I felt compassion for all; My Heart, almost exhausted to the limit, throbbed for all. From My Cross, I have guided everyone: I guide the perfect and the imperfect. Whether the good or the bad, those who are near or those who are far, I call every one of them, and they should all hear My Voice, so filled with warmth and Love.

Why do so many of you resist the sight of your God nailed to a Cross? You have no pity for Me, and I am filled with pity for you.

Mérida, March 29, 2005 – The Lord

Oh, beloved men and women of the twenty-first century, who seeing Me crucified, do not realize that I am also their model and thus, they do not make up their minds to imitate Me. And when someone appears who wants to imitate Me, they do not succeed because they do not become humble.

Then they experience anger and do not recognize that the annoyance they experience is a gift of Mine for the purpose of making them see their weakness, their inconstancy, their reluctance to accept suffering. What do they obtain from that? By seeing themselves powerless, they will gain a great deal when they find peace therein. Only there, only then, do I newly overwhelm them with gifts.

I am always worried about all of you, and that comes from the immutability of My Love, which does not wait for requests but proceeds and offers of its own will. When it seems to you that I resist giving you something, you should think above all about whether I want what you desire and ask for. Then think about the fact that I want you to ask Me so that you will feel your need of Me. Reflect lovingly on all this and feel the urge to abandon your own miseries in order to clothe yourselves in real riches and be filled with the fullness of Me.

April 2, 2005 – The Lord

This was the evening of Pope John Paul II's death and vigil of the Feast of Divine Mercy. A day of mourning and of Grace for humanity; of mourning, because there will no longer be among you a righteous man, My Vicar, the humble, impartial, wise, charitable messenger of Love and Peace. Tonight, when the bells ring, a great many men and women, old people, young people, and children, some of them for the first time, will again feel the weight of orphanhood.

It will be a night of Graces because finally, the one who loves Me will be freed from that tired and painful body in order to be clothed in immortality. Like Me, he did not mind dying on the

Cross. It is important to Me that you listen to My Voice and that at the foot of My Cross, with My whole Church, you truly understand the great drama of Calvary.

I have called you again through My Vicar. Listen to Me! May your ears be attentive to the voice of forgiveness that I offer you spontaneously without your needing to feel ashamed.

You do not know what you bring about when you offend Me. When you sin, it is as if My Heart were being pierced by a great many blows from a dagger. When you wake up tomorrow, come to your crucified God. I have saved so much for you! While My Heart is destroyed, at the same time, it remains intact in order to Love you, because it is not liable to decrease in spite of your deafness and very scanty affection towards Me.

Bells of the world, toll sorrowfully, because you will no longer see the Righteous Pilgrim. Bells of Heaven, ring out your Glory because My beloved is near, the Son who comes holding the hand of Divine Mercy.

(Tonight the Holy Father, John Paul II, passed away as the Lord said this morning, and truly the feeling of orphanhood is dreadful (...) my guide on earth has left me alone and has returned to the House of the Father).

Mérida, April 12, 2005 – The Lord

My children, let Me call you passionately, with My Soul filled with desire to see you at the foot of the Cross. I am anxious to see you calm and at the same time grieving for having caused Me to die. Do not be afraid. It is not My desire to increase your sufferings. On the contrary, I want to sweeten them. I only ask you to think about Me, crucified, sorrowful, and covered in so much of My innocent Blood.

LENTEN SEASON OF 2006

Mérida, April 3, 2006 – The Lord

My Passion and My Cross have for centuries concealed the faults of human beings, especially of those who oppose My Divine Will. Yet this does not produce the final effect desired by Me if human beings do not choose and decide to make of their own personal cross the altar of their own immolation.

Cochabamba, April 12, 2006 – The Most Blessed Mother

Beloved little children, I am going to tell you something that you will talk about in future years, and this gift, which is so great even in Heaven, will be enjoyed because I bring it to you by request of Jesus.

That night at the Last Supper, I was with the Apostles in the Upper Room where all of us were welcomed. This has not been referred to in the Gospel because of the Jewish mentality of that time—which God Himself wanted to make use of—which only took males into account.

Thus, you can also observe that when speaking of the multiplication of the loaves and the fishes, the Evangelists only mention the number of men.

That night, in the midst of Jesus and His Apostles, I was first in the mind of Jesus, Who never failed to honor Me in public and in private. I was the happiest person when it came to the institution of the Sacrament of Love because I already knew that it would be instituted.

Just imagine! I, who engendered Jesus in My virginal womb, now, upon receiving Him, was rewarded for all the sadness that I had endured up to that day. It had to be thus: only Mother, only Son. Only Love united Us: Me to Him and Him to Me.

Meditate frequently on these mysteries and remember that, upon being the Mother of the Sacrament of Love, I would be pleased for you to remember Me as the Mother of the Divine Sacrament (the

Eucharist). To those who believe and to those who thus invoke Me, I promise the most beautiful spiritual as well as material Graces; the latter in order to confirm the former.

I want to extend to all of you My sweetness as Mother glorified and placed at the side of Jesus, My glory and your glory. This sweetness is the infinitely sweet Love that is poured on Me and on all of you through Jesus.

At dawn on this Holy Thursday, I bestow My maternal Blessing on you.

LENTEN SEASON OF 2007

Cochabamba, April 5, 2007 – The Lord

During the enormous loneliness experienced by Me the night before My death, I was only alone in appearance. While it is certainly true that the effects of My situation were abandonment by all, heartrending agony, and the greatest of bitterness, you should know that My Father, while permitting Me to feel such enormous loneliness and human weakness, bestowed on Me the companionship of faithful souls who through the centuries would share in My greatest of suffering, which was to feel Myself abandoned by the Father.

That suffering was much greater than having assumed the sins of all mankind.

Therefore, all of you whom I call to unite with Me at Gethsemane, receive this Will of Mine as an immense gift, and as such, accept it as coming from My Heart. I have not chosen many because I know what My choosing means for all of you. But those who are meek and make an effort not to depart from My Peace experience an understanding of the reason for their loneliness.

Cochabamba, April 6, 2007 – The Lord

Today My Church commemorates and renews My Passion precisely through all of you. Unfortunately, there are many men and women who do not like pain, or the memory of Me, and even less, to feel sorrow or experience suffering!

For that reason, they forget My suffering; their thinking about My suffering is quickly clouded over because they have to be more concerned about their own suffering.

Who is preventing you from uniting My suffering with yours?

Remember that if you have to suffer, it is because I Myself allow it, so that you may gain Paradise. I repeat to you that without the cross, you cannot call yourselves Christians. Remember this and take heart by taking refuge in My Wounds. Stay protected by My sufferings: those that wounded My Spirit to the point of causing Me to sweat My Bodily Blood.

Little children, do not remain strangers to the action of My Spouse on earth, My Church. Instead, allow yourselves to be led by Her and by Me to the great ocean of My Passion. If all of you perform the renewal of My Sacrifice with great desire, perform it in Memory of Me.

LENTEN SEASON OF 2008

Mérida, March 16, 2008 – The Lord

Holy Week is beginning, and when all of you reflect on these pages, I want you to prepare yourselves for the Great Celebration of Easter. Meditate on My Goodness and on your own faults, on My Mercy and on your indifference and resistance, on your few good joys in the past, and on My inconceivable and terribly sorrowful suffering on the Cross. Think about yourselves and think about Me.

You were gone astray, but I am firmly on the Cross and I allow Myself to be seen by all of you, remaining silent, practically beseeching you, so that when your resistance is overcome, you come and seat yourselves beside Me, in the triumphal carriage of the One who overcame death and sin, in that carriage of light and flame, which moves closer to the shining goal which is Our House and will be your Paradise.

Once more, I ask you to warm up My Heart, injured by the frozen hearts of so many human beings, wounded by so many betrayals.

My beloved, if you speak of My suffering, My Crucifixion, My death, with every word you utter, you enkindle sparks of Love in this Heart that loves all of you so much. With that Love, I cause words and thoughts produced by My Passion on the part of each one of you to be transformed into Divine fuel, which enkindles many flames of compassion and repentance in your hearts and in the hearts of others.

All of you, look at Me on the Cross; really look at My Face; look at My eyes which I can scarcely open, My jaws so stuck to My cheekbones that they deform My Face.

Do you see My beard? If it has kept a little of its normal appearance on My Face, it also is red with Blood. How much of it has been torn by the soldiers of Pilate and by those who, along the Via Dolorosa, allowed themselves to commit such savage acts of evil!

You, whom I have been attracting to this Work in order to shape you through all the stages of My Life, be compassionate to Me. Accompany Me during the days that recall My Passion, while many, a great many, forget Me.

Being compassionate to Me will lead you to have compassion on your brothers and sisters, and thus, your apostolate will be more fruitful.

Mérida, March 23, 2008 – The Lord

My little children, during this time, I also wish to make the Sign of the Cross over you in order to separate you from the world and to offer you a special sign of My satisfaction.

I am happy to be among you because everywhere, they are casting Me out. And if I present Myself with the Cross on My shoulders, those whom I also called with so much Love, even though they be few, offend Me more.

They are afraid and they hide instead of asking for forgiveness and making straight their path. They are afraid and they hide, or else they slam the door right in My Face.

Can you imagine how disdainful they are? To suffer, to die, to desire their good—the good of those who reject Me—and then to be renounced.

Little children, I do not want to stir up in you vain feelings, pious sorrow for Me and for them. You know little of the enormous thorns that some people in the present time pierce Me with.

LENTEN SEASON OF 2009

Mérida, February 24, 2009 – The Lord

My daughter, now finish writing in this notebook so that it will reach My children and your brothers and sisters, so as to enable them to prepare themselves spiritually for Holy Week.

In this way, I want all of you to understand that in order to be in union with Me, you need to keep watch over yourselves, to restrain yourselves often, and to pray more with a steadfast and calm will.

The ignominious end to which I was condemned by those who represented the then Sovereign Pontiff was the crowning of My Life of absolute abandonment to the Paternal Goodness, Who, like Me, wanted to save humanity by offering the greatest Sacrifice that could be made: I Myself.

My Passion contains everything that you need today and tomorrow, and it works marvelous miracles on all those who forget the world and themselves in order to think of Me.

When everything is subordinated to My sufferings, to My Will, then My Passion brings great benefits to souls.

In the world, many words, too many, are uttered! But if greater reasoning about Me, especially about My sorrow, were introduced into the world, My Love would soon enkindle flames in your souls.

Yet I am deprived of this delight: the stirring of souls to unite their sufferings to Mine in order to attain comfort and strength, generosity, and patience—all that which is lacking in men and women of these times.

They remove Me from nations, from households, from schools, and even from many Christian installations. They do not want to exalt Christ crucified; they prefer to show Me to new generations as Christ Resurrected, as if Tabor could be separated from Calvary!

Many do not understand that those who love Me as Christ crucified and acknowledge My sufferings will also love My Presence in the Eucharist. But those who are ignorant of My Passion will be unlikely to believe in and to love My Eucharistic Presence, alive among them.

About the Editor

Tim Francis is a nationally known speaker/evangelist and founder of You Shall Believe Ministries in Fort Worth, Texas. After years of addiction, he was thrust into a search for truth after witnessing a lady experience the stigmata, the wounds of Christ. Discovering centuries-old scientifically documented miracles and supernatural happenings, he set out on a quest in 2009 to share these findings with the world.

As the father of three children and has been married for twenty-five years, Francis travels the United States today, putting on multimedia presentations that show the biblical, historical, and supernatural evidence of Jesus Christ's teachings and practices up until today. He is currently working on a major motion picture, inspired by true events, of a priest & exorcist who was abused by a priest as a child and became a self-absorbed Wall Street banker before having a riveting conversion that led him back to Christ's church to serve as both a Pastor and Exorcist.

Here are samplings of thousands of testimonials after attending his presentations and/or watching videos:

"I wanted to thank you for changing my life. My mom went to day 1 of the 3-day mission… she got me to attend the second day… I was an occasional Mass attendee, mostly holidays. After your talk I made a good confession and now attend Mass DAILY…."

"I thank you from my heart for the 3 days of 'Science Tests

Faith'... Because of ignorance, I was bringing pain to Jesus just as those who beat and crucified Him. No more!! After over 40 years, I received the Sacrament of Confession again, and will continue from now on...I am so fired up to do as much as I can for Jesus and to spread what I've experienced."

"Without hesitation, nor exaggeration, I can say it was this presentation that was the pinnacle of my return to the Catholic Church...Two days after the event, my 10 year old daughter asked if we were going to start going to the Catholic Church. I told her, I think so, but did she understand that...they taught that the bread and wine actually become the body and blood of Jesus Christ. Without hesitation she stated, 'Well they do, remember, we saw the video.'..In that moment, through the eyes of a child, I was given clarity of purpose and my family and I returned to the Catholic Church."

"My wife noticed the video "Science Test Faith" in the back of St. Mary's several days ago... Over the past 73 hours, I feel as though I have undergone a religious transformation. Once you watch the video... there is no going back. As a doctor, I consider myself a scientist of sorts... (who) utilizes evidence-based clinical decision making whenever possible. You and your colleagues are providing an awesome service... truly life-altering and, I think, ultimately soul saving. Thank you very much and God bless you all!"

You can reach Tim at

www.ScienceTestsFaith.com

francis.tim13@gmail.com

866-671-7284